ALL MINE

PETER EDWARDS

PETER EDWARDS

Also by Peter Edwards,
BUSHMORE'S DARK SECRETS

Peter Edwards lives on the Surfcoast, along the Great Ocean
Road in Victoria, Australia, with his son and daughter and
their dog named Sue.
This is Peter's first work of fiction.

Follow me on Instagram
peteredwardsallmine

Website: allminestories.com
Email: allminestories@bigpond.com

Liked my book, then please like my page,

www.facebook.com/PeterEdwardsAuthor
Twitter: Peter Edwards@allminestories

PETER EDWARDS

ALL MINE

For Sol and Jen,
and my parents, John and Judy.

PETER EDWARDS

Prologue

South of Griffith, New South Wales
The Mid-Eighties

The engine drained the last drop of petrol and died. Jimmy dumped his trail bike in the bush and tracked west along the riverbank. He reached a wire fence and rested in the heat, scouring gaps between the red gums ahead, sucking in a couple of heavy ones to calm his nerves, drown out the fear. It was not too late to leave. He hadn't entered their property yet. Fingers clung to the wire, the mind wrestled with decisions.

He could make it out to the road before dark, hitch a ride home. His mother would be worried by now.

If he came back and got the bike tomorrow, no one would ever know he was here. They'd sell up, just like his parents had said.

Then he pictured his father's steaming rage, the vicious words, the shotgun at his hip poking out the farmhouse door. The Italians had driven off the property in an air of confidence and dust barely an hour ago.

Decisions.

His mother had worked too hard for five long years. He had to reach Franco Caruso. Surely the man would talk. He's a businessman, after all.

'Fuck 'em,' he mumbled to no one, then cast a final glance over his shoulder before climbing through the fence, careful to avoid the electric strand on the inside. He slipped between the trees keeping a watchful eye on the open paddocks to his left. All he saw was cattle, until a tiny wooden hut appeared in the distance. He reached it and took cover on the blind side, checking past the corners.

When it was safe he edged around to the front. A sign on the padlocked door read,

CARUSO IRRIGATION PUMPHOUSE 2
TRESPASSERS PROSECUTED

Prosecuted? He mused. Yeah right. Shot and dumped in the river, maybe. Chucked in a hole, buried, also much more likely. Even the dogs in Griffith knew that much about the Caruso family.

The property stretched for many miles along the Murrumbidgee. He walked for hours, careful not to stray from the bank or the protection of linking shadows beneath swaying river reds. On dusk, tired eyes caught a dim light from a small house, possibly a fishing shack. He knew the main house was located away from the river, closer to the road, perhaps even further west. He crept up onto the verandah, peered through the corner of a window. The light came from a lamp standing beside a brown, silver studded leather couch, finer than he'd ever seen. At the sound of pitched laughter his eyes fell on two naked bodies gleaming with sweat, stretched out on a thick rug. The woman's back was arched upwards, her neck stretched long. Top teeth bit into her bottom lip with pleasure as she gazed up at the man pumping inside her. The right breast was exposed, almost flat, wobbling like jelly with each thrust. He became instantly hard staring into her eyes.

Her eyes.

She had rolled her head.

He ducked, hoping he hadn't been spotted, but was unable to resist looking again, raising his head just a little. Never had he seen a woman in the flesh before.

The man was already pulling up his jeans. Jimmy cursed his foolishness and sprinted toward the bank where a canoe was tied to a trunk. Frantic fingers worked the knot. The line freed just as he heard footsteps and was grappled from behind, driven head first into the shallows. He tried to resist but was spun over easily and punched twice in the face. Arms were pinned by knees. A hand latched onto his throat.

Jimmy expected another blow. When it didn't come he looked up, surprised to be staring into the fierce eyes of another teenager with the muscular physique of a man. Veins tracked up each arm.

'What the hell are you doing here?' the heaving, bare-chested youth said, the tone sinister, fist cocked.

The woman ran toward them, screaming. 'Carlo, let him up. Let him up. Now!'

Jimmy spat blood and water, mud crunched in his teeth. 'Carlo. You're Carlo Caruso?'

'Who wants to know?'

'I must speak with your father.'

A sour laugh returned. 'Why would my father bother with a little pervert like you?'

'I never meant—'

Carlo struck him in the mouth again.

'Don't hurt him,' the woman said.

'Get back inside, Anita. Get dressed. Go!'

The woman left. Jimmy ran his tongue along throbbing teeth to check they were all still in place.

The youth glared down. 'Do you even know who my father is?'

'I know he is the boss of—'

Knuckles slammed down hard between Jimmy's eyes. His nose cracked, hurt engulfed him.

'Say that again and you're dead.'

Jimmy ignored the threat, the pain, the helpless anger. 'If I can't speak to your father, I'll find him in Griffith or at the meat works, I won't stop.'

'What's your name?'

'Jimmy.'

'Who's with you?'

'No one.'

'If I find out you're lying—'

'I'm not.'

A cold moment passed between the two youths before Carlo relented. 'All right. Get up.'

Jimmy was hauled up by the arm, led over to the house and shoved onto the verandah.

'Don't move. If you're not here when I get back, I'll find you. Count on it.' Carlo and the woman drove off in a car, taillights disappeared over a small rise in the paddock.

Jimmy sat and waited, holding his wet tee shirt to his nose to stem the bleeding. He was in. He felt in. How could this go wrong?

When darkness finally surrounded him, two cars arrived. Doors slammed, men wandered about brandishing shotguns and lit cigarettes. Carlo stood in the headlights next to an older, shorter man dressed in dark pants and a white shirt with rolled sleeves. A thickset man holding a pistol walked past into the house. Jimmy was careful not to meet his eyes. Despite the warm and still night air, he pressed his elbows into his thighs to stop his body shivering.

He heard the man trampling about room to room.

The older man strolled over and stood on the verandah. Jimmy looked up, unsure. He guessed who the man was, though he had no idea what Franco Caruso looked like.

The other man came back out of the house and spoke in Italian.

'Grazie, Marco. Leave us,' the old man said and sat down next to Jimmy. Deep folds stretched across his brow neatly, spaced like foolscap.

'Why do you request a meeting with me, Jimmy?'

Franco's accent was heavy, but he spoke slow and clear. The precision in his words surprised Jimmy, relaxing him out of his terrified state, just a little, but enough so he could look Franco in the eye. Jimmy knew he had to do that before he began.

'Men came back to our house today, sir. Our farm. They told my father it was his turn to grow their marijuana again.'

Franco nodded. 'I see? Do you know these men?'

'No. But my father has just done five years—'

'These men are Italian.'

'Yes, sir.'

'I see. Tell me more.'

'They paid for lawyers, protected my father in prison, made sure we stayed on the land. Now they say he must show loyalty.'

'Loyalty, uh.' Franco locked his fingers together, placed them under his chin and took a moment as the slow, dark Murrumbidgee waters passed by toward the moon, full and low.

'Your father, does he know where you are?'

'No ... sir.'

'How old are you?'

'Sixteen.'

'Sixteen uh, and you came all the way up the river to my house because your parents were threatened.'

Jimmy swallowed hard, his throat dry, but this man let him speak his mind. 'You ... I ... I know you can help. They told my father he has one week to decide. If he goes back to jail we'll lose the farm. My mother can't go through this again. We'll do anything.'

Eyes turned down on him. Wise eyes. Not the eyes he'd expected of a man with such a fearsome reputation.

'You should not have come here Jimmy, but you put your family first. There is no stronger loyalty. What is your last name?'

'Riggs, sir.'

'Jimmy Riggs. Franco.'

11

A hand was extended, Jimmy shook it making sure he returned a solid grasp.

'Tomorrow I will meet with your father, first, let me teach you what my own father once taught me when I was a boy.' He raised a finger. 'In Sicily we say the squeaky wheel, he gets the oil.'

'I … I don't understand, sir. What does that mean?'

A firm hand clasped his shoulder. 'Ahhh, the meaning is different for every man, Jimmy. I will teach you that over time. I promise. But for you now, it means those men will never trouble your family again.'

Part 1
Murder,
And The
Homecoming

PETER EDWARDS

1

Coogee, Sydney
2004

Welham woke to that incessant, awful rattle only hard plastic vibrating on a glass table can make. He reached out, fumbling blindly onto one handset. The buzzing continued until his hand slapped down on the second phone just as the noise ceased. He flipped the top open, raised his sunnies and waited for his eyes to adjust. Blurred words became crisp.

A missed call from a private number, he knew it was Ingliss.

He rubbed his eyes, yawning. Down below the chatter of Coogee beachgoers rose on the soft sea breeze that had kicked in while he slept. Wind also tickled the chimes on the neighbouring balcony. Welham was yet to meet the new couple who'd moved into the apartment only a week ago. Shooting the string on their annoying ornament was probably a little premature. A slight mention about the chimes and the fact he was on the building's body corp committee – while they waited at the lift – would be more appropriate.

Behind him the balcony door slid open.

'Went inside, you were snoring,' Tracey said.

'I'm rooted,' he replied. 'Really needed that little snooze.'

'Whose phone was that, sweetie?'

'Mine.'

She lifted her mobile off the table, checked it and took it back inside.

Matching phones. What next?

Such a delightful woman, yet so many annoying traits. Just last week she needed a new phone and bought the same model as his, a Motorola. *"They looked cute together,"* had been her comment.

Another sharp vibration in his palm. Sunlight forced him to angle the screen to read the blunt text from Ingliss.

—PICK UP BENSON AWAIT FURTHER ORDERS—

Ingliss was still pressing ahead with surveillance. Three days ago they received a tip off. A container carrying Mexican cocaine would be moved off the Botany Bay wharves today, placing detectives from Strikeforce Phoenix, Federal Police and Australian Customs on full alert. Yet the shipment had not been located, it was now late Sunday afternoon. Welham had hoped for an easy night, suspecting it had already been moved or might not even exist at all.

Glancing over his shoulder to make sure the door was closed, he rang Ingliss and confirmed he was about to leave, then called his partner. Benson answered.

'It's Welham. Be ready in fifteen.'

'Yeah, just got the message.'

He was about to hang up when he detected Benson's puffing. A high-pitched voice hung in the background.

'Carn Daddy, hurry up n' bowl.'

'We interrupting cricket again?' Welham said. Each time he visited, Benson's son Jake tried to rope him into a game.

'It's stinking hot, can't get the cheat'n little shit out.'

Welham chuckled. 'Get yourself fit old son.'

'That train's left the station mate, see you when you get here.'

Welham snapped the handset shut. Stiffness made him groan as he hauled himself up off the sun lounge, a reminder of the *"welcome to the back nine"* card he received from his golfing mates on his recent fortieth. Inside, he filled a glass of water and switched the air conditioner off.

'What 'ya do that for?' Tracey said. She was lying on the couch, facing away, typing into her new phone.

'Off to work.'

'Seriously, this late, thought we were doing dinner?' She held up her empty glass. 'Be a darling.'

He grabbed a fresh wine bottle from the fridge, carried it over and jammed it in the ice bucket on the coffee table, then quickly shoved it under her bikini top.

Squealing loudly, she jumped up holding the phone at arm's length. The bottle tumbled onto the carpet. 'You're so going to pay for that,' she said, half seriously through a tensed jaw, flicking icy droplets off her chest.

'Have to get you moving somehow,' he said, laughing. 'Take it with you.'

'Can't I stay? My place'll be roasting.'

'Go to the beach.'

'Can't be stuffed.'

Earlier in the day she whinged about her air conditioner playing up again, he felt a little sorry for her. She lived in a rented apartment, west side of the building four doors down the road.

'What about dinner?' Tracey asked, gathering her clothes. 'How long will you be?'

'Who knows, I'll call if I feel like something.'

'We should try the new Greek place on Dolphin Street.'

'Along with every other arsehole in Coogee. Maybe during the week when it's quieter.' He wandered off to his room, strapped on his holster, checked his gun, changed into better shorts, a shirt and boat shoes without socks. When he returned to the main room Tracey waited by the door, her handbag was slung over a shoulder, the ice bucket and wine nestled in her other arm.

They kissed.

Eyes followed her to the elevator. He tapped his pockets, felt only keys, his wallet, no phone, and he couldn't see it on the outside table where he thought it was. Instead he found it on the coffee table beside the small pool of water from the ice bucket. With no time to wipe up he locked the door and left.

———

The traffic lightened as Coogee trailed off behind. When he arrived at Benson's Newtown address, young Jake sprinted out the front door and across the lawn around to the driver's side. Welham dug into the ashtray for a coin.

'Hey Craig,' Jake said through a gap-toothed grin, elbows stretched uncomfortably up through the open window.

Welham shook his hand. 'Getting stronger little man.'

'Yup, sure am.' He focussed on Welham's left hand.

'Been helping your mum?'

'Yup, doing what she asks.'

He winked, handing over two-dollars. 'Remember the deal?'

'I know, don't tell the old man.' The wink came back.

'Good boy.'

Benson's wife appeared carrying a bag to her car.

'What's your mission soldier?'

'Going to Grandma's, Daddy says you're coming for dinner.'

'Is that so?'

Benson climbed into the passenger seat, placing a camera bag in the back.

'Get going buddy,' Benson said to Jake, 'see you later if you're still up.'

'Sure Dad, bye Craig.' He raced away with the coin clutched in his fist.

'Got plans tonight,' Welham said, driving off.

'Come on, you're leaving this week, Mum's worried, might never see you again.'

'She'll find me. What if we're late?'

'Few expansion cracks in the gravy, plastic tasting veges, nothin' that'll kill ya, least it'll be warm.'

'Guess I'm locked in,' Welham said.

His partner's mobile rang. Benson took the call and listened. 'We're on the move, I'll put him on.' He held his hand over the microphone. 'It's Ingliss. He called before. Head to the Norfolk Arms Hotel, Botany Road, I'll fill you in on the way.' He passed the handset to Welham.

'Detective, why can't I reach you? Been trying your number,' his boss said.

'No Idea.' Welham glanced down at his own phone face up on the console, turned on. Radio silence had been ordered for the operation. 'You brass keep telling us how good this digital system is. Who am I to argue?'

'Just hurry up, get to that pub, Purcell and Cornes need to be relieved.'

'Only a few minutes away.'

'Good.' Ingliss hung up.

Welham passed the mobile back and picked his own up. 'What's he on about? Got five bars of reception.'

Welham turned onto Botany Road, dropped Benson off a block away and parked across from the Norfolk Arms Hotel.

Inside, he bought a beer then shouldered his way back through the crowd and found a quiet space beside the front window. Memories of younger days sprung to mind, bluing wharfies, live music, nicotine clouds at eye level. Walls now had a fresh coat. Gold stars dotted the carpet leading to an opaque glass door separating the pokies.

Detective Cornes sat at a table next to the back wall. Purcell stood at the bar. When he saw Welham, he drained his beer and walked outside where he met Benson on the smokers' deck. They chatted like old mates before Benson entered, heading straight to the betting counter where he studied a form guide pinned to the felt wall. He scribbled on a betting ticket, crossed it out, marked up another card and took it to the bar, paid for his bet, bought a beer.

Welham moved quickly to the betting counter, lifted the first ticket, turned it over and read Benson's scribble on the back — *pool table, red tee shirt, dark hair, glasses.* Over the other side of the bar, pool balls cracked from an opening break.

Welham picked out a short figure with familiar thick lips, puffy, olive cheeks, oily hair. He wore a red polo with ripples in the collar and warped at the hem by a perfect potbelly. He looked harder to make sure.

Little fat Joey Avola was lining up the white ball.

What are you doing in Sydney? Welham thought.

Purcell's partner Bruce Cornes left. Several minutes later a woman at the bar smiled, half attractive, her better days gone by. Welham strolled over and struck up a conversation, ignoring Benson's glare from the end of the bar. Avola moved to a corner, answered his phone and plugged a finger in the opposite ear. Welham caught the sudden rise of his partner's brow before Benson departed through a side door. The woman mentioned live music in the bar later that evening. Welham concentrated over her shoulder, Avola left through the main door.

'Got to go.' He downed his pot. 'Music starts at nine, yeah?'

'You'll be here?'

'Sounds good.' He needed an excuse, Benson's mother dished up crap.

Outside, his partner stood impatiently at the driver's door, a hand stretched. 'Hurry the fuck up.'

Welham tossed the keys, they settled into traffic south bound towards Botany Bay.

'The white van,' said Benson.

'Name's Joey Avola.'

'Know him?'

'Family's known, crossed em' years ago.'

'That all I get? From Sydney?'

'Griffith. Don't lose him.'

'Mafia?'

'Family's connected, Joey's the try-hard.'

'Try-hard, huh. Just like you. What the hell were you doing in there, anyway?'

'Surveillance.'

Benson shook his head.

'Oh come on Sammy, she was passable. You're just jealous women don't hit on you, those hairy guardrails on that bald scone of yours, scare the bejesus out of anyone.'

'I'm happily married, dipshit. What about Tracey?'

'Who?'

'Tracey ... Tracey, you're a real moron sometimes. Settle down instead of tappin' anything breathing. She gets along with the missus for Christ's sake, must be all right.'

'They've met once.'

'First impressions work on my wife. I know.'

Welham laughed. 'Always thinking of yourself.'

Benson returned a hot glare. 'You can talk, when will you man up?'

'Don't go there mate, Tracey's an okay chick, not the be all, monogamy's not for everyone.'

'Yeah, right, sooner you stop referring to women as *"okay chicks"* and start treating 'em like real ladies. I warn ya, don't speak around my wife like that again—'

Welham's mobile rang. 'Working now,' he said, glad to be rid of the subject. He answered.

'Detective Welham. Superintendent Mersche. Your exact location, please?'

'Botany Road, we just passed the airport. The man we're tailing is Joey Avola—'

'Let him go.'

'What? Does Ingliss know?'

'You have your orders, Detective. Inspector Ingliss is in a briefing as we speak. Janis cannot be compromised. Another team will pick him up.

Welham listened to Mersche's further instructions and hung up, staring off to the right. Clumsy looking, towering red dock cranes never failed to remind him of Tripods from John Christopher's Tripod trilogy he'd read as a boy.

He thought about calling Ingliss, but Mersche was right. Operation Janus, the largest organised crime investigation ever undertaken in Australia, was poised to commence within a week. Welham's team would re-ignite investigations into Italian businesses and superannuation funds throughout the Riverina district of Southern New South Wales. 'Gotta let him go, Sam.'

'Serious?'

'Orders, mate.'

'This to do with your little upgrade?'

'Yeah.'

'Be stuffed if I'm calling you sir.'

'Day's coming, smartarse. Left into this business park up ahead, before the roundabout.'

Benson grinned as they entered through black iron gates onto a common driveway, paved with serrated bricks the colour of sunburnt skin.

Welham pointed. 'Head right, looking for Asian Pacific Logistic Solutions.'

They drove down the business park between reflective glass offices, freight terminals and warehouses. Long trailers minus the rigs rested on front hydraulic legs in the centre island of the commonway. No other cars visible.

'That's it there.' Welham pointed to the letters A. P. L. S. on the roller door. 'Get a visual.'

They found one, five buildings away. Benson reversed beneath cantilevered offices and cut the ignition.

ATTENTO SEAFOODS TERMINAL FOUR was sprawled in block across the roller door of the warehouse directly opposite.

'What are we looking for?' Benson asked, reaching behind for the camera bag.

'Don't know yet.' Minutes later a canary yellow transit van pulled up at A.P.L.S. The driver remained inside. Benson fitted a long lens and began snapping. Welham reached into his pocket for a notebook. Benson read out the number plate.

'What's he doing?'

'Fuck all,' said Benson.

'Recognise him?'

'Nuh.'

Movement came, up in a window on the second level of Attento Seafoods. Welham concentrated hard, only a glint of sunlight bounced back. He returned his focus to the van. The driver hadn't moved. A glass door in the front of Attento Seafoods opened. A man appeared wheeling a luggage bag, tall, thick set, jet-black hair. With his back to them, he twisted keys in the door. A navy blue office shirt fluttered between broad shoulders, a lengthy black coat was draped over his left arm. Mascot Airport was less than two kilometres away. Welham assumed he was an executive ready to fly out to a colder climate. The man walked off toward the end of the court. Welham saw only the side profile of the face, he disappeared behind a parked trailer with a blue shipping container on the back. Benson's camera clicked furiously. The driver now stood at the side door of the yellow van. 'Com'on you piece o' shit, turn around,' Benson said. Only the driver's back was visible. 'Might have to get closer.' 'Wait'll this guy pisses off.' Welham looked toward the far end of the trailer, expecting the executive to appear. Instead, he stepped out from the front corner, the bag and coat gone. Instantly Welham recognised the face. Carlo Caruso marched forward, black-gloved hands grasping a dark muzzle.

'Get down,' Welham yelled, sparks flew, bullets pinged off the bonnet puncturing the windscreen. He wrenched his gun out, slid down, another volley strafed the car, squares of glass and bullets rained, thumping the seat above his head.

The firing ceased.

His heart thrashed. Lungs heaved, gasping frantically. He was alive.

Benson's chin rested, dead. Welham let off six rounds up through the vacant screen. No fire returned. He raised his head, far as he dared. Silence. Was Caruso down? He found the door handle; it clicked open, a stream of bullets thundered into the outer skin. Metal ripped metal, bullets spat and bounced. Many others penetrated.

———

Carlo released his finger. A mild puff of smoke drifted from the insulated silencer of the MAC 10, yet it felt cool to the touch. The Mexicans were right about the powerful muzzle climb. Thousand bullets a minute, they said.

The passenger's left arm twitched. A finger lifted. Carlo eased the Glock from his belt, fired into the side of the head, then slipped the pistol back and crossed the commonway towards Reynolds, the driver of the yellow van. The roller door of A.P.L.S. let out an oil deprived screech as it slid up to reveal the truck. The engine turned over, the truck shook, idling. Reynolds' empty hands hung at his side. Sweat beaded like shingles on his forehead.

'Who's in the truck?'

'Your replacement.'

'No, Carlo … we had a deal.' A hand moved to his back. Carlo fired, relishing in the man's disbelieving gaze. He studied the weapon. Impressive.

The man hired to kill him took the full impact of at least fifteen bullets, perhaps in under a second. He made a circling motion above his head. The truck shunted forward over the body.

2

Aspen, Colorado
Seven Years Later

From behind the window of Lecky's Diner, Carlo chuckled to himself when he recognised Jimmy Riggs, clad in a dark blue snow jacket. A little older, carrying a little more beef.

The chairman of L'ombrello Superannuation Funds had just stepped out of the hunting shop on the other side of East Main Street. Carlo had expected to see his older brother Nicky – the only member of his family he'd seen since leaving Australia – definitely not Jimmy. They hadn't seen each other since Sydney. Jimmy turned his collar against the wind, jammed his hands in the pockets and crossed the road.

Suddenly nerves took hold. Carlo became awash with different emotions. Excitement, fear, trepidation, guilt. Jimmy, his father's most trusted adviser, *is* family.

How would he treat me now?

Head craning forward, Jimmy walked to the window peering straight at Carlo. He waved, feeling like a goldfish until Jimmy's confused look began to wane. A wary smile emerged and he entered. There were no exuberant greetings, instead he simply slid out the opposite chair.

'Carlo,' he said in a low voice, portraying doubt, his hand extended forward.

'Hey Jimmy.' Carlo nodded, grasping the hand. He placed his other hand on top to warm the gesture. 'Great to see you, mate.'

'It's really you?' Jimmy's eyes ghosted with moisture.

'Course it's me. Not such a big deal, is it?' Then Carlo tried to imagine old photos, he hadn't seen one in seven years, only a face in the mirror. 'Nicky showed you photos, didn't he?'

'Sure did, but jees, you look different again, somehow.' Jimmy stared hard, nodding, unconvinced. 'Guess I'll get used to it. So good to see you too after all these years.' Jimmy's genuine smile helped his fears dissipate.

'This is a real surprise,' Carlo said.

'You're looking well. Despite living it up, you've kept fit.' Then Jimmy pointed his finger. 'Don't deny it. I pay the bills, remember.'

'It's all good, what about the face, huh?'

'Bit of panel beating, did a good job. Better than the alternative.'

'Guess so, but take a look at you. There's an extra chin under there.'

'Fuck you,' Jimmy said, twisting his face, acting serious. 'What if I reckon you don't look Italian no more?'

Carlo laughed. 'Don't be like that James.' Jimmy only liked being called James amongst business circles. 'Thought you might've learnt to take a joke on one of your many chins. And it's about time we fixed that nose I busted all those years ago. Can put you in touch with a very good surgeon, Israeli guy.'

'Expensive one too.' Jimmy's old smirk rose. 'I ain't going under a knife, don't have to.'

'Guess so. Nice jacket. Come here.' He motioned to Jimmy, who leaned forward. Carlo reached behind his neck and ripped the tag off, then patted his shoulder. 'You look like the Michelin Man in that thing.'

'Was going to buy one of those redneck moose hunting jackets.' Jimmy mocked a serious look. 'You know, the checkered ones with the matching cap, dickie looking ears down the side like a regular Elmer fuck'n Fudd.'

'Elmer Fudd hunts wabbits you idiot. Come to Aspen looking like that and I'll shoot you myself.'

Jimmy thrust his head back laughing. Carlo saw the warm glint in the eyes he'd missed so much. The waitress came, poured coffee. 'Can I get you fellas some lunch?'

'Give us a minute,' Carlo said, she walked off.

Jimmy threw up his hands. 'Aspen hey!'

'Wanted to get in before ski season. Once that fires up they reckon you can't even breathe in this joint.'

'Didn't know you could ski?'

'Why'd you think I spent all those winters in the Alps, huh. The women, mate … it's a smorgasbord.'

'I bet. Where's your place round here? I can imagine your street. Bruce Willis up one end, Demi … Demi …' He clicked his fingers a couple of times and before Carlo could help him, his eyes lit up like a light bulb had turned on. 'Demi, that's it, Demi fuck'n Moore up the other, you running amuck in the middle.'

Carlo laughed. 'Sharp as a nut sack, Jimmy. Take you there after lunch, it's not far. Haven't seen one celeb yet, except for you. Not that I'm looking. How'd you get here? Through Utah or over the Rockies?'

'Did the mountains. Hit New York first, business, flew into Denver, drove straight here. Sensational drive, but I can never work these yanks out with their numbered highways. Surely Roaring Fork River or Twin Lakes Highway is a far more attractive name than a number?'

'No arguing good sense to the Yanks mate, you know that, but they sure know how to build a highway. Eisenhower Tunnel, how good's that, huh?'

'Didn't do it, mate. Took the truck route instead. Had to stop for an hour, backtrack a bit. Don't want the F.B.I. up my arse.'

'Good move,' Carlo said. 'Hey, I can't believe you put your hand up for this? Means a lot to me.'

Jimmy shrugged. 'Had to get the idea past Benny first.'

'Benny … what?' Then he saw his friend's eyes widen.

'The Chin.'

'Benny the Chin? What's Benny got to—?'

'You're coming home.'

Carlo struggled with the reality of the words. 'Jimmy ... don't.'

Jimmy reached inside the snow jacket and passed over an envelope. 'Courtesy of the Chin. He's got your passage all worked out.'

Carlo wiped his hands down his face.

'You're shittin' me—' It's what he hoped this meeting *might* be about – now the realisation hit him.

'No kidding, mate. Your father wants you home. Benny wouldn't step up for anyone else ... personally overseeing the whole operation. Everything's planned.'

'The Chin? Can't believe it.' Carlo thought of his mother, fighting back more emotion. He saw Izy's face. Twenty-seven now. She would be more beautiful than all the women in the world.

He suddenly realised his fists were pressing together in anticipation. He relaxed them, then had to ask. 'What about Izy?'

'What?' Jimmy glared back. 'Are you fucking crazy? Surely you've forgotten about—'

'Course not. How could I?'

Jimmy shook his head. Eyes narrowed. A questioning look surfaced, mixed with confusion, disgust, anger, disbelief. 'She helped the cops. That woman's gone from your life, mate.'

'She still in Perth?'

'Last we knew, but ... oh ... shit, seriously! I know what you're thinking. You must be mad if you think she'll come back.'

Carlo perished the thought as best he could. Perhaps Jimmy was right. But then his mind turned over. He would prove Jimmy wrong. Prove them all wrong. 'When am I coming home?'

Jimmy tapped the envelope. 'It's all in there.'

'Sounds good, hey, how's Donna?'

Jimmy leant back in the chair, a smile spread. 'She's great. We have a boy now. Can't wait for you to meet him.'

'I heard. A belated congratulations, my friend.'

'Thanks mate.' Jimmy reached behind, pulled out his wallet and showed a photo. 'Four years old. We named him Frank. Gets Frankie.' His face swelled with pride.

'Yeah, heard that too. My father would be so proud. He's good looking like his mother … and his father.'

'You'll meet him at Christmas. Can't tell him much about his Uncle Carlo.' He shrugged. 'You know—'

Jimmy's words cut deep. There would be so many other obstacles. Carlo's thoughts returned to his mother. He wanted to ask earlier. His mother, an inevitable crossroad he must confront. In his gut he knew what this was about. 'Mama. How is she?'

Jimmy sighed. 'Not well mate, not too well at all. I'm going to call out to the farm when I get back. Franco wants you home before Christmas.'

A great sadness washed over him, he fidgeted with the envelope, then began tearing open a corner.

'Don't—' Jimmy raised a palm '—don't want to know what's inside.'

'So why'd you come? I was expecting my brother.'

'Volunteered. Nicky okay'd it … and you know I'd never let your parents down. Your father gave me the opportunity of a lifetime.'

'You forget Jimmy, I gave you that opportunity. Could've tossed you in the river, perving on me like that.'

Jimmy laughed. 'You got lucky. Was about to twist your nuts till you whistled Waltzing Ma-fuck'n-tilda.'

'Like I haven't heard that a thousand times.' The two friends laughed aloud until their eyes glazed over.

'Seriously Jimmy. Thank you. I wouldn't have trusted anyone else, either.' He was touched his good friend had risked everything he ever worked for to deliver news halfway around the world.

'Cut the sentimental bullshit. Roll me in blow and honey and toss me down a pit full of bow-legged women.'

'Keep saying that, one day I will.'

'Can't wait. Let's have some fun.' Jimmy's grin broadened even more. 'And seven years ago I shouted you lunch, too. It's your hook. I'm starving. Get me the most expensive thing on the menu that's got potatoes in it. Helps with the jet lag.'

Carlo chuckled and signalled for the waitress.

3

St Claire,
South-west Coast of Victoria

White-walled tyres were roped to the sides of the Princess Jenny, protecting the shiny new aluminium hull as the passing wind gently bumped and swayed her into the pylons.

At the cabin door Big Steve packed beer into an esky. From up on the pier Lucas Maddigan winced at the grotesque sight, more than he ever wished to see of his lifelong friend. 'It's true what they say, big fella,' he said. 'When you bend over the sun comes out.'

At the stern Steve's main deckhand, Thumbtack tossed his head up from the bait board. Hard laughter rolled out over the calm waters of Fishhook Bay. 'Warned him, Lukey,' Thumbtack said. 'Here lies Big Steve, dead from crack burn cancer. Deadly stuff that, lemme tell ya.' He wore his traditional red windcheater, cut off at the shoulders displaying tattoos down short, stocky arms. The faded blue teardrop dripped beneath his right eye.

'Can see it on his tombstone,' Lucas replied.

Steve yanked his trackies up, not a hint of embarrassment. 'G'day mate,' he stretched the words sarcastically, flicked his spiralling, sandy hair back while squinting into the morning sun barely a hands width above the horizon. 'Thought you'd be all snuggled up beside that mysterious lady of yours.'

Good old Reno, Lucas thought. 'Reno's got his fish already, huh?'

Lucas's girlfriend, Carmen had driven down from Melbourne the previous night for the weekend. They dined at Reno's restaurant. Her company was laborious at best.

'Nuthin's sacred buddy.'

'Don't I know it?'

Thumbtack's knife sliced through the bait like warm butter before scraping it into a burley bucket. Keen eyes of Clyde, Lucas's dog followed his every move. Muscles pressed, shuddering with anticipation beneath the short coat. Thumbtack scooped the one remaining fillet onto the fat of his blade and slung it up onto the pier. Pandemonium filled the air as a flock of squabbling gulls attacked, but Clyde pounced. He licked the old planks clean and chased the birds to the sea wall at the end of the pier.

Steve slammed the esky lid shut and cleated it down. 'So when do we get to meet this new lady? Must be what, six, eight months? Gotta answer to the missus, mate.'

'Yeah I know. Horry and Connie are bringing their boys out for a barby tonight. Bring the family. We'll crank up a fire, too.'

'Can't do.' Steve nodded toward the foot of the pier. 'Shiny arses from Fords, three hundred bucks a head. Chasing Bluefin.'

Lucas had noticed the new sedans parked on the street. 'Bit late in the season, isn't it?'

'Got me spots, mate. Might chase Blue-eye out deep. Should've set this chartering business up years ago. Licence to print.'

'Saw 'em heading over to the café for brekkie,' Lucas said. 'Looked like they're dressed for golf rather than a fishing trip.'

'Won't look like that when we're finished with 'em,' Steve replied.

'Let's just eat at Reno's tonight instead.'

'Gotta be another time, mate. Little Thumbtack's first day skippering. He's all grown up now. Just got his ticket. Makes me the shitkicker and I'll be too knackered. Be gorillas in the mist by then, too.'

Lucas chuckled at the rhyming slang. 'Thought you banned drinking on the boat.'

'Rules for some, mate.' Steve gave a wide grin.

'Congratulations Thumbtack.'

'Cheers Lukey, glad it's all over. Never read much other than a charge sheet. Almost had to learn words again.'

Despite Thumbtack's sometimes strange and uneasy presence, Lucas always had time for him. Steve relied heavily on him because he lived in town, unlike most of the blow-in deckhands.

'Hey listen,' Steve said, 'the girls are working in the shop. Grab some fish on the way past.' He sold his fish from a wooden stall at the base of the pier.

'Can't, I'm walking, might drive back later on.'

'Sure, buddy. Weather's gonna turn faster 'n Elton John overnight. Let's catch up tomorrow?'

'Have to be early, Carmen's heading home straight after lunch. Call me.' He began to walk off.

'Okay … hey,' Steve called, 'another boat's coming in soon. Couple of bludgers called in crook this morning, wanna help unload? Otherwise, gotta delay the charter for an hour.'

'Can't do, sorry. Not going home stinking of fish.' He shrugged. 'I'm off to find Horry, need anything from the bakery?'

'Sandwiches. Tell that useless Afrikaans to get his arse into gear and bring 'em over.'

'No probs.' Lucas headed back down the pier. Clyde watched Thumbtack to see if there was more fish coming his way before trotting after his master.

———

Forests of kelp streamed on the current beneath the pier, reminding Lucas of the days when as kids, he and Steve and another mate, Nat squid jigged and pried abalone off the rocks surrounding the pylons on days of no surf.

Cloudbanks now hid most of the sun, allowing only shafts of sunbeam to hit the surface, casting a wintry smear the colour of burnt silver. A handful of surfers waited it out on the bank in front of the lifesaving club. Further out a longboarder searched for a distant set, but the swell was nothing more than a pulse on a flat ocean.

He crossed the Great Ocean Road to the hub of St Claire. A block down, Horry's white ute was angled in front of his bakery. Lucas found him seated outside Tom's café dressed in whites, hands tucked behind his head, no sign of being awake beneath the sunnies until the boyish grin stretched a little.

'Had coffee yet?' asked Lucas.

'Nuh.' A hand came down. Clyde accepted a pat.

Inside, Tom was serving breakfast to the businessmen taking up the largest table. Laughter and pitched voices dulled to murmurs as they tucked in.

'Hey Tom. Morning Betty,' Lucas said with caution to the cantankerous old bitch who always sat alone near the counter. *"Good morning"*, was more than most locals would dare say to Betty. Any tirade might be unleashed, any given day. Only a grunt returned without raising her nose from the paper. Lucas dropped coins in the till, left open for tax reasons during the early hours of each day.

Outside, Clyde had two paws up on Horry, licking jam off his apron.

'Shouldn't let him do that.' Lucas took a seat.

'I'm done,' Horry replied, 'Connie's in the shop.' After almost twenty years in St Claire, his South African accent was still as broad and clipped as the morning air was brisk.

One of the businessmen came out and tipped some bacon rind on the path. Clyde ditched Horry.

'Thanks,' Lucas said.

'No probs,' the man replied. 'What type of dog is he?'

'Ridgeback mostly,' Horry said.

'Yeah, can see a bit in him.'

'We don't really know,' Lucas said, 'Vet reckons maybe greyhound, possibly mastiff too.'

'He's nice looking.' The man went back inside, Tom brought their coffees out.

'How's Carmen?' Horry asked.

'Okay.'

'Just okay?'

'Tired from the long drive,' Lucas replied, trying to convince himself. When they'd arrived home from Reno's, she dozed off on the couch within minutes, despite them not having seen each other for three weeks. Perhaps she really was tired. Might've been the four glasses of wine. When he woke she was in the bed, but he let her sleep in, thinking it best to take Clyde for a walk into town.

'You guys still coming out later on?'

'Ja. Connie's put food out.' They heard a familiar rolling noise. Ca clunk ca clunk ca clunk. A teenager rounded the corner on a skateboard, carrying a surfboard with a wetsuit slung over the nose, taking no notice of the men as he passed.

Lucas had an idea. 'Hey kid.'

The boy turned his head, but rolled on, arching his back to balance.

'Grommet,' Lucas called, a little louder.

The kid slammed down the tail of the board and skidded. 'You gonna tell me off for riding on the footpath?'

'No, thought you might want to earn some cash?'

The face lit up, the attitude left. He skated back. 'How?'

'Got any other mates in the water?'

'Won't be far away.'

'All right then, keep an eye out for the next fishing boat to come in. Big Steve needs a hand to unload. Take your mates out to the pier.'

'Sure, I know Big Steve. How much does he pay?'

'You tell him no less than twenty bucks an hour each,' Horry said, grinning. 'Cash.'

'Awesome. What's ya name again?'

'Lucas,' Horry replied. 'Ask for thirty and work down.'

Lucas slapped Horry's arm.

'Awesome, thanks heaps.' The boy skated off down the path.

'Made that grommet's day,' Horry said, laughing.

'Reckon so. Steve wants those sandwiches, too.'

'Connie's got it sorted,' Horry said, leaning back. He stretched his arms over his head, groaning in frustration. 'No waves Lukey boy, driv'n me nuts sitting around. Let's go on tour down the coast.'

'Next week maybe, swells about to pick—'

'What are you doing out here on your own?' A concerned female voice caught them both off guard. Their table was the third along the shop front, several metres from the door where the woman, wearing a fawn coloured turtleneck was crouched down, stroking Clyde beneath the chin with long pink nails. Smiling in ecstasy, his tail whipped the concrete, eyelids closed over. The woman appeared young, although a dark wall of straight hair shielded her face like the teeming curtain of a waterfall.

'You're such a beautiful boy,' she said. The tail thumped harder.

'Reckon he's in love,' Horry said, under his breath.

'Don't take much.'

A white and black pug tied to the bike rack started up a jealous snarl. 'Hush Dimi,' she said over her shoulder, then turned her attention back to Clyde, speaking louder.

"You could get hit by a car out here.' She tucked her hair behind her ear exposing the high cheekbones, a jaw line cut perfect like a hockey stick. The whitest row of superb teeth gleamed back.

'Why isn't he on a lead?'

Before Lucas could answer, she continued, 'He could get killed on the road.'

Lucas rolled his eyes up and down the empty road.

'You guys know whose dog he is?'

Lucas found his tongue. 'He's—' *bugger it,* '—he's Andy's dog.'

'Andy?' She pointed into the café. 'The cook?'

Lucas raised his eyebrows and nodded, choosing not to say yes, holding back a grin.

She patted Clyde on the head. 'You stay here, boy. Don't move.'

As she walked into the shop, Lucas noticed her tight denims and how tall she really was, such a dominating physique. Shoulders were naturally pinned back, six foot, maybe six one despite the flat beach shoes sporting a white rubber strip around the bottom, similar to the old gym boots his dad favoured. The businessmen all looked up, mouths open, chewing slowly. She spoke to Tom at the counter.

'What the fuck did you do that for?' Horry said, laughing.

'Touros, mate, I'm over 'em coming down here, telling us what to—'

'Oh hoh, you dickhead. She's no touro, works in the pub. Connie talks to her in the bakery all the time.'

She *had* known who Andy was, straight away. Lucas rarely went to the pub, but he did know that when Andy wasn't surfing or working, he'd be found in the Triple Finn Hotel, the town's only pub. Andy was British.

A warm flush of guilt tinged his brow. 'Can't be local?'

'Been round for a while mate, you really have to get out more.'

The TV on the café's back wall showed a weather map. She marched straight past through into the narrow brick hallway leading to the toilets, and the kitchen. Lucas guessed she was not going to the toilet. 'Why didn't you say something?'

'You're kidding me. And miss that.'

'Yeah. Real funny. Think we'd better clear out.'

'Ja, I reckon so.' Horry hurried off toward the bakery. Lucas walked beside him. 'Piss off. Don't follow me.'

'Gonna stick my head in an oven,' Lucas said. He turned to Clyde who stayed beside the door, staring into the café, drooling. 'Hurry up, you.'

_____

A short time later Lucas left Horry's bakery and crossed over to the beach. Clyde ran ahead chasing gulls beneath the trees lining the foreshore. With a loaf of bread swinging in his hand, he strolled toward the Yellow Rock, a small semi-detached section of the Bluff which continued out as reef below the waterline, forming the eastern tip – or the hook as the locals called it – of Fishhook Bay.

The moment his feet hit the sand, eyes were upon him. He glanced back at the café. The little white dog towed her across the road toward him, so he waved, apologetically.

Best option for now, he figured. Maybe she's got a sense of humour. Perhaps she's just walking her dog. Instincts warned him both were unlikely. He crossed Modey's Creek, barely ankle deep as it cut walls through the sand toward the ocean. Without looking back, he hurried along the short stretch of beach to the Bluff. He'd have to run for a bit to make it home before the rising tide cut him off, he didn't want to have to swim. He reached the Yellow Rock and began to climb.

_____

Twenty minutes later Lucas waded through knee-deep shorebreak, passing the last section of cliff beneath the Bluff. He rounded the corner and trudged up the beach to his house. A towel fluttered on the deck wiring, he used it to dry off Clyde. The light easterly pressed his damp shorts. Thoughts turned to a warm shower before hopping back into bed with Carmen.

He leaned forward, resting his elbows on the deck rail, gazing out across the ocean.

'It's as flat as a shitcarter's hat out there, me boy.' His grandfather's voice flooded his mind. He turned, half expecting to see the old rocking chair moving back and forth inside the window. A silhouette appeared through the glass. Carmen stood inside the door, dressed.

A bag at her feet.

4

Lucas checked the rear mirror, the car behind was still tailgating, a deadly game often played by impatient drivers on the tight bends of the Great Ocean Road.

A haunting reminder of the accident sprung to mind.

But he knew this stretch better than anyone. As the car behind closed the gap again, he slammed the stick back to second and pulled away. Headlights traced out over a black ocean. He accelerated the old Porsche through the first high, sweeping bend, down into the hairpin. The car behind couldn't keep up. He eased through the last corner before negotiating the turn off to his property.

Springs creaked and moaned, water leapt out of potholes along the bush track. Clyde greeted him at the house. He lifted his board and wetsuit from the front seat and together they climbed the stairs.

Missed calls, all from Carmen. Last night Horry and Connie came out and shared a consoling beer, but real solace was only found in the water, a Sunday evening surf at Boneyards with a troubled mind for company. A new swell meant a new beginning, again, despite the guilt he felt for not taking Horry.

Sue stared back from the wall unit. Outside, the ocean roared. Inside, the heaviness crammed his mind, that other faithful dog. He didn't believe in Gods or spirits, nor did he believe the souls of his family lurked in dark corners. Carmen had returned some form of life to the house.

The instant he opened fridge he decided against cooking. Reno's would have to do. Company was required. He threw a chicken neck on top of the dry food, it got sniffed, but instead

Clyde stood on his back legs and stretched up, digging his front claws through Lucas's tee shirt. The dog could already sense his moods.

He slapped Clyde's flank. 'You stay here boy.' A sorrowful look returned and Lucas left, ploughing back up the track. Within minutes he crossed the bridge over Modey's Creek where the sign read,

WELCOME TO ST CLAIRE
THE JEWEL IN THE CROWN OF THE GREAT OCEAN
ROAD

Despite the bricks life kept hurling, he never tired of his hometown's serenity.

The main street was quiet, void of weekend tourists and day-trippers. Reno had only two tables occupied, a middle-aged couple and a pair of young lovers seated in a dim corner.

He nodded at Lucas while serving the older couple. The blonde wife rocked back, laughing at a comment Reno had made. His magnetic personality, a quintessential trait for the survival of business through the quieter months along the coast. Lucas found an opened Shiraz at the counter, poured a glass then pulled the kitchen curtain aside and said hello to Stella, Reno's wife. He ordered a Caesar and sat beneath the window overlooking Fishhook Bay and the pier lights. The moon cut a slivering path, broken only by fresh swell. He thought of Carmen. Sue's face appeared.

"Reality, son. Face it full on. It's always behind you, always in front of you," came the ever-grooming, crackling voice of his grandfather. *"The sooner you face the reality of what's happened, the sooner you can start to shape your future. But you can't do that if you're buried in the realities of the past. I've known too many men killed by war, decades after it finished."*

Lips in the glass moved, he realised he was talking to himself repeating the old man's words of acumen. With a tinge of embarrassment he looked across the room. The blonde woman instinctively met his gaze. He shied away toward the young couple. Beneath the table the girl's foot rubbed the young man's ankle.

Sue.

He turned back to the window pondering the dark waters of life.

————

The bell over the door tingled, though it barely registered in Lucas's mind. Nor did he pay attention to the excited group of elderly women shuffling in, until he heard a familiar voice.

'Lucas, oh Lucas, my God is that you?' Sheila Blaxland approached wearing a long golden top over orange slacks, a matching shawl draped over her shoulders. Bronzed cheeks and a vibrant smile lifted his mood.

'Sheila.' They embraced.

'Oh Lucas, darling.' Her eyes glistened. 'How are you, dear?'

'Fine, thank you. What a nice surprise, you look wonderful. Still living in Melbourne?' He recalled his grandfather's funeral; the last time they spoke.

'Thank you, dear. No, just moved back, divorced.'

'Sorry to hear—'

'Don't be, nothing but a cheating bastard.' Then her demeanour changed as caring eyes searched him up and down, betraying sadness. 'Of course I've been meaning to … oh Lucas, I'm so sorry I haven't visited.'

'It's okay.' Everyone took the news of his family's accident differently. Sheila, his mother's dearest friend had never been back out to the house.

Shedding her emotion with typical bravado, she said, 'Join us dear, you must.'

'Course I will.'

The other women crowded in the small foyer studying Reno's wall of fame, as he liked to call it. Anyone famous from Italy made the wall. Models, actors and actresses, sports men and women, even Fangio, though Lucas often pointed out he was Argentinean. *"Italian descent,"* Reno would boast.

He and Lucas set two tables together in the middle of the room.

'We're being joined by one more, Reno,' Sheila said and he placed another chair.

She introduced Lucas to the ladies. Two lived in Melbourne, the third, Mona Braidshaw resided in town. Mona explained to the other women how Lucas had designed and built the house she and her husband purchased when they first arrived in St Claire.

'Remember that house quite well,' Lucas said. 'A most challenging site, spectacular views.'

'We love the house,' Mona said. 'My husband has a telescope on the front deck, we can see whales passing right out at sea.'

'You're a designer, Lucas?' The voice came from the lady at the end of the table. Lucas had forgotten her name already. Clearly drunk, she reeked of cigarettes and wore the drawn face of a lifelong smoker. She stared with drunken innocence, mashing refreshed lips together, reminding Lucas of how Sue had told him beetles were once crushed to make dye for expensive lipsticks. He pictured a big stainless steel vat in some Eastern Bloc country, normally used for making cheese, only this one churned live beetles to a cherry red mush.

'I'm an architect,' he replied.

'Oh. My husband and I want to build a holiday home near the golf club. Can you come and take a look sometime?'

He cut a smile but didn't answer, she was already scrounging through her bag, then retrieved a pen and looked up, straight past him.

'Hello dear, so nice of you to join us,' Sheila said, addressing a much younger woman. The vacant chair slid out opposite Lucas. The chair stopped midway. His turbulent mind raced. The encounter had been so brief he'd somehow suppressed his idiocy at the café the day before. He wondered how. This lady was stunning.

And God-angry.

She remained standing. The chair, gripped by hands, firm as the piercing blue eyes. Lucas thought she was about to push the chair back in but instead she took her seat, smiling uncomfortably at the ladies. Sheila glanced at him. The old hawk had seen the exchange.

Reno held the bottle of red in front of the lady, 'Yes, thank you Reno,' she said, eyeing Lucas.

Sheila cleared her throat. 'Lucas, I'd like you to meet Isabelle. Just finished her shift at the pub.'

She held out her hand, a coy smile. 'Nice to formally meet you, Guv'na.' She pronounced *Governor* in Andy's cockney accent. Tom's cook nicknamed Lucas the *Guv'na* a few years ago when he found out Lucas owned the café building.

A guilt-ridden cord tightened across his shoulders, they shook hands. The touch light, her glare hot. His forehead warmed. 'I didn't realise you're a friend of Sheila's.'

That sounded pathetic.

She pounced. 'So, had you known that I knew Sheila, you wouldn't have lied to me. Are you for real?'

'Excuse me.' Sheila's pencilled brows lowered like a drawbridge.

'I can—'

'No, no, no, Lucas. I can explain, it's okay.' Isabelle's manner was self-assured, even upbeat. 'He lied to me yesterday, Sheila. We spoke briefly at Tom's. According to Andy the cook, you lease the café. *Roight Guv'na.'*

Lucas struggled for words.

Sheila interrupted. 'His grandfather owned it, ran the grocery—'

'Perhaps his grandfather should've have taught him better manners.' She told the ladies her version of the events from the previous morning that had ruined her weekend.

A cauldron of eyes descended on the male.

'I know how bad it sounds … and I do apologise, but—'

'This is all true, Lucas?' Sheila asked.

'Look I can explain, really.' He couldn't, there was a block, couldn't even recall his emotions over the last two days.

'My word you will,' the older lady warned.

'I … I was with Horry, just mucking about, that's all.'

'Andy thinks I'm some sort of a nutcase,' Isabelle said. 'Tom and half the town probably think the same. Haven't been back since.'

'Horry? Horry was with you?' Sheila said. 'As a kid you always blamed Steve, or Nat, now it's Horry.'

'Horry's the nice one,' Isabelle replied, 'the one that *didn't* lie to me. You going to blame your dog next?'

Sheila came to his rescue, somewhat. 'This is your father coming out in you, God rest his soul.' Lucas recognised the old look of disgust. She turned to Isabelle and spoke as if he wasn't present. 'We all loved Lucas's father dearly, but he possessed a twisted sense of humour. Quite often he'd be the only one laughing, too. Used to tell him it's like Tourette's – you know, when they swear and don't realise it. Well, Lucas's father was being un-funny, and didn't know it. They haven't got a name for it yet, surprisingly enough, Christ, everything's got a name nowadays.'

This brought on light-hearted chuckles from the elderly ladies and for the first time that evening, Isabelle smiled; a warm smile, only she directed it at Sheila. Lucas was captivated, the corners of her mouth dimpled into her cheeks. Her tongue sliced provocatively between pristine, white teeth. He remembered the teeth, arranged so orderly, organ pipes filled his mind. She turned her eyes back on Lucas, took a meaningful sip from her wine. Lucas plunged into deep regret. Three simple words, *"it's Andy's dog"*.

'Look I can explain, we get—'

'So … what?' Her head rose, neck lengthened, the shape of a vase. 'Dog laws don't apply to you?'

'The dogcatcher knows Clyde, it was early.'

'Doesn't matter, he should be on a lead. Could get hit—'

'There you go again, telling me what to do.'

She screwed her face. 'What the hell?'

A different tack was required. 'Look, please … please. We cop this all the time. You people come down from Melbourne, tell us how to live, how to drive, how to behave in the surf.'

'You people!' she retorted. 'You obviously have a problem with people from Melbourne.' Her gaze shifted around to the other ladies. 'Or perhaps anyone that exists outside your precious little town.'

He held his palms out in submission, trying to pacify the lady. Thoughts of returning to his own table crossed his mind.

'Guess that didn't come out too well, did it?'

'No.'

'If you just let me explain for a second.'

Isabelle opened her mouth. Sheila raised a hand. 'No dear, let him finish.'

Isabelle sat back, arms folded, silent. All eyes waited on Lucas, again.

'Guess what I'm trying to say is things are a bit cruisier down here. My dog's not used to being on a lead, he behaves himself, you have to understand our way of life.'

Don't say *people like you*, or *you people*. He took a breath.

'My Grandfather used to tell me you can only draw on your own life's experiences, most times, anyway. Of course we don't like it when crew come to our town, trying to impose their ways.' He shrugged. 'It's human nature.'

They stared at each other, finally her gaze wilted. He picked up the bottle, used it as a peace sign by hovering it over her already half empty glass.

She nodded.

He poured the red.

'Is he right?' she asked Sheila.

'On that note, yes, however there's no excuse for rudeness. You will apologise, Lucas.'

'I've been trying to apologise. When my dog rips the bin apart he rolls on the floor and begs forgiveness. I can do that if you like.'

'Not in the restaurant, dear, although … Isabelle, would you—, because I'm sure—'

'A proper apology will do. Might be fun though, watching him roll around.' She licked her finger then looped it through the air causing a sharp uprise of laughter from the women.

'Alright,' Lucas said. 'I'm sorry, really sorry. I did the wrong thing. Sheila's right. I must have had the wrong head on—' He wanted to tell her of a bad weekend. 'There's no excuse.'

'Accepted.' The eyes softened, an upward flicker, the smile began to shine, the savage intent to crucify him, gone. She sipped her wine. He wanted to tell her she had the most beautiful smile, wisdom caught his tongue.

'Can we start again?'

'That's a good idea.'

Silence descended over the table before beetle lips burst into laughter. 'What the hell was all that about?' she asked, handing Lucas the paper. 'Here's the address. My husband would like to chat sometime.'

———

'Are you going to call that woman?' Isabelle asked Lucas. They were strolling along Roy Street through chilled air, up the hill away from the beach. Lucas offered to drive. Isabelle declared she'd much rather walk home, turning her nose at the sand and mud caked on the Porsche. Mona Braidshaw's husband picked up the other ladies after dinner.

'What woman?'

'June. Wants you to design her home. Aren't you excited?'

'Not particularly, I'll recommend a colleague. I don't work for clients.'

'You're an architect, don't you design houses?'

'Sure, but I source my own land and build the house I know will best suit the site.

'So you're a builder too?'

'Yeah. Currently building over on Gloucester Street. Use my own contractors. My mate Patto's a carpenter, does most of the work and I sell through an agent. That way I don't have to deal with clients.'

'But wouldn't you get so much more work from clients?'

'Do all right on my own. Most people have no idea what they want, or what's best for them. Then they tell *me* what to do.'

'That old chestnut.'

'Guess we've run that river dry tonight, huh. Something tells me you enjoyed that, didn't you?'

'Just a little, maybe a lot. We're starting again, remember.'

'Sorry. My father was a builder too. Watched him deal with clients for years. Most were okay. It's the demanding ones that stain your memory. One woman in particular from the Bay, Dixon was her name. Hassled dad for months, changed the plans constantly, pushed and pushed until the contract was finally ready, then got a cheaper quote off another builder. Like Dad's time wasn't valuable. I'd rarely seen him so angry. I was studying at the time, put me right off working with the public. I pitched my ideas to him, he liked them, but kept on building until—'

He knew he had gone too far.

'Until what? He's retired, is he?'

Her question was innocent, still, the dark batch of heaviness rose.

'No.' The wind lifted a gust. Hairs bristled on his neck. 'They died.'

'*They*?'

'Lost my wife, my father and my mother. Car accident in Melbourne, bit over five years ago.' He breathed in and out through his nose, a technique he'd learnt to help ward off a little of the debilitating head pain that could rise further at any second.

She gasped, a hand leapt to her mouth. 'Oh my God. That's terrible, I'm so sorry.'

'You weren't to know.'

'So you ... you were left all alone?'

'My Grandfather died eight months later. Don't know how I would have gotten through without him.' An entire block passed in silence. Of all the responses and sympathetic comments over the years, silence was easier.

Dotted lights from the St Claire District Hospital poked the darkness up ahead. He read the street sign as they passed. 'Roy Street, know who Roy was?'

'Walk down this street every day, never thought about it.'

'The ocean road was built by World War 1 diggers. Roy was a Scottish engineer they brought out.'

'Doesn't seem a good reason to name a street after him.'

'It's not. Old Roy was famous for building a six-hole golf course in the forest, up ahead, along this road. You been for a drive up there yet?'

'Yeah, but didn't go too far past the hospital, bitumen stops just past it.'

'That's where it turns into Bluestone School Road. Only other road out of town, a slow drive, rainforest all the way.'

Isabelle shrugged. 'Would never have guessed there's a golf course up there, given there's already one in town.'

'It's gone now, reclaimed by the forest. Old Roy was a fanatic golfer, never beaten on the old course, so the story goes. Built it with the help of the road workers on their days off. Then the club got the grant for the land in town.'

'So what made you think I'm from Melbourne?'

The question surprised him. She obviously had little appreciation of the effort to hack a golf course out of the rainforest. He'd spent hours listening to his grandfather's stories of the course and the diggers, but like everything that didn't exist anymore, it was just another old story to her. 'Most people that come down here are from Melbourne. Just assumed, that's all. Got that wrong too, huh?'

'Sure did. Drove all the way from Perth.'

'Wow! One hell of a trip. Done it a few times, got mates down south of Perth.'

'It's a stunning coastline, like this one.' They turned the corner of Roy and Surfview. 'This is my street. Hey, can I ask you something that's been bugging me?'

'Anything you like.'

'Yesterday, when you left the café, in a rush I might add, you climbed over the Yellow Rock. Where were you going?'

'Saw you watching me.'

'You even had the gall to wave.'

'Came after me, didn't you?'

'We've moved on.'

' Yeah, okay, my house is down there.'

'On top of the Bluff?'

'No. It's on a small beach in a valley at the end.'

'Oh! I climbed the Yellow Rock once. There's no beach at all, just water and cliff face, far as the eye can see.'

'The Bluff stretches for about two kilometres. You can only get past at low tide, even then it's dangerous.'

'Why do they call it the Bluff? It's just a long wall of cliff face.'

'Who knows? Not even my grandfather knew the answer to that.'

Isabelle stopped at a single fronted brick home. 'Well this is my house.' The blinds moved, the white dog started barking behind the window. 'And that's Dimi. If I don't hurry he'll wake the neighbours again. Don't want my landlord to find out Dimi's inside. Thank you for walking me home.' They shook hands. 'It's been fun. Goodnight Lucas.' She turned and hurried up the driveway.

'Hey, I really am sorry, you know.'

She spun on her heels, walked backwards. 'Forget about it. It's really weird though, bumping into you tonight, after yesterday.'

'Small town syndrome, bites you on the butt, huh.'

'Guess so.'

'Can I call you, do you mind?' He managed the words, despite fearing frayed nerves would trip his tongue.

She stopped, shoulders slumped. 'Can I be honest with you?'

His heart sank.

'After yesterday, I warned myself to avoid you. Didn't want to make a fool of myself, again … and well, I enjoyed tonight, but you told Sheila you've just finished a relationship. So maybe just a drink, sometime, coffee?' She smiled, lifting his spirits.

'Meet you at Tom's.' Was it too forward to ask for her number?

'Okay.'

'Bye.' He concentrated on not breaking his ankle on the curb, walked over the road, waited beneath the street lamp.

A final glance back at her door.

It opened. The light flicked on. She jogged over with a piece of paper.

'My number, for coffee.'

5

The East Coast of Tasmania

The trawler motored past an outcrop of smooth, domed white rock. A strange looking algae, orange, almost rustic in colour clung to the face. Carlo watched the approaching land through the cabin window. A town sat deep in the bowl of a large bay beneath pockets of mist loitering in the surrounding trees. The boat manoeuvred sharp left. A narrow passage led to a hidden inlet. Calm waters. A welcome contrast to long days on a furious ocean. They docked at a small concrete jetty.

Australia.

Where would they come from?

As this day approached, he'd resigned himself to surrender rather than risk being shot by cops. Let them prove who he was.

Banging on the cabin door startled him. Seated on the end of the bed, his head snapped back, eyes fixed on the lock.

Relief came through the skipper's voice, 'Let's go.' Other than at mealtimes they'd hardly spoken since he boarded, somewhere in the middle of the Tasman Sea.

Finally he could put his seasickness to the backburner. Carlo grabbed his bag and stepped out into the icy wind, wiping salt scabs off his face.

Tasmania.

The trees, the hills, and no idea of his location other than somewhere on the east coast of the island. A lone fisherman in a red spray jacket studied the tip of his rod, showing no other concern. Carlo scanned the ramshackle bunch of Colorbond sheds where more trawlers were dry-docked.

FRESH FISH was painted in large letters on a wall of the main building.

No one appeared.

His mother leapt to the forefront of his mind.

Would she forgive?

Would she even accept him?

Today was the only day he hadn't thrown up on the voyage, he'd been doing okay, until now. Fluids suddenly rose, he spat over the edge, breathed in deep and slung his bag over his shoulder, eyeing off buildings, gulping down spit so full of bile it felt like he was swallowing razors.

'Watchya self, gunwale's slippery as shit,' the skipper said. Carlo clung to the ladder rail. Either he or the wharf swayed momentarily, a hand found a rounded bollard, legs found themselves.

A low grunt from the skipper acknowledged the fisherman as they passed. Tobacco smoke drifted by. Carlo focussed down on the concrete jetty. Faces would be remembered like fine weather in this God-forsaken joint. They headed up a ramp between two decrepit walls bricked about three metres high from small, square offcuts of stone with jagged ends, the only remnants of an old, unknown structure claimed by history. He was pleased to see the only car up in the car park was a small blue hatch facing the ocean. A woman would be inside.

They trudged up between a cluster of sheds and down a small, stepped dirt embankment, past a water tank and a shipping container dumped on the ground. From inside the iron box came the monotonous hum of a generator, possibly a cool room. He eyed every corner, every tree, every gap, no boots, no guns, no cops.

They brushed through sodden bracken fern to reach a tiny shed with faded palings. The skipper unlocked the door and motioned with his palm. Carlo ducked beneath the frame.

A garbage bag sat on a chipboard desk under a window frosted by salt and spider webs. 'Get changed, leave the crap ya wearing in that bag.' The skipper left, closing the door.

Forced to memorise in semi-darkness, Carlo managed to dodge ropes, cray pots and old tyres to reach the desk.

Wearing fresh clothes, he emerged back into the bleary afternoon. The sun loomed behind clouds of lead. If it broke, ten degrees might become eleven, regardless, he pulled his sunnies down.

The last pair of woollen socks warmed his feet, first time in a week, although moisture from the long grass threatened to penetrate his leather boots. He longed for a car heater and gave the blue hatch an eager glance.

'Shit,' he whispered.

A tall, skinny-arsed man with a blond ponytail was leaning through the window chatting to the woman, although Carlo couldn't see her.

Anger boiled, he slipped out of sight behind the shed. He assured himself it wasn't a cop, but still dug into the bag for his gun. He slid it inside his jeans beneath his shirt, then moved across the bitumen stretch, stepping over a low, weed-infested cement block wall retaining the car park. As he strolled past the back of the car, the engine started. Carlo kept moving. Gravel crumpled beneath tyres.

'See ya later on in the pub, maybe,' Ponytail man called out, sounding enthralled.

A glance to the side saw the man head off down to the wharf.

The woman had blown it.

He had to contact Benny, find another way to the mainland.

Benny would deal with the woman.

For now, he had to get out of here. Without turning back he moved fast, head down, eyes up, reaching another grass bank. He followed a narrow track leading past the beachfront through scrub between a rock fall and a small fibre cement sheet building. Another carpark, vacant, except for a pile of wooden crates and a fishing boat angled skyward on a trailer.

Dogs barked. His head snapped left. Fit chocolate coloured bodies bolted from the scrub, bounding through shallows, over rocks, chasing. His mind relaxed. He'd grown up with Kelpies. Whether they were working on the farm or fishing the Murrumbidgee River, dogs always accompanied Carlo and his brother Nicky. An elderly couple appeared on the beach. One of the curious dogs ran up to him, its tongue lolled about and hot breath escaped in short clouds. Carlo patted the dog, it was wet, he jerked his hand back. The hatch rolled up alongside as a whistle filled the air. Ears twitched, eyes lit up and the dog ran off.

An uncomfortable sense of not belonging in his homeland washed over.

'Get in,' the woman said.

Carlo hesitated. She was tiny, yet attractive, despite the stern face. He opened the door, squeezed himself in and she drove off.

'Chuck your bag in the back.'

'It's fine where it is.' The pistol jammed into the small of his spine. He pulled it out and rested it on top of the bag between his legs. 'Who the hell was that guy?'

She glanced at the weapon. 'No one.'

'He's someone.'

'Just a local pisshead,' she said, an air of defiance. 'Benny would expect me to fit in. That's what I did.'

Carlo decided not to pursue it here.

After a cold pause, she asked, 'How was your trip?'

'Shithouse, had enough of boats.'

'Bad luck, we're on our way to catch another one.'

'That's a car ferry.'

'Still a boat.'

He disliked her snappy answers and she drove below the speed limit. They passed a town sign. He tried to read backwards in reverse through the mirror but wasn't quick enough.

She dug into her pocket and handed over a small, blue velvet bag. Out dropped a wedding band into his palm.

'Put it on.'

'Shouldn't I propose first?'

'I'll say no. You don't have that option.'

He slid the ring on, stretched his fingers out. 'Feels like I'm wanted.'

'Oh I'm tipping you're wanted all right. Don't get too sentimental, I'm not the type.'

'No chance, hardly know you.'

'I haven't introduced myself. Nadine. Your wife.'

'My wife, huh,' he said. 'Wayne. Apparently.'

'We're the Scunthorpe's.

'Who the hell came up with that?'

'Yeah well, Wayne wasn't my idea either,' she replied. 'Sounds like a backroom office clerk twenty-five years into a forty-five year career. Never sees the sun cause weekends always piss rain for him.'

'And Nadine?'

'Favourite character from a Stephen King novel, left an indelible imprint on a young virgin.'

'A while ago?'

'Long time ago.'

She reached into the console and produced a wallet. 'Tanks full, next stop Devonport. Go through your I.D., give me anything old.'

Carlo did as asked, admiring the manner in which she had assumed control, knowing that would be important before re-uniting with the family.

He turned toward her. 'Indulge me. Who was that man?'

'Nobody, don't worry about it. You stink like fish.'

'That's either spew or wet dog. Don't bullshit me.'

'Look, I checked the place out last week. He's a barstool.'

'You have compromised everything, the whole operation.'

'What the hell are you talking about?' She raised her tone. 'If I screwed him, *then* you could accuse me of compromising my position but you just have to trust my judgment. That boat is from this town, was meant to come in further up the coast until I went and found out the cop station is right across the road from that dock. So I brought you in here.' She sighed. 'Look, he's a fisherman, had to do my research. Best place in a dump like this is the pub, right. He's the only guy in there, except for a couple of old drunks goggling at me full on. We played pool, talked races. Banged on about his ex-missus and miserable fuck'n kids, and most importantly the weather. It's my responsibility to know the weather so I could tell you were on schedule. It's called research. Get used to it. Everyone else in this shithole's working, and this guy's pissed off cause the boat he works on left without him a week ago. Work it out for Christ's sake.' She calmed herself a little. 'He happened to recognise me on his way down to the pier because his boat just got in. So go through your wallet, get to know everything. Address. Credit cards. If we get pulled up, you don't open your mouth. Got it? Not risking having to shoot some nosy cop.'

Carlo ignored the irony and shuffled through the cards. 'What's this orange one?'

'Supermarket loyalty card, get caught without one of those and they'll know your shit's a hoax.'

She checked her watch and turned the radio on, already tuned to the races.

He switched it off.

'Hey. I got a horse running in three minutes.'

'I don't care. Do you know what the Chin will do to you when he finds out?'

'*When*?' She spat.

Carlo absorbed her icy stare and chose not to reply.

'You don't have to worry,' she said. 'Benny and I are thick. He trusted me to bring you in.'

Carlo found himself enjoying her anger, her passion. He relaxed and decided the bag could go on the back seat after all.

But Nadine wouldn't let up. 'I know what you're trying to do. I have no idea who the hell you are, and you must be pretty important for Benny to get involved.' She flicked the radio back on. 'Don't touch it again. I'm in a prick of a mood and got an interest in this horse. He won't win cause he's set for a big race next weekend.'

'What's his name?'

'Mr. Majestic.' She gripped the wheel so tight her knuckles turned white. The horse ran fourth.

Carlo decided not to upset her anymore. His feet were warm.

———

They reached the northern city of Devonport and lined up behind other cars ready to board the Spirit of Tasmania. Night had fallen. The gaping floodlit hull resembled the haunting, square cut mouth of an evil wooden puppet, threatening to deliver him across Bass Strait to a prison cell on mainland Australia. Once they were on the ramp, nerves tightened. No turning back. A stark contrast to the pleasant drive up through the hills on a road called the Elephant Pass from Tasmania's east coast.

'What's wrong with planes?'

'Don't worry about a thing. They don't ask questions and there's no quarantine entering Victoria. You're just another passenger crossing a state border. Take two of these.' She passed a bottle.

'What are they?'

'Seasick tablets, not having you puke in the room.'

An attendant in a fluorescent jacket with silver reflective bands directed them through a lane.

'Any flammables or weapons?' the man asked.

'No,' Nadine replied. She had shown their tickets at an earlier booth.

'Drive straight through.' They drove up the ramp and left Tasmania behind. Carlo wiped the sweat away. Another man directed them in behind the line of cars. She parked and cut the engine. He cracked his door open.

'Close it. Wait till the hull clears, then follow me.'

He hadn't made up his mind whether he liked this officious little woman, her sharp tone, abrupt manner, but he had to accept she was doing a job. After ten long minutes, they had the elevator and then the hallway to themselves. She found their cabin. Inside, a double bed took up most of the room.

'You can't move from here till we dock in the morning. And of course you don't answer the door to anyone.'

'Not going anywhere.' He dumped his bag on the floor, slumped on the bed and closed his eyes. Engines hummed through him.

'What do you want for dinner?'

'Eye fillet, chips, gravy, vegies, salad, whatever, medium rare.'

'You read my mind. I need meat too. Have a shower while I'm gone, get rid of that smell, whatever it is.' And she left.

Beneath the coffee table stood her canvas bag, a lime green sailor's sack with ropes for handles.

She was really taking this sailing thing seriously.

He got up off the bed, spread the top open, dug through the clothes and found a black leather handbag. Inside was make-up, a box of tissues, an envelope stuffed with fifties.

He brushed the envelope aside and almost missed it, except for the dull pink bubble gum coloured frame. The chamber, the snub nose barrel, the grip, all matte finish, gunmetal grey, absorbing light rather than reflecting it. *THE PINK LADY* was stencilled into the barrel – worn from use. Practice, he assumed. The lightweight piece, a 38 fitted neatly inside his palm, possibly made from high strength aircraft grade aluminium. The perfect accessory for a girl who may find herself in a situation she may be forced to defend.

He rolled open the chamber. All five bullets sat neatly in their lethal arrangement. 'Serious little girl,' he muttered, placing the gun back.

She was right; he needed a shower. The water warmed quickly, he rinsed the salt from his stubble and hair. Thoughts turned to Izy.

Would he be able to convince her of his innocence after all these years?

He blocked the thought, focussing on the enjoyment of hot water tingling his skin.

A door clicked. His body tensed. Engines still idled. The boat hadn't left the dock. There were no cries of police, no thudding of boots, his own gun, useless in his bag.

Nadine slipped through the curtain, naked. The cubicle was tight, cramming his shoulders. She craned her neck back. Water cascaded over already pert nipples, surrounded by small, fleshy goose bumps.

'Food will arrive in the next hour.' Fingers strode the length of his cock, already hard. He guessed her to be only a little over five feet tall. Her head reached his chest. 'When you hear a knock, come straight in here, I want to hear the toilet seat drop. Had to bribe the kitchen staff. Cost me two hundred bucks. Told 'em your thalassophobia brings on incontinence, you have to eat in the cabin.'

'My what?'

'Fear of the sea. Research, remember.'

'How sweet,' he replied, rising fully in response to teeth almost puncturing his chest. Moving closer, she expertly caressed him, forcing him to concentrate on not exploding. He lifted her easily, her body lithe and supple, taut, smooth. Her head almost touched the ceiling before legs wrapped around him. She lowered herself gently onto him, sinking teeth into his shoulders. All ten fingers dug into his chest threatening to pierce the map of blue veins. Groaning came as he bit her nipples gently, one after the other, delicious, wet. His eyes closed over, Izy's face appeared.

———

When Carlo woke, early dawn was pouring through the porthole, the blind had been opened. City lights streaked on the still waters of Melbourne's Port Phillip Bay.

His body ached. He longed for a good night's sleep after so many days at sea, but Nadine was a gifted animal; insatiable, and also gone. Terror seized him.

Had she sold him out? Would cops storm the ferry?

He envisioned a prison cell, then consoled himself with thoughts of the many opportunities authorities already had. The flight into New Zealand. The voyage across the Tasman Sea. Engines droned without end. Tense fingers gripped the windowsill. Down on the pier, dock lights picked out workers.

Positive thoughts surfaced. His father had sought out the Chin, for the same reason Benny had chosen the delightful Nadine.

The door clicked and sprung open, his heart skipped.

'Good morning.' She wore a cheery smile, her hair in a bun. 'I've had breakfast, a slave to the metabolic clock routine, but you can wait till we get off the boat.' Her manner was all business. 'Get dressed and pack, then stand by the door.'

Carlo obeyed. She wiped everything down. He became hard again, and sore, just from watching her, relieved she'd returned and also impressed when thirty minutes later they drove off the wharf, through security, no questions at all. She turned left into a nice place called Beacon Cove, reminding him of a gated community in Florida he once stayed in, only without the gate. One minute later they were safely inside the garage of a modern, double storey brick home. Nadine had performed her task well.

6

Touches of mid morning warmth between cloud breaks were disrupted by onshore gusts. Despite the extra care fighting off the dried, split ends since living on this coast, Isabelle preferred the view from outside Tom's café. She still smelt the ocean's drifting scents, heard whispering leaves in the foreshore trees. Sounds – she'd been told – that would leave her after a time.

Sheila's car pulled up.

'Good morning dear,' she said, taking a seat. 'Sorry I'm late.'

'That's okay, just ordered. Long black, right?'

'I'm impressed.'

'Can't take the cred.' Isabelle flicked a glance inside the café. 'Wow! Nice outfit. Shows off your figure.'

'Don't start, things aren't where they used to be. Bought a whole new wardrobe on his card, same day I caught that mongrel in bed with the very same mistress who ruined his last marriage. Funny thing is, I knew not to marry a salesman and still went ahead.'

Isabelle speared a helpless grin. 'Sorry, didn't have much of a chance to chat last night.'

'That's okay.' Sheila was in the pub through happy hour and they arranged breakfast. 'I know Friday's payday, but I've never seen the pub that flat out. The eyes of those young tradies followed your every move like you were a chocolate-coated pizza. Let me guess, your boss has got you working weekends, too.'

'Not every weekend, got today off.'

A young girl served coffees.

'Shall we order?'

Sheila put a hand up to the waitress. 'Not yet, thank you.'

'Speaking of chocolate-coated, how'd you get such a tan around here?'

'Oh, we get plenty of sun,' Sheila said, 'just have to know where to sit, move around a lot, too. You've still got a little colour. Stay down here long enough, you'll turn a lovely white shade of Scottish blue.'

Isabelle giggled. A baby wailed like a siren at the next table. 'Haven't seen you around for a while.'

'Been up in Melbourne, stripping that bastard for every cent. Like peeling skin off his back. Divorce and knowing what's in front of you at sixty-four hardens you right up.'

'What will you do now?'

'Nursing's all I know. Spoke to the hospital, they sound keen.'

'I hope you're okay.'

'Tough as cowhide, dear. Say, we haven't caught up since dinner, what, four weeks ago?'

Isabelle knew the subject would surface soon enough. 'I haven't had a chance to thank you properly for inviting me.'

'My pleasure, we needed the spark of youth and boyo, what a spark you provided. Handled that situation remarkably well.'

'He didn't mean it, we're good now.'

Sheila leaned in close. 'Soooo?'

'Soooo what?'

'Soooo, cut the crap. We all saw him walking you home.'

Isabelle frowned, inside she laughed. 'And nothing else.'

'Settle down. Just have to report back to the girls. I'll make something up, not a problem.' She sipped her coffee, trying to drown her grin.

'Better not,' Isabelle warned.

'Would you prefer they make stuff up themselves? That's how rumours start, you know.'

'Small town syndrome, hey.'

'Exactly, don't get mixed up in the politics round here. Can get weird. They once held a meeting in the Finn to decide whether the pub or the pier should be the town's landmark.'

'The Triple Finn? Why the two N's and how can the pier be a landmark?'

'That's what I said about the pier. You're not just a pretty face. Turned out to be just another excuse for the whole town to all get pissed. And the two N's. The pub was built by a couple of Finnish immigrants, came out after the war. One had a Russian wife but we called her a Finn anyway. New owners come along in the eighties and changed the name. Bit of marketing, that's all ... you know ... a play on the surfing thing. Now, stop changing the subject. What do I tell the girls when they ask?'

Isabelle tried to keep a serious face. 'Not even a peck on the cheek goodnight, tell 'em that.'

'Sounds like your whole sex life would fit on the back of a postage stamp.'

Isabelle winced, despite knowing Sheila was only kidding. If only she really knew. She brushed off the comment. 'I have boundaries, write that down.'

'Boundaries,' Sheila said. 'Let me tell you about boundaries. Boundaries are on the outside of town, not the inside. Everyone knows everyone's business round here, if they don't, they ask me.'

'Not those boundaries.'

'I know what you meant.' Sheila's eyebrows tweaked. 'Those boundaries got me married to that lowlife. My first husband died on me, you know.' She took another sip of her coffee.

'Oh, I'm sorry.'

'Have you seen him since? Lucas?'

'Nope.' He hadn't made any effort at all to catch up. On the morning of the dog incident she'd gone for coffee earlier than usual after a sleepless night. Normally she went to Tom's mid-morning, just before work, and she kept to that routine and hadn't bumped into him again.

'How strange. You two seemed to be getting along so well. On a serious note dear, Lucas is a very, very special man in all of our lives.'

'He told me about his family. It's extremely sad.' Her heart felt heavy, she thought of Lucas often.

'The accident's the worst thing to ever hit St Claire.'

'I can't begin to think,' Isabelle said. The baby fired up again, Sheila's eyes clamped shut, cheeks lifted, scrunching her brow. Isabelle knew the hung-over look too well.

'I feel like exploring,' Sheila said. 'Heard of a new winery up in the forest. We'll be able to eat in sunshine out of the wind.'

'Sounds good, I'll drive, you look like you need a wine.'

'Where's your car?'

'The red one in front of yours.'

'I'm not going in that thing.'

'That *thing* is my Hyundai, got me across the Nullarbor from Perth.'

'Well my Lexus goes back soon, part of the settlement. Until then, we're travelling in style, dear.'

Isabelle relented. They headed east across Modey's Creek and out of town. The ocean road snaked up beneath a cutting wall so close to Isabelle's window she could almost reach out and touch it. In some sections where water seeped down the wall, wire mesh held the face to prevent rockfalls.

'What's the name of the winery?' Isabelle asked.

'Batten Hill.'

'Haven't heard of it.'

Sheila didn't elaborate. Instead she concentrated on slowing to as much as twenty kilometres an hour through the tighter bends. 'Lucas's driveway is just up ahead. Let's call in, see if he's home.' The road twisted away from the ocean, lush vegetation thrived on both sides. Sheila began to brake.

Isabelle became unnerved, yet excited. Since the night at Reno's she'd kept her eye out along this section, but hadn't picked out a driveway on the ocean side, only endless bush stretching to the cliffs. Her caution came to the forefront. 'I really think we should have phoned first, and I'm hungry. We can't just call in.'

'Course we can.'

What the hell are you up to? Isabelle wanted to ask, instead, what came out was, 'Look, we really should keep going.'

'Don't be silly. Believe me, this is something you'll never forget.' She rounded the next bend, slowed and veered over the double white lines onto the wrong side of the road in front of a blind bend. Isabelle gripped the armrest, terrified.

———

Carlo's eyes had closed over while relaxing beside the pool. Nadine's voice interrupted him from inside.

'You ready?'

'Half hour ago, now I'm comfortable.'

She had left at eight a.m. for the hairdressers, returned at nine and taken another hour to get ready for the races. Cox Plate Day was big in Melbourne.

Sun drenched the yard over the hedge guarding the perimeter from neighbours. He liked it here. He had to. This was the first time she was allowing him to leave since arriving a week ago, and the house had a gym.

'You can get comfortable at your meeting.' She appeared in front of him wearing a dress of uncharacteristic white with a laced hem, patterned above the waist with pink and red roses. Tilted sideways on her head was a wide brimmed hat complete with a matching floral arrangement. 'How do I look?'

Anything but an escort, he thought.

'So good I could toss you over, spank you red.'

'Slow down cowboy, right answer wrong time of day. Seriously?'

She pirouetted.

'Stunning. Glamorous. You'll raise tents, not talking about marquees, either.'

She laughed, high pitched. 'Not sure that's just what a girl wants to hear, now fix my hat.' She showed him how to clip the hairpins, then locked the house.

Benny had replaced the Festiva with a blue Landcruiser. They drove through manicured streets boasting shiny SUV's and houses with orange terracotta or grey tiled roofs, no eaves, no flair, no variation. Cardboard cut-outs tended their gardens. Financially plotted monochromatic lives sucked dry to their credit-ridden bones by institutions, governments and the pressure to keep ahead of the mirrored faces next door. They passed a row of apartment buildings and headed away from the bay through a crowded Port Melbourne shopping strip. Nadine found a side street, then another, and another.

'Know where you're going?'

'Course I do. These streets are all the same, Benny owns houses in every one.' She squeezed up yet another narrow car-lined street and parked outside a fake-brick sheeted home with an overgrown garden, a lean-to carport. 'I'll wait here until you're inside.' She leaned over. 'Give me a kiss, make me feel like I matter.'

He laughed and kissed her cheek.

'Wish me luck.'

'You won't need it. You look amazing.'

'Another compliment, how sweet, must be doing my job right. Now off you go.' He walked up the driveway, grinning.

———

'Sheila! What the hell? You can't do a U-turn here.' Isabelle expected another car to sweep around the bend and T-bone them, but Sheila steered in behind a thick bush of blooming white spring buds. Native grasses, along with the bush hid the start of a dirt track.

'Boy! Thought we'd get cleaned up for sure.'

'All under control, dear.' Sheila dodged the potholes with experience past an open gate rusting off its hinges, a letterbox and a private property sign. Trees strangled out the sunlight. Black boys and shin-high ferns thrived in the shade, scraping the undercarriage.

'These trees are creepy,' Isabelle said.

'Moonahs, stringybarks, I s'pose, nuthin' but weeds his grandfather used to say. Anytime he wanted to do some work, half the job would be trimming the damn things to get trucks in.'

The car stopped at a small rise, the track dropped away. Sky and ocean opened over a deep valley. Isabelle gasped.

'What do you think?' Sheila said.

'It's breathtaking.'

'Sure is.' Sheila pointed through the windscreen. 'Take a look at the cliff, left hand side.' In the distance, a towering, monolithic face of jagged ledges defied the ocean. Perched on top was a crown-like rock formation, seemingly poised to topple into the sea at any moment. A line of greenery showed where a creek flowed to the ocean beside the cliff.

Sunrays glinted off a roof amongst the trees. On the opposite side of the valley, the wall of the Bluff ended at a dramatic corner, retreating away from the ocean, eventually becoming one with the bush. The drop seemed much higher here than back at the St Claire end.

'Hard to believe,' Sheila said, 'between the wars no one wanted this hunk of land. A farmer owned the whole area for miles. When they built the road this section was cut off. Lucas's great grandfather picked it up for a song.'

'How tall's that cliff?'

'Hundred, hundred and fifty feet I guess, maybe more. Decent old climb.'

'You've been up there?'

'Not since I was a kid. Lucas's mother, Liz and I knew every inch of this land.'

'What's on the other side?'

'Just rocks and sand. The cliff continues further east and rings behind the entire beach. There's a track leading down from Lucas's side. Only other way in there is from the next point, couple of miles away. Long walk though.'

Isabelle focussed on the view. 'What are you up to?'

'What the devil are you insinuating? This is a part of St Claire not many people ever get to see.'

Isabelle rolled her eyes, catching Sheila's mock look of surprise. 'You're setting me up, you cunning old—'

'Watch your mouth. You don't know me well enough yet. Cunning, I can handle. Old. Don't start. Let's see if he's home.'

Isabelle smirked, Sheila accelerated down the slope. They emerged into a clearing past a wooden shed. Its roof was coming away in one corner, peeling up toward the sun leaving a gaping hole. 'One of the workers' huts, over 80 years old,' Sheila said as they approached the home constructed of timber panelling allowed to grey off and weather. A popular trend Isabelle had noticed in this district. Slatted timber shades strung on chains protected large windows, even extending around the butt jointed corner panes. The only other structure was a concrete water tank with drainage pipes running from the roof. The blue Porsche was parked in shade beneath the outside stairs.

'Car's there,' Isabelle said.

'Can't believe he's still got that heap of junk. Must be thirty years old. Look at the mud.'

'Does he ever clean it?'

'Appears not.'

Up on the deck the dog from the café had his head stuck through the wiring, barking profusely. When the car stopped it raced down the stairs and circled with a stiff tail, hackles raised on the short, fawn coat. Curled lips shuddered, menacing teeth were exposed.

'Must be the dog you two were discussing at dinner?'

'Yeah. Only patted him once at the café.'

The dog prowled outside Sheila's window. 'I'm not moving until Lucas comes down.'

They waited. No one came out.

'You sure he's home?' Isabelle asked.

'Perhaps not, heard he's still got his father's four wheel drive.'

An unexpected release of tension washed through Isabelle, though her curious side wanted to see this private beach. 'We've come this far. Hope he remembers me. Wait here.' She opened the door a little.

The dog snapped.

'Get back in,' Sheila said, but Isabelle stepped out.

'It's okay boy.' She spoke in a hushed tone. Fear rose, so did the thrill of the challenge. The snout retracted, the dog growled, but in a slightly less threatening manner.

'He remembers me ... I think.' She held the back of her hand forward, as her father had taught her.

Rear paws scraped the sand in bull-like fashion, ready to charge.

She crouched, fearful, cautious, yet trusting. 'Hey boy ... it's okay.'

'Be careful.'

'We're connecting here. Aren't we boy.' She rubbed the tips of her fingers together. 'Andy the cook mentioned his name ... I can't remember it ... come on, boy.' The tail swayed once, the dog took a step forward, growling softly, whining too. 'I think it's Clem or Clarrie; Cliff, maybe, some silly old – Clyde!'

The dog's ears pricked, the tail wagged.

'That's it, Clyde, come on, Clyde.'

Clyde walked up and accepted a pat, leaning his body against hers. She stroked his back, the tail whipped. He whined and sniffed, licked her hand. 'Good boy, Clyde. You're beautiful. The roof of my mouth is tingling. It's like there's an energy passing through him. He's just as scared of us, too.'

'You sure he's okay?'

'He's fine.'

'Positive?'

'Yes, come on. Hop out.'

As soon as the door opened, the dog took off around the car and started barking once again before Isabelle could grab hold. Sheila slammed the door shut.

'Clyde! No!' Isabelle chased the dog. He succumbed easily. She grabbed the collar, stroking his back. Though she felt bad about it, she couldn't help giggling.

'What are you laughing at?' Sheila snapped through a gap in her window.

'Oh, he's just a big pussycat.' She ruffled the dog's ears, he returned a lick to her face.

'Get back in the car. We're leaving this minute.'

'You're the one who wanted to come here. I'll take him around the front, see if anyone's there. Come out when we're gone.' Isabelle ran beneath the deck toward the beach calling the dog. Clyde followed.

———

The old fly wire door cranked on a rusty spring. Benny the Chin stared up with his traditional, passive Chinese game face, round and ageless, lips firm. Carlo was reminded of icons

Nadine downloaded onto his phone. Thin streaks of hair were combed over liver spots. Except for a tuft of whiskers on the point of his chin there was little evidence of ever knowing the requirement to shave.

'G'day Benny,' Carlo said, patting his shoulder. The other hand accepted a wet-fish handshake.

'Everything okay, you late,' Benny said, slaughtering his R's and L's, though few people mistook Benny's broken English. He held the door open, always watching. Despite his age, Benny's eyes shone with the serene superiority only the Chinese could portray. Stories behind those eyes could sell newspapers, bestselling underworld books, fill prison cells with politicians and the affluent.

Carlo turned his shoulders so not to catch his shirt on the timber frame. 'Got lost Benny, instructions weren't too flash, mate.'

'No, no. Instructions good. She my best girl.'

'Not wrong about that.'

'Uh, uh.' He grunted, pointing down.

'Sorry mate, forgot the old custom.' Carlo slipped off his boots.

'Custom. Customs uh. How customs treat you?' And Benny laughed the strangest sound, re-igniting Carlo's memories of the many times Benny visited his father over the years. The laugh normally fired up after he'd sunk his first glass of grappa. 'Hi hi hi hi hi.' His face came alive with his jittery laugh, segmented, syllabic, each ridiculous noise spent a breath on its own.

Carlo grinned. 'Thank you so much for everything, mate.'

Benny's face took on a sharp expression. 'Follow me.' He bowed, turned, padded in his socks silently through a living room. Carlo followed into the kitchen and was confronted with a force field of pungent cooking odours. 'For God's sake Benny, for all the money don't tell me you live in this stinking place.'

'Hey!' You can't say that. This is girlfriend's house.'

'Aren't you married?'

'Yeah, sho sho.' He pronounced *sure* like *sho.* 'Wife not come here. This is girlfriend's house.' The peculiar laugh ignited again. He enjoyed his own jokes, laughter continued down a narrow hall, Carlo followed. The light fitting hanging at eye height reminded him of a speedball, he dodged it left. They reached another living room, another odour, this time cigarette smoke.

A familiar voice greeted him. 'Carlo. Get your arse over here.'

———

When Isabelle reached the front of the house, or the back – she didn't really know – it surprised her how isolated this valley was.

She knelt in the dampness at the apex where the beach fell away to the ocean. Only her footprints existed here. Waves lined up and crashed on the sand and on outcrops of shiny black rock with checkered fissure cracks, found on nearly every beach along the ocean road.

Above her the oppressive peak of the Bluff seemed to overhang the ocean. Tide lapped up high, no sign of the beach Lucas used to walk from town. On the face were dark stains several metres high. Never before had she seen swells like those lashing this coastline through winter. They swamped the Yellow Rock on the biggest days, cascading over the sea wall in the tiny harbour. Locals in the bar told the most amazing survival stories of the Lock Ard and other shipwrecks further along this coast. On certain days she couldn't believe how anyone could survive this wildest of oceans.

The Bluff wall facing the sea ended at ninety-degrees, continuing inland past Lucas's house. To her left the cliff on the east side bore exactly the same streaks.

ALL MINE

Epochs came to mind. She'd learnt of epochs at school. Times scaled in shaded lines of age, equal in height. The cliff looked much higher up close despite being at least a couple of hundred feet away. The base cut into the ocean like the bow of an icebreaker ship.

This was the real St Claire. She could feel it. Almost touch it.

Through her modelling days in Sydney, she experienced many photo shoots on private beaches. At the time they were amazing. None had provided a nostalgic joy like this setting.

There was simply nothing here. No false, controlled environment. Only peace, raw, untamed, secluded, secrets of time hidden amidst waves and their relentless continuity. She wriggled further into the sand, delighting in the contrast of warm sun and cold wind through her hair, struggling to remember such happiness.

Since the murders she had not picked up a magazine. No longer did she have to force herself to shy away from a newsagents stand. She cast the thought, folding her knees to her chest. Her dress was damp, though it didn't matter. Clyde appeared, leaning his bulk in, she slung an arm over. 'For a guard dog, you fail miserably.'

Something moved high up on the Bluff wall where sunshine raked the face. The only shadow was in a crevice, her neck hurt. She was about to turn away, it moved again.

A bird?

Several feet to the right of the crevice, steps were carved into the sandstone. Half way down they disappeared behind the scrub ending somewhere at the base. She checked the crevice again – nothing.

Next impulse was to feel the ocean. Visiting this paradise would not be complete otherwise. She approached the water's edge, lifting her dress, stepping in up to her knees, surprised to feel reef and slimy weed beneath her feet. A wave heaved and clawed, foamed and retreated, soaking the hem of her dress. A squeal of delight came as she darted back.

Sheila sat up on the deck, now. It stretched across the home's width, continuing down both sides around the entire perimeter, supported by angled steel posts into the sand. Beneath the deck was a glass door next to a small wooden boat. Two magpies were perched on the side wasting warbles into the wind. No concrete pathways, no pavers, not even a step down from the door, just golden sand.

'Anyone home?' Isabelle called out.

Sheila ignored her, so she called out again, this time louder. The distance wasn't great. She must've heard.

Something was wrong. Isabelle climbed the stairs to the deck and peeked through the windows. The interior seemed spacious and modern, her gut tightened. 'Should we even be up here?'

No answer came. Side on, Sheila wore a vacant, perhaps troubled, expression.

'You okay?'

'Yes. Yes, of course.' She made an effort to smile. Isabelle caught her face, awash with grief.

'You've been crying.'

Sheila turned away. Clyde sniffed her. 'Get away from me,' she snapped.

'Umm. He likes you.'

Sheila relented, gave him a wary pat on the head.

Isabelle sat down on the edge of the lounge, a tentative arm slipped around the older woman.

'What's wrong?'

'It's fine, really.'

'Please, we're friends.'

After a moment Sheila finally said. 'I didn't know if this would happen, so many good times, so many years. I knew this would be difficult. After the funerals … I … I've seen Lucas, of course, but couldn't come to this house. Should have been here for him, I wasn't. We used to say St Claire looks after her own.' She wiped her eyes dry. 'I ran off to Melbourne.'

'You got married.'

'That's no excuse, I grew up here. Lucas's mother, Liz and I would walk home from school along the Bluff top every day. There's a track, leads into town. We'd swim out to the rock pools. You can't see them at the moment because the tide's up, and there's this reef, such a long way out. Lucas and his friends surf this huge wave, even have a name for it.'

'A name for a wave? Heard they do that. Seems a bit silly, not as if it's a cat or a dog.'

That's what I reckon too, but the size, oh it's incredible. Liz would be petrified, but those boys are so skilful, so fearless.'

She poised, her lips moved slightly like she was thinking aloud, before she spoke again.

'You know ... there was a time, four or five years, can't quite remember, when I actually lived here with Liz and Lucas's grandparents. My father, bastard of a man, slept out here as often as I could at first.' Her tone sharpened. 'He'd come looking for me. Ron, Lucas's grandfather wouldn't make me go. They would argue, eventually I stayed. Last time I ever saw my father they stood almost toe to toe at the track behind us. Ron held a shotgun, warned my father to take one more step. I remember willing him forward. Ron was the most honourable man, yet hardened by war. My father knew he'd shoot.'

She burst into tears, dropped her head, sobbing. 'And I prayed he would.'

Isabelle hugged her, wondering if her own life wasn't so bad after all.

Sheila drew a breath and gathered herself before wiping her eyes. 'We ... we all lived in a tiny old house Lucas's grandfather and great grandfather built between the wars. Lucas and his father built this one. Liz and I were like sisters.

Used to top and tail in a single bed. His grandmother – she died not long after Lucas was born – would have rows of timber crates beneath netting on the old deck where she grew all her own vegetables. Only natives survive in the dirt around here, they trucked in soil, fruit trees grew in big pots behind the house. Ron built a timber fence so they'd get all day sun and protection from the wind. Even grew enough to sell in the grocery store. Liz and I worked there as kids, and see that old rocking chair inside the window. That was his grandfather's. Can still see him rocking on the old deck, smoking his pipe, puffing away, boy, those old windows rattled a tune.' She huffed out a small laugh. 'I was upset when Lucas and his father tore the old house down. My blood was on that deck, nails'd pop up everywhere.'

Isabelle rubbed Sheila's hand. She felt great sympathy, also, part envy. Thoughts of her own upbringing entered – a strict religious environment, then modelling. 'I think I would have liked to have grown up here.'

'It was a lifetime of fun. I'm half expecting Liz to walk through that door with a bottle of chardy. Never had to chill it in winter. This coast can be the coldest place on God's earth, but it's our home. Sorry to put you through this, dear.'

'It's okay, really. Why did you come here, if you knew it would affect you like this?'

'Didn't think I'd get this upset. Drive past all the time. Thought a tough enough old broad could put it behind. I should have been here for Lucas.' She sniffed, fighting back more tears.

Isabelle tried to console her, rubbing the hand some more. 'You were grieving too. He would have had his own friends to help him through.'

'Oh, he did, they're such a close-knit group, the young ones. Shouldn't say young; all mid-thirties by now, baby-sat them all. After the funerals it was much easier just to leave.'

'Grief changes us. Don't be so hard on yourself.'

Sheila's face tightened. 'Can you not get angry at me if I tell you something?'

'Of course not.'

'Thought it might be easier if someone came out with me. It was. Thank you.'

'Don't mind, really.'

'Look at you, so young. Don't make the same mistakes I've made in my life. Love the people who love you. Give the rest their due, if they're nice, be nicer back. If they're not, then you stand up for yourself. Seen you do that in spades, young lady. But love the ones who love you, most important thing in life.' A gust of wind lifted thinning hair across her cheeks. 'I let someone down who I love so dearly. Not everything is as it appears to be.'

"Not everything is as it appears to be."

Bloodied bodies punctured her mind, bullet holes, like singed ink spots, photos, imbedded sounds of the penthouse door being busted down. Guns, arrested, handcuffed.

"Should drag you down the morgue myself you rich little harlot. Show you what he did to our men. Where the fuck is he?"

The raining spit she couldn't wipe off, the smell of the detective's hot tobacco breath.

"Not everything is as it appears to be."

'Are you all right?

'Isabelle ... Isabelle ...'

Hands on her shoulders. A chilly gust on beads of sweat awakened her senses. 'I'm okay.'

'You went blank, dear.'

'No, no, I'm fine,' she replied, not really knowing what had happened, or for how long. 'Some sort of a hot flush, I guess.'

She paused to collect herself, but the older lady's caring eyes penetrated, they searched. 'There's something I don't understand, dear. How is it you're here on your own? Looking like you do, so much love in those eyes.'

Instincts told her that had been coming. 'Guess that's the way life is.'

Sheila wasn't satisfied. 'There's worry in you. What is it, dear?'

Isabelle could only stare back, unable to lie to this lady. All she could offer was an unbreakable silence.

Sheila didn't press the point. 'Maybe we can talk about it someday.'

'There's just ... some things I have to let go of.' She collected her composure, changed the subject. 'The night at the restaurant, why didn't you tell me about Lucas's family? You could have taken me aside.'

'Perhaps I did throw you in at the deep end. Sorry.'

Isabelle nodded and tapped Sheila on the knee. 'Let's go and get some breakfast? We can come past on the way home, maybe he'll be back by then.'

Sheila's face lit up. 'He'll have something. Let's go inside.'

'What? We can't just—'

'We do whatever I say round here.' Sheila stood and tried the door handle. 'Hmmm, locked, we'll fix that.' Clyde let out a low growl. 'Don't you think of biting me now, you upstart.' She raised a finger at the dog, Isabelle found herself grinning again.

'Come and help me.'

Isabelle followed to the far end of the deck past what appeared to be an office, two bedrooms, all with sliding door access. At the far corner stood a large clay pot with a plant struggling for life. Sheila rubbed the dirt. 'Hasn't been touched for years, I bet.' She knelt down. 'Lift up one side.'

'Why?'

'Just do it.'

Isabelle heaved, the pot lifted enough for Sheila to rummage around.

'Got it.' She held up a rusty key. 'Some things never change.'

She marched back up the deck. Isabelle peered into a glass door at an unmade bed. Clothes were strewn over the end rail, a golf bag full of clubs stood in the far corner. The bedroom was otherwise clean.

'Come inside.'

Isabelle followed back along the deck, they entered through the main glass door.

'Classy Lucas,' said Sheila.

Isabelle grinned when she saw the older lady's point of focus. Beside the fireplace stood a clothes rack with boxers and socks drying by the window on the opposite side of the room. 'Are you telling me I wouldn't see that in your house?'

'God help you,' Sheila said.

The home was tidy, natural light gleamed off timber floors. Cabinetry along one wall ran the length of the room, photos – *his family, all dead* – sat below a flat screen. The furniture consisted only of a white modular suite, an eight-piece wooden dining table and the rocking chair beneath the corner window overlooking the ocean.

'Don't know much about architecture,' Isabelle said, 'but an interior designer once told me that black, tan, white and grey is the most easy-on-the-eye colour scheme.'

'All subjective. Me, I need a bit more colour. He's re-decorated since his mother passed, thank God. Liz was terrible with décor. And this is new.' Sheila strolled over to the fireplace and rubbed her hand along the sandstone hearth.

'Same stonework they used on the Park Hyatt.'

Sheila looked up. 'In Sydney, right on the Harbour, I've stayed there. Aren't you from Perth?'

Isabelle cursed her tongue. 'I, uh, I grew up in Sydney. Moved to Perth when I was twenty.' Hunger gripped. 'Let's find some food.'

But Sheila wasn't swayed. 'You've made some big moves for a young lady.' Isabelle walked away into the kitchen without answering, ignoring the look of concern. Relief flooded through when Sheila seemed to brush it off by saying, 'Find some bread, I'll see if he's got eggs.'

Isabelle began searching the pantry.

The fridge snapped open. 'Oh look what he's left, just for me.' Sheila held up a bottle of white, half full. 'Might have one now. Trick is to only have one more after lunch, then a snooze, keeps me ahead of the pack. I'm meeting the girls for a five o'clock chardy at the Finn, you're welcome to join us.'

'Might just do that. Sticking to coffee for now, and there's no bread in here.'

'Stop looking, found it in the freezer.' Sheila closed the fridge. Clyde gave a dejected look, waited, then wandered away.

'Open the fridge again,' Isabelle said.

'Why?'

'Open it. You'll see.'

Sheila pulled the door, Clyde moved and sat next to the fridge, his tongue fell out and he thumped the floor with his tail.

'There's something in there you want, isn't there boy?' On one of the racks sat a bowl of chicken necks, she tossed one to Clyde. He caught it mid-air, wolfed it down, then wore an innocent face like the neck never existed, expecting more.

Isabelle laughed and walked over to study the coffee machine on the bench. 'Any idea how to use one of these?'

A scuffling noise. Clyde ran out onto the deck and took off.

'You're the bar worker.'

'Never had to make coffee.'

'Don't have to.' Sheila held a bag of instant.

'Fat chance. If we're breaking into someone's home and there's a coffee machine, I'm doing real coffee. Can't be too hard, seen Tom do this, there's a filter, somewhere?' Isabelle stuck her head under the machine, grabbed a handle and twisted.

'That's right, it's a filter,' he said, followed by a blinding crunch.

———

'Tell me all about Mamma,' Carlo said.

Sadness swept his older brother's face, he took a lasting drag and crushed the butt. Nicky stood a foot shorter, three years older than Carlo. He'd aged poorly since their last meeting two years ago in Italy. Jowls had drooped. Skin had taken on a sallow tinge.

'She was dying.' Smoke trailed from Nicky's nostrils, small puffs escaped with each word.

'Dying? What do you mean, *was* dying?'

'In and out of hospital all year.'

'Any idea what it is?' Carlo leaned forward, resting elbows on his knees.

'Depression.'

'Depression? Come on Nicky. Mamma? In the eighties they called it stress, now depression. Just a modern day name for being pissed off. That's not Mamma.'

'That's what I reckoned too, doctors couldn't work it out. Major organs were failing. She lost so much weight.'

'So ... what, she's getting better?'

'Signs are good. She's eating well. Before, she'd throw up most of what she ate, now she gets through half a meal.'

'What happened?' Something must have happened.' But his denial masked the real answer, which he knew, but didn't want to hear.

'We have a good doctor looking after her. You remember the Serafino family? Worked for us at the abattoirs, uncles, brothers, cousins.'

Carlo shrugged. 'No.'

'One of the sons is now a doctor. Studied a lot about how this serotonin stuff in your body can control things called—'

Nicky paused to recollect '—called fuck'n neurons or somethin', how all this shit in the brain makes other parts of the body suffer. Reckons there's these connections, emotions and the gut. It's how the mind controls the body.'

'You believe all that?'

'Thought it was a load of crap, but he did tests, looked into her diet, asked about whether she got enough sun and vitamins. You know what she's like, everything's from the garden. Then he asked about you.'

Carlo was about to take a sip, the arm froze just short of his lips. 'Why?'

'Everyone wants to know about you, Carlo.'

'What did you tell him?'

'He's a doctor. His family are loyal. Told him you're overseas. He understood, asked if you're ever coming back. I said I don't know and that's when he reckoned Mamma was dying of a broken heart. She couldn't touch you, couldn't speak to you, a mother has to feel the skin, you know. This doctor says it's the same as you being dead.'

Carlo knuckled tears away. He had longed to ring her every day, especially when he received the news of her illness.

'You've always been her favourite, huh. The whole family knows that, you fuck'n Pazzu.'

Pazzu, a nickname dubbed on him by his father, meaning mad, crazy. Carlo heard it a lot growing up.

'At least when you moved to Sydney she could talk to you and visit any time. She doesn't believe you knocked those two cops. We told her other families were responsible, you were already overseas, but cops have been out to the house. She reads the papers too, people talk. Worry is eating her like a cancer.'

'She knows I'm safe.'

'Of course, but it's not the same. The doctor wanted to put her on anti-depressants. Papà refused, instead he decided you must return. I remember sitting next to her bed, I held her hand, promised to bring you home.'

'What happened?'

'Her eyes shone like gold Carlo, only the eyes. I'll never forget her words. *"You will do that for me, you will bring my baby boy home?"* Her grip tightened, she found strength, and her smile, man you should have seen her smile. She came alive and that instant I knew the doctor was right. She had bottled so much in.

'I was due to fly to Sydney but cancelled my meetings. Next day she got up, I found her down in the kitchen with Anita, who's still with us. Mama was busy telling her off, one of her chickens had died. Like the old days, huh. Anita was so happy, she saw the change too.'

Carlo smiled fondly at the mention of Anita, the family's cook, his first lover.

'We ended up putting her on a small dose of meds. Every day she improves and asks about you.' Nicky paused to light up, took a long pull and stabbed the two fingers holding the cigarette at Carlo. 'You mess this up and you will spend the rest of your fucking life in jail, if you're lucky. I won't be able to clean up again. You know what'll happen to Mamma.'

Carlo nodded. 'When can I see her?'

'Papà wants you home for Christmas.'

'Why so long, that's two months away.'

'The doctor said while she's still weak, anything emotional could trigger a heart attack, or a stroke. He's happy with her progress. We don't want you near the house until Mamma is strong enough, she knows her Christmas present, she's doing a little better every week. It's like she's getting ready for you. Anita and Angela spend their days looking after her.'

'Angela? How is she?' Carlo had been so absorbed with news of his mother, he hadn't asked about his younger sister.

'Oh Carlo, she's grown up so beautiful. Getting married. Here, I have pictures.' Nicky reached into his back pocket, passed an envelope over.

Carlo flicked through the photos of Angela with a young man, they looked happy together.

'Good Sicilian boy from Griffith,' said Nicky.

'Couldn't give a shit how good you reckon he is, you tell him if he fucks up, I'll break his fuck'n legs too.'

'He knows what you did to that Priarto boy. Anyway, you can tell him at Christmas. They've been together for four years. He's working for us, I'm grooming him to replace you, huh.' Nicky held a serious face until Carlo spurted out laughter. The two brothers then enjoyed a light-hearted moment together.

'Can I keep these?' Carlo asked, as he spoke the words he realised what he'd said.

'Of course not you fool.'

Carlo nodded toward the kitchen. 'How'd you get him involved? Thought Benny was finished.'

'He and Papà go too far back. We couldn't trust anyone else to bring you in. Made sense not to use our own people.'

'Used our people overseas.'

'That was different. There's so much pressure from the cops. Papà barely held on. Things changed, Carlo. We had to work hard. But there are families who now see us as vulnerable again. Like fuck'n vultures. After all Papà has done for them. I keep telling him we don't need them anymore. Beef markets are strong, L'ombrello's funds have provided us with opportunities we never would've had. Investments in mining, shipping, Asian gambling, too.'

At the mention of L'ombrello, Carlo smiled. 'It was good to see Jimmy.'

'You'll see him on the farm at Christmas. He's a great asset, the way he's controlled the super funds. Some on the board wanted to invest in Europe and America, Jimmy took us into

Asia instead. Looks like we've avoided a lot of trouble. Like everyone else, Jimmy's pissed off at you, knows you were set up.' Nicky waved his finger again. 'There are families desperately trying to gain control. Papà and Jimmy stand in their way. If you think Papà's tough, Jimmy's a fuck'n iron bar. With those two it's not about money no more, it's about respect, and the way Papà wants L'ombrello funds to be administered after he's gone. If the wrong men gain power they will change everything he's built, and if you were around, they'd never dare treat Papà like this.'

'Why not send Marco,' Carlo said. Marco Sabina was his father's bodyguard who trained the brothers in weapons from a young age. Other than his father, Marco was the only man Carlo feared.

'After the mess you left, it's not like that no more.' Nicky raised his chin, the gaze hardened. 'I see that look in your eye. I don't like it.'

'But you know what happened. You know what they did—'

'No Carlo. No way. You can never make things right, understand that. I warned you not to get involved, as usual you didn't listen. What went down was business. It's done. Over.'

'What went down was nearly eight years of my life.'

'You can believe all that bullshit, but you pulled the trigger. Plus, the trade-off was a fucking big earner, paid for your holiday a thousand times over brother. What's done is done. Jimmy's in control, that's all that matters. They need the funds as much as we do, but enough of business, you're pissin' me off. You will stay in Melbourne until Christmas.' He passed over a wad. 'Forty grand, just in case.'

Carlo tossed the bundle up, then caught it. 'Why not Griffith, or at least somewhere in the Riverina? Why Melbourne?'

'Think yourself lucky. I wanted you on one of our cattle stations in outback Queensland. Benny wants you here. Cops find out you're back, you'll be a fucking sprinkler system.

Half of 'em believe the rumours you're dead. Others don't, they wanna be the ones to finish you off. You listen to everything Benny says. Don't leave that house till he gives the nod, he'll look after everything, yeah. You understand me?'
'I think so. You staying in town?'
His brother's jaw tightened. Lips twirled in anger. 'You think so, eh. You fucking think so!' Spittle flew. Nicky had always possessed a hot temper. 'After all I've told you about your mother, is that all you can say, you fucking think so.' Nicky was one step from yelling. 'The lengths we have gone to, the money we've spent. All you can say is *you think so.* You have to fucking *know so,* Carlo! There is no *I fucking think so* no more, you got me? If you stuff this up, it's the last time. The last fucking time!'

He calmed himself by running his hands down his face, but anger was still simmering near the surface. He lit another cigarette. 'Gave 'em up for three fuck'n years, huh. Then Mamma got sick, and well, you know.' Nicky slapped Carlo's back. 'It'll be okay brother, Mamma's also seen photos of you.'

Nicky was right. Carlo knew all of their father's work throughout his entire life in Australia had almost been undone in one selfish act. He had a lot to make up to his father, but he was only brought back to see his mother.

'Now listen,' Nicky said, 'no one can recognise you, you gotta be a fox, just like those pricks in the media say. That's what you gotta be, smarter than 'em.' He took a long swig of beer, eyes firmly locked on his younger brother, content he'd gotten his point across.

'It'll be fine, Nicky.'

'Good. Papà doesn't trust any of the families down here anymore. If something goes wrong, they will see to it that we all go down with you this time. Papà has stayed on top all these years cause he knows how they think, he knows how to control them, that's why you have to stay down here till

Christmas. Benny's a man who can't be compromised. I hear he's got you a nice girl, uh.'

Carlo grinned at the thought of Nadine. He didn't hear the padded steps, Benny simply appeared in the doorway. 'That buddy of yours still the Mayor, Benny?'

'Oh, hoh! You been away for a while,' Benny said.

'Don't matter.' A wry smile lifted the corner of Nicky's mouth. 'Between those two they still own half the fuck'n Docklands, eh Benny.'

The Chin gave a gentle, calm nod, his expression also firmed. He rarely discussed business.

'Appreciate everything, Benny,' Carlo said.

Nicky cast his eyes at the Chinaman in the doorway. 'If you knew what this is costing me, there's no need to thank him. Benny has arranged another house in case there's a problem.'

Carlo sniffed the air. 'Hope it's an improvement on this joint.'

Benny raised his chin, lowered his eyes.

'Sorry Benny,' Carlo said, grinning.

Benny offered only a smirk. Nicky laughed, beer glistened on his lips. 'Where are your Italian manners, Pazzu? I should slap you. Papà always taught us to be polite to our host.'

———

Isabelle's head hit the underside of the machine so hard it lifted off the bench.

'Ouch,' she squealed. Even with her face contorted she looked extraordinary.

'Ouch,' Lucas repeated in sympathy. 'Didn't mean to scare you.' A snigger came from his mate, Nat, standing behind. 'Not funny, Nat. You okay?' He asked Isabelle.

'I think so.' She rubbed her head. 'Hi Nat.'

'Hey,' Nat said.

Lucas spun around to face Nat. 'You two know each other?'

'From the pub,' Isabelle said.

Horry's right. He had to get out more.

Sheila examined her. 'No blood, you'll live.' She turned on Lucas. 'Look what you did, sneaking up like that.'

'It's my house.'

'I didn't want to be in here,' Isabelle said, clearly embarrassed.

Sheila walked over, kissed him on the cheek.

Then she kissed Nat. 'Nice to see you, dear.' She bent her wrist towards Isabelle, 'Don't know if I'd want to be in the trenches with this one.'

'She gave you up pretty quick,' Lucas said.

'Let's not gang up on her. She really is a sweetheart. Handled your dog just like she handled you at the restaurant. Thought we'd get eaten alive.'

Lucas eyeballed Clyde. 'Serious?' The dog stood on its back legs, the front paws dug into Lucas's chest. He slapped Clyde's flank, then pushed him off. 'Trade you in for a cat.'

'We're about to cook breakfast. Want some?' Sheila asked.

'I'll cook,' Nat said. 'Been surfing all morning. Could eat a horse between two mattresses.'

'You're on the job then,' Lucas agreed, eying the wine bottle on the bench. 'You've obviously found everything.'

'Absolutely. Glasses—?' Sheila pointed to a top cupboard.

'You know where they are.' He walked over and placed a concerning hand on Isabelle's shoulder. 'Want me to take a good look at that?'

A nervous twitch happened, his right thigh muscle shuddered just above the knee. It was the first time he'd touched her other than to shake her hand.

'I'll be fine,' she said. 'Totally embarrassed. Feel like I've broken into someone's home.'

The leg wouldn't stop. He didn't want to look down in case her eyes followed to see his shorts fluttering like a leaf, so he ignored it. 'Half the town walks in here unannounced. Quite often I come home and find Horry's wife, Connie sitting on the deck, kids running wild, no food in the fridge. Just make yourself at home.'

'That's a strange thing to say to someone you don't really know.'

'I'm a good judge of character.'

Their eyes met.

Why didn't I call? His mind cursed.

'Let me show you around ... unless she's already taken you through.'

'Sure.'

He led her through to the study. Earlier that morning he'd been detailing the kitchen for his project home in Gloucester Street, when Nat arrived to go surfing. Plans were strewn over the desk. 'This is my office.'

"DO YOUR WORK" drifted back and forth across the computer screen.

'I can see why you need the motivation.' She nodded toward the ocean. 'So called room with a view.'

'Gets tough.'

She walked to the sidewall and read his plaque aloud beginning with the capitals, *"HOW IN THE HELL"* written in large red lettering.

'How in the hell could a man enjoy being awakened at 6.30 a.m. by an alarm clock, leap out of bed, dress, force feed, shit, piss, brush teeth and hair and fight traffic to be at a place where essentially you make lots of money for somebody else and were asked to be grateful for the opportunity to do so?'

She turned. 'That's funny, so true when you think about it. I'm impressed. Really like it.'

'I live by it. The very idea of working for someone else can make me violently ill.'

She laughed. 'Bet that's not the truth.'

'True enough. Had a job once, in a studio in Melbourne after completing my degree. Nine to five's really only a name.

More like six to seven. I quickly came to realise I could only enjoy working for myself.'

She stared at the name at the bottom of the quote. 'Who is Charles Bukowski?'

'An American writer and poet. He's dead now. Hated the thought of jobs and being told you had to be somewhere, so he became a great writer. He inspires me.'

'Everyone's got to have a job.'

'Doesn't mean you have to be told what to do.' And then he realised what he'd said, reminding him of their first meeting.

A flat smile returned.

He moved on to his parents' room – now a guest room – and then his own bedroom.

She wandered over and lifted his 3 wood up halfway out of the golf bag. 'You play golf?'

'Not any more. Used to play with my dad and my grandfather.'

'Always wanted to try.'

She nodded toward a black and white photo of three men resting on shovels. 'Which one's your grandfather?'

'In the middle. The older guy on the right is my great grandfather. On the left is Roy. Remember—'

'Good to put a face to the name … to the street, I guess.'

When he started dating Carmen, he moved Sue's photos into the living room. It had been a tough decision. Afterwards it surprised him how much better he'd felt. He led her downstairs. 'This is where I lived with my wife. Now I just keep my boards down here.'

'What's in here?' she said nudging open the door to the second downstairs bedroom.

'Careful. I've been repairing a couple of guns. There's one leaning—'

Isabelle gasped, a hand thudded her chest, the door opened fully and the board crashed to the floor. She stepped back, distraught.

'Guns,' she whispered through a short, tight breath. He reached for her elbow. She jerked away, her face, drained of colour.

'Long surfboards, called guns, they've got narrow tails, we use them for big waves.'

'Oh ... oh, okay,' she said, clearly relieved.

'You sure you're okay?'

'Yeah. I'm fine. Just don't like guns, that's all. The other ones, of course. Sorry about your board.'

'Don't worry, just a ding, it'll take a minute to fix.' He'd never seen anyone react like that and took her elbow again, this time more gently. She didn't pull back.

Through the downstairs living room other boards lay about in covers. 'Just step over them,' he said then pointed to the third bedroom. Don't touch that door either, full of junk too.' He opened the sliding door, she followed out onto the sand beneath the shadow of the deck.

'My backyard.'

'Love the landscaping.'

'Took a few million years.'

Voices and the barbeque, already sizzling, could be heard further along the deck up above. Though his nerves had quelled slightly, Lucas knew he had to wait until they got back inside before he could ask her out for a drink, to avoid being overheard.

Dinner might be too forward.

Then why was she here?

The damn knee started up again.

'It's so close to the ocean,' she said.

'Hey?'

'It's close ... to the ocean.'

He replayed her words. 'Exactly forty-nine metres back from the high tide mark.'

She rubbed her head again.

'You sure you don't want something—?'

'Just a small lump.' Scrunching her eyes she focussed up at the Bluff, pointing. 'Saw something move up there before. In that crevice.'

'Peregrine falcons nest up there.'

'You're kidding. Wow! Never seen a falcon before.'

'Now you have. This place is teeming with wildlife. Kangaroos, wallabies, we all co-exist except Clyde. Possums on the roof drive him nuts at night.'

He led her back inside, up the stairs.

He'd thought of her many times since the night at Reno's. After the first week he noticed these thoughts caused the heaviness to lift a little. He rarely thought of Carmen, instead he feared Isabelle, with her looks would start dating another man before he worked up the courage to call. She'd become just another ripple that would die on the shores of reality. Such was his predicament, shoulders would tense, he'd put the phone down after punching in only a few numbers.

The thigh stammered. He pushed his foot into the step, it didn't ease, he stopped on the stair above, last chance. Under normal circumstances she was taller than him. He tried to lock his knee. The thigh went crazy. She didn't seem to notice.

'Hey, I intended to call.' He searched for signs of disapproval in her face. To his relief a smirk arose.

'Oh … sure.'

'Let's do that drink tomorrow night. Reno's maybe?'

'Reno's? They say Reno's is for eating, the pub's for drinking. So, is this a date?'

He pushed weight through the leg. 'Everyone knows your business at the pub, besides you work there. So it's Reno's, unless you want to go out of town. We could do dinner, maybe?'

She twisted her lips in thought. 'Got plans tomorrow night.'

'Plans? I'm sorry.'

Plans? He tried to remain upbeat.

'Have to work.'

Relief came, confidence shot up again. 'What about tonight then?'

Idiot, he cursed, knowing it was too soon.

'Okay. Let's make it dinner.' Her smile appeared.

His spirit elevated even further. 'Okay then.'

It's a date. His mind celebrated.

Sheila's voice interrupted. 'Food's ready.' Tension left the small confines of the stairwell. Lucas began to walk up the stairs, when a thought re-entered. 'Hey, how'd you two happen to be out here, anyway?'

'Do you know a winery called Batten Hill?'

'I do. About an hour's drive away.'

She raised her eyebrows. 'Is that right?'

7

'Bar work, doesn't really suit you,' Lucas said. They were seated next to the window at Reno's Restaurant.

'Half way through a childcare course,' Isabelle replied, 'might pick it up again soon, be fun to own my own bar one day, too.'

'So why'd you leave Perth?'

Questions, she thought.

'Escaping issues, I guess. Needed the change.'

'Relationship issues?'

'Sort of ... itchy feet.' Not really a lie. 'So glad I found this place.'

'I was going to ask, why St Claire?'

She studied the man opposite, a nice guy, get through it. There's always going to be questions no matter who sat in that chair.

'Just Googled it. Even sounded friendly. Always wanted to live in a coastal town, do the Great Ocean Road thing.'

Suddenly Lucas became distracted. Something out the window had caught his attention, eyes widened into a look of dismay.

'Is someone out there?'

He tossed his head sideways. 'That big guy, you know him?'

A bolt of fear struck. Her heart skipped, but common sense kicked in and snapped her out of it. The face of evil could not be out there.

Not here. Not in St Claire. He's dead.

She shrugged it off, just as she had trained herself to do, and also because Lucas now wore a bemused expression.

'Take a look.'

She leaned forward to see a middle-aged woman beside the unmistakable Viking like figure, beaming a smile, waving. A mobile phone held to his ear. 'Sure, I know Big Steve and Wendy, from the pub.'

'Too late, he's spotted us.' Lucas shook his head, dejected. 'And they're joining us.'

'They're friends of yours?'

'Sure are.'

'Well I, uh, guess it's okay.' She liked Steve, he always gave her the ten per cent locals discount on fish.

The doorbell tingled, a booming voice floated across the room. 'Lukey Boy!'

Heads spun, many diners smiled, greeting the fisherman as he squeezed between the tables in scruffy denims and five-dollar thongs. They made a flapping noise. Sleeves were rolled up on his flannelette shirt, stretched over his gut like he was hiding a small atomic bomb under there. Wendy wore faded jeans, a lime green top.

They reached the table. Isabelle took note of the affection when these two men clasped hands. Steve winked, a large hand fell on her shoulder. The smell of beer and his inquisitive gaze hovered.

'Isabelle? What a surprise. Met my wife before, Wendy?'

'Many times. Hi Wendy.'

'Hi,' Wendy said, twinkling her fingers. They'd spoken on occasions in the pub when she picked Steve up, normally late at night. She kissed Lucas and ran an endearing palm down his cheek. 'We interrupting something here?'

Steve dragged another table over. 'Pay attention luv, course we are. Didn't you see his car's clean.' Lucas winced, clearly embarrassed. Isabelle had noticed the streetlight gleaming off the Porsche when he picked her up.

Steve sat beside her. 'This is cosy. Heard you're from Sydney.'

Isabelle sat back in her chair, stunned. Everything happened so quickly. *Sheila.* 'You've been talking to Sheila in the pub.'

'No flies, huh. Good guess.'

Lucas mouthed, *"Sydney?"*

'I grew up there, just haven't had the chance to tell you yet.'

'Is this what, a date?' Steve asked.

'Kinda was,' Lucas replied.

'How come I'm always the last to know? Might as well pack me shit up. No one tells me nothing no more. What happened to what's her face?'

Wendy slapped his shoulder. 'I told you about the breakup.' Then she turned to Lucas. 'Connie told me.'

Steve threw up his hands. 'How am I supposed to remember? S'pose Horry might have mentioned something but if *you* told me Lukey, I'd know. Been avoiding me, haven't ya?'

'Avoiding you means avoiding questions. It's simple.' Lucas turned to Isabelle, gave a boyish grin. 'See how it works round here?'

As an architect she looked upon him as a professional, but there was an unlikely history between these two, a warm mateship she would not have imagined. They seemed so different. Lucas never came into the pub. Earlier in the day she had picked up on his nervousness, now she saw a different side, the boy behind the man.

'This isn't right,' said Wendy.

But Isabelle sensed adventure. 'No, no, we don't mind, do we?'

'Like we got a choice,' Lucas said.

Steve shot a glance past her out the window. 'What a coincidence?' He rose, grabbed two chairs off a vacant table near the far wall and returned.

'What's he doing?' Isabelle asked.

Lucas gave Wendy a stare. 'He's called Horry, hasn't he?'

'I'm sorry,' Wendy said, shrugging. 'He's been on the punt all day, somehow found out you guys were here, and you know it's useless trying to stop him.'

Isabelle rolled her eyes. 'Sheila again.'

'Wait till I catch up with her,' Lucas said. 'S'pose Thumbtack's on his way too?'

'Only let him out of his cage for work or the pub,' Steve said.

Isabelle's lungs deflated, an exhale of relief. Thumbtack and that teardrop tattoo made her very uncomfortable.

'You sure this is okay?' Wendy asked her.

'Course she is, luv. What are friends for?' Steve leant in toward Isabelle, then shot a cheeky grin at his wife. 'My God, why can't you be this beautiful?'

She gave Isabelle a solemn look. 'Used to be very pretty before I decided on a career as a fisherman's wife.'

Steve's rich green eyes lit up, dancing in wide sockets. 'Never looked back have ya?'

Isabelle held a hand over her mouth to halt the threatening laughter. She'd seen Steve drunk many times, though never obnoxious. First impression had been of a fearsome, almost interrogating type of man. She found him to be quite the opposite, always polite with a firm control over his workers in the pub. He even knocked a guy out late one night for abusing a staff member. Isabelle had turned to pour a beer, heard glasses smash and a table hit the floor. By the time she knew what happened, Steve was already dragging his barely conscious deckhand out the door.

He helped himself to the red and poured a glass for his wife. 'Cheers,' they all tapped glasses.

The bell tingled, Connie entered, followed by Horry who clearly tried to smother his embarrassment behind a reluctant grin. Since the morning of the dog incident, he'd deliberately not made eye contact in the bakery, and had been noticeably scarce from the pub during her shifts.

Horry sat at one end, Connie at the other. 'What's going on here?' she asked.

'We *were* about to have a quiet dinner,' Lucas said.

'You two?' She gave her husband a look that would melt cheese. 'Horry. D'you know anything about this?'

'How the hell do I know what's going on? You were at home with me when he rang.'

'So, let me get this right,' Isabelle said to Horry. 'Steve phones you to say Lucas is on a date, and you decide to come down.'

'Ja. I was almost asleep on the couch.'

She grinned at Lucas. 'And these are really your mates?'

'Used to be.'

Steve turned to Isabelle. 'You do know he's an architect, yeah?'

'What's wrong with that?'

'Difficult bastards to get along with, weird too.'

'Is that so? You call him weird, he's on a date, you're stalking him and you reckon he's weird.'

Steve's mouth shot open, then froze. He glared at Lucas, eyes almost to bursting. 'I got nothing!'

They all laughed so loud the entire restaurant turned again.

'Don't listen to his crap,' Lucas said. 'He likes to put down those more educated than him.'

'He's right,' Steve agreed, winking at Isabelle again, nodding toward Horry. 'Notice I don't hang shit on our little guest from Boer land.' He bellowed more laughter, they all joined in again.

All except for Horry, who said, 'Ha fucking ha. Been hearing that dribble for too many years, stop acting like the big galoot. You need a human side when we meet new people.' Isabelle giggled uncontrollably. She was the centre of attention and for the first time in her life, perhaps it wasn't for her looks.

'Just put up with it,' Connie said to her. 'Let 'em get the insults out of the way first. The night 'll only get better.'

'That's right,' Steve said, 'and it's on me tonight, too guys.'

'Why's that?' Horry asked.

'Guess what happened to me today, Affffreeeekaaaans?'

'Oh no, you're about to brag about something, ja?'

Horry's strong accent somehow suited his eager, carefree manner.

'Glad ya asked,' Steve said. 'Fella walks into me shop this morning, must've been six-thirty. Wasn't open, but served him anyway cause he's connected. Guy's loaded, I'm talking serious kanga. Worth millions.' He pointed at Lucas. 'By the way Lukey boy, gave him your number. Name's Jack something or other, Gillings I think, chasin' an architect. Wants a house designed near the golf course. Expect a call.'

'Gee thanks.'

Isabelle grinned at the sarcasm from Lucas.

'Glad to be appreciated,' Steve said, raising eyebrows. 'Anyway, so he gives me this tip right, race four, Mr. Majestic paying twelve bucks. By the time I got to the pub it had come in to eight, chucked a dollar on the nose, didn't I. Damn thing shit it in.'

Horry's head slumped. 'Ohhh, fuck me. Know how long I gotta work for that kind of cash?'

'Yeah, I do,' Steve said, belting out more raucous hysterics.

Isabelle became confused. 'So you won eight bucks, big deal?'

'No, no,' Horry said, shaking his head. 'He doesn't talk zeros – eight grand.'

'Oooh, that explains it.' A chair scraped, Horry left the table and went over to the counter, spoke to Reno and returned with two bottles. Isabelle recognised the labels of a dusty Grange Hermitage and a Leeuwin Estate White. She wondered if

Steve really knew the value of the wine about to be uncorked, but kept her mouth shut.

Reno came and took their orders, and when he left Connie swung her finger between Isabelle and Lucas. 'So you two, how'd you meet?'

Horry and Lucas suddenly wore sorry grins like school kids who'd been busted smoking.

'This won't end well, mate,' Horry said.

'Hmmm,' was all Lucas offered.

So Isabelle took a long sip and proudly told her story of the dog and the café, this time she told it with glee. Steve paid out on his mates all night, Connie told Horry off for not being honest. He defended himself by saying he had not said one word to Isabelle that morning, and when the last of the diners left, Reno locked his doors and joined them with more wine. Isabelle was rich with laughter and food and stories of St Claire and this crew, as people in St Claire often referred to themselves. She couldn't remember such a night in her torn memory, and also struggled to take her eyes off this freewheeling, ruggedly handsome architect opposite.

8

South Melbourne

Carlo stepped out into the midday sun, glad to leave that dingy internet café with its greasy haired, rude owner and Goth customers. He folded the paper, tucked it in his pocket and strolled toward the car. Thoughts turned to coffee. He searched around for a decent café when a red brick building on the opposite corner caught his eye. Workers in khaki overalls and Hi-Vis shirts filed through the roped entrance beneath a glittering sign,

MAXINE'S

He decided on his first tap beer since arriving back. Benny encouraged him to get out and drive each day to gain some confidence for his integration back into society. Nadine was at the Oaks Day races. Melbourne's Spring Carnival was almost over, and although Carlo enjoyed horse racing, he'd become sick of hearing about a place he couldn't attend. He slipped coins into the meter, waited for a tram to pass and wandered over. For the first time in his life he paid an entrance fee.

Inside, a tricked up version of Carly Simon's *You're So Vain* pumped the room. On stage, a dancer writhed around a pole and a group of office boys hollered in front of the crowd, balancing beers. Carlo found a stool in a quiet, dark corner, furthest from the stage with the entrance doors in full view.

A barman approached. 'What'll it be?'

'Middy of lager.'

'New South Wales lad, huh?'

Carlo gave a lean smile. 'Make it a pot.'

The barman poured the beer. 'Enjoy.'

While listening to the crowd he recalled how as a young man, the strip bars of Kings Cross had fascinated him when he moved to Sydney from the Riverina.

He unfolded the piece of paper, angled it toward the light and read it again. It was too good to believe. He'd been prepared to travel the country, but Jimmy's information would be correct. Izy worked in a hotel down on the Victorian coast only a few hours drive away.

Daylight spilled in. Through the mirrors between the shelving on the back wall of the bar, he saw four bikers enter. The first was a slob of a man with long hair and an anvil-shaped, untidily clipped black beard. He moved straight to the bar and slammed down his palm. An array of rings clacked loudly on the wooden top, the barman held up four fingers, the biker raised his thumb. Four stubbies were retrieved from the fridge, placed in an ice bucket and handed over the counter. A sign dangling from the ceiling above the tap advertised four beers in a bucket for eighteen bucks.

Not a bad deal – although no cash was exchanged.

The barman motioned to Carlo who nodded back. Another beer was poured. As he sipped the beer, he noticed on the top shelf of the mirrored wall stood a statue of a man with the words, 'YOUR CREDIT IS GOOD IN HERE', printed beneath. The statue had his palm extended towards a pig's arse.

To his immediate right a door burst open behind the bar forcing Carlo to sit back in the stool. The door was cut so neatly into the dark wooden panelling, he hadn't noticed it. Bouncers appeared, he relaxed again. They walked by without looking at him, then lifted up a flap in the bar top and moved out amongst the crowd.

Several minutes later excited voices in the crowd raised a notch. A troupe of dancers had entered through the front door. Carlo knew the ploy, often used in the Cross. Parade the girls past desperate men, desperate eyes. A flash of a smile or a wink would enhance sordid lives, ensuring repeat business.

Bouncers escorted the strippers along the length of the bar through a rear stage door. Another group of men emerged from the same door. Stage lights caught the necklaces and bracelets. Carlo recognised the Lebanese gang instantly. They scanned the crowd, elbows out, rubbing fists into palms. Most probably armed. One Lebo caught his attention, a tall, lanky man, the pencil thin moustache reminded him of many years ago.

———

Lebos had moved into the Cross and began dealing inside the territory of an associate, kneecapping two men. Carlo was asked to settle the dispute and arranged a meeting in the aptly named suburb of Punchbowl. The gang chose the restaurant, a Lebanese establishment on their own turf, thinking they were safe until Carlo's men entered through the kitchen. Gang members were quickly disarmed and Carlo thrashed their leader, A.K., a strong, arrogant man, to within inches of his life. He threw the bloodied pulp through the front window and his men escorted the remainder of the gang to their car. But one young member with a similar pencil thin moustache threatened reprisals and was quickly led back in to face Carlo. Instead of beating the kid, Carlo befriended him with cocaine and prostitutes and money, along with the promise of a better criminal life, convincing him of the error he would be making to side with his gang. Within a day the kid had spilled information on suppliers and addresses where the gang kept their arsenal of weapons and drugs. Carlo then had him taken out to the desert and shot.

———

His daydreaming ceased when two more security men emerged from behind the bar. One walked outside, the other engaged the bikers. The stage burst to life with music and multi-coloured circles of flashing lights, almost blinding at first and spiralling across the ceiling and down the walls. The show had begun.

External doors swung open again. Carlo was drawn like a moth toward the light, but his gaze fell on the bikers. The fat one with the black beard passed the bouncer a bag of powder. Carlo knew to turn away, but his eyes met Blackbeard's. An eerie smile crept over the biker's face.

Carlo focussed back on his beer.

How in hell did I get into this? His mind cursed, hoping, against all hope as seconds later, dark shapes loomed. Two men stood behind. Blackbeard propped his hands on the bar to Carlo's left, straight-armed. The fourth guy, a giant of perhaps six foot eight took up a position on the other side of Blackbeard. He leaned on the bar, shoulders the width of a pick handle's length screened Carlo from onlookers. The Sons of Cain M.C. was sewn on his leather jacket around the insignia of a bloodied knife. Carlo knew he could take the other three, but also knew where he would be stopped.

Unwittingly he had sized up the men earlier. Blackbeard was roughly the same height as Carlo, around six four, oafish, a hundred and fifty kilos or more. Of the two men behind, one was tall and skinny, the other, stocky with an eighties style mullet haircut. The only thing that could save him now was if Marco Sabina, his boxing teacher and mentor walked through the door. With Marco by his side and their backs to the wall, they would cut their way through the bikers, and the bouncers.

But there would be no fairytale today.

Carlo recalled the promise to his brother, *always the family first.*

If he retaliated, not a person in the bar would witness a blade slip neatly between his ribs.

"You're a jellyfish," came Marco's put down. *"Tighten up, Piccolo."*

Blackbeard leaned in close shaking his head, he'd seen this a million times. Carlo focussed on the mirror in front and pressed his elbows into the bar, stomach tight, rigid, clamping his right hand around his left fist beneath his chin. Biceps tensed, hard as cricket balls.

Creepy fat fingers ran through his scalp, twisting hair. The hand pushed down hard, tearing roots. Carlo grimaced but held firm. A face plant could be expensive.

'Strong boy,' Blackbeard said in a gravelly voice. Hot, rancid breath puffed in Carlo's left ear. A jab came below the ribs. He braced, fists struck three more times on either side of his midriff. The hand pushed down again, fistfuls of hair were ripped. Carlo resisted, digging his elbows harder into the woodwork.

Forceful blows ripped up into his kidneys. Air burst from his lungs, he arched his back, pain spiked his insides. Instinctively he thought of tucking his elbows in to protect the body but they'd simply work on other areas.

Blackbeard sighed. 'No matter how fuck'n strong ya are there's always men like us. Meet Squash, ugliest man alive, aren't ya Squash.' Another punch pounded into his right flank from the man named Squash.

'Must be depressin', do all that workin' out, then ya meet us. Fuck'n talkin' to you. Look at me.'

Carlo eyed him through the mirror. The hand on his head released its grip, the acidic taste of blood and bile sliced the back of his throat. He swallowed hard.

'Here for the show?' Blackbeard asked.

'Just a beer.'

Blackbeard shifted his weight to his left. Carlo glanced up as the spider web tattoo on the lethal point of the elbow crashed into his temple. His head rocked back spinning and swirling. Darkness fell over amidst exploding pain. He could almost feel his brain sloshing about in matter similar to an oil compass looking for true north, or true anything. A hand steadied him from behind. He was unable to decipher the music, it lost its beat, reminding him of the times when he and Nicky used to put their mother's cherished opera records on the wrong speed.

'Don't fall off ya chair,' came a nasally voice in his right ear with a similar, unwashed stench followed by a bizarre hissing, snivelling and exasperated wheezing. Senses had returned. Carlo thought they may have punctured a lung then realised the wheezing wasn't coming from him.

Blackbeard tried to slam his face into the bar again. This time the action was quick and even more forceful with plenty of weight behind it, still Carlo had the strength to resist again.

The man gave a sickening chuckle. 'Told you to look at me.' The hand twisted his hair sideways this time, forcing Carlo to stare up into Blackbeard's laconic eyes. They portrayed a man resigned to having to dish out a beating. Dark stumps, the last remainders of teeth bore evidence of a lifelong gluttony of speed or meth. The busy tongue traced back and forth over his gums like he was chewing a bag of marbles.

'Now tell me why you were minding my business and not your fuck'n own?'

'Look, this is some sort—'

Fists full of steel rings worked him deep, either side. Carlo cried out, agony rocketed through him.

Ruptured organs came to mind, spleen, kidneys, liver.

'Some sort of what?'

'Mistake—'

They hammered his sides again. A torrent of spew burst onto the floor splashing Blackbeard's boot.

'Watch where ya fuck'n spit.' Blackbeard wiped his boot on Carlo's jeans. They allowed him a moment.

Sucking in air, he gritted his teeth, raised a hand.

'Look—'

Fists thumped into his lower back. Pain rifled up his spine, more puke, this time a rack of clean glasses on the other side of the bar copped the lot.

'Ya getting the picture here?'

Carlo didn't answer, just wiped his lips.

'Good. A fast learner. You do the listening son. Ain't that right, Squash?'

'Fuck oath,' came the nasally voice. Followed by more grunts, another blow to the ribs. Carlo tried to gather his vision by focussing on the statue and the hand addressing the pig's arse.

Blackbeard placed his arm around and tapped Carlo's cheek. 'Now your eyes have got you into a lot of trouble today, son. Never look up from ya beer. And never come back to this fuck'n pub.'

Carlo focussed on the silver rings filled with grime or grease. H.A.T.E. was tattooed across the knuckles. It mystified him why criminals, of all people, branded themselves with tattoos.

'I spoke to you.'

Carlo only nodded.

'Good boy.'

He dropped his head, despite the boiling rage he willed himself through. Never had he been on the receiving end of such a speech. If they were finished, it meant he'd contained himself for the first time in his life, because he had to. Through wracking agony he calmed his mind, further.

Marco's voice came again. *"Get out alive, but don't show them fear, Piccolo."*

With all his remaining stamina he lifted his head and locked onto the biker's vacant eyes. Life was a waiting game for these men. Another blow came. Though his body rocked, his eyes never left Blackbeard's face, committing to memory every wrinkle, every thin red capillary lining the cheeks, the blue star on the right earlobe.

More fluid rose. He forced it down. Blackbeard's tongue zipped back and forth again beneath yellow-stained hairy lips like a cat with birth contractions. The constant need to clean his gums, driven by a mind fuelled by drugs.

The biker's stare broke first. In a calm, controlled voice he said, 'You're a lucky man. When I'm not on parole, been known to hack a man's fingers off. Works well. No one's ever come back. Recommend you do the same.'

Carlo thought of his mother and felt glad he'd left the gun in the car. Blackbeard raised his eyebrows.

An answer was required.

Carlo nodded, obediently. Blackbeard slapped his shoulder like there were no hard feelings. The three men walked off. Only the big man, the screen, remained, fingers twisting wiry hairs on a narrow goatee. Carlo absorbed the cold, evil eyes and wiped his mouth with the back of his hand again. More vision returned. On the front of the man's jacket was the badge of the club's Sergeant-at-Arms above the name, Tinny.

———

Over at the stage the theme song *Maxine* blasted out. Carlo knew the song. No longer would it be buried in the annals of his youth.

'Let's go, tiger.' Hands tightened on his forearms, bouncers helped him outside. Sunlight only added to his injuries. He put one foot in front of the other, grimacing, straightening his battered body with each step. He reached the car, opened the door, got in, waited a few seconds and threw up what was left in his stomach. Nadine would not be impressed. First priority was to reach the house and call her. She'd have to leave the races early. He drove south toward Port Phillip Bay, his mind split in two. A weak presence told him to keep driving. Pride ordered him back.

The other side of the road was clear, he braked, yanked the wheel around, tyres screeched on the tram tracks and he accelerated back toward Maxine's. After passing the doorway, he took a left down a side street filled with old weatherboard houses. Roses bloomed in front yards. A gap appeared between two white picket fences. He entered a cobblestone lane, turned left into another and reached a dead end. Four gleaming Harleys were parked alongside a stack of kegs in a loading bay. He opened the glove box, pushed the gun aside, found a pen and paper.

Jimmy would find out more about these men than perhaps they knew about themselves.

9

Lucas jammed the knife hard, breaking the suction. He prised the abalone off the canyon wall, dropped it in the netting and kicked toward the surface. Suddenly he felt resistance. The net had snagged. Cutting it meant he'd lose his catch in the depths of the narrow canyon in the reef. Clamping the knife between his teeth he worked fast. Lungs were at bursting point, energy sapped away on the current. He calmed his mind, twisted the bag free and headed for light.

Under for two minutes ten, not bad, about the maximum of his lung capacity. The longboard was still tied to the reef only a few metres away, he swam over and began the long paddle in. From about a hundred metres out he saw her on the beach. She was early.

He'd invited her out to lunch but there was at least another hour's work cleaning abalone.

Clyde and Dimi played along the water's edge. Onshore winds pressed against her skirt. Hands were tucked into the sleeves of her woollen jumper. This coast was much colder than Perth or Sydney, her resolve was admirable.

To her face, Big Steve described her as *"a bit of a trooper"*.

"Ballsy," he said behind her back.

As he rode a small wave in she flashed her warm, infectious grin. 'Hi.'

'Hi.'

He dumped the board on the sand. A thought of kissing her cheek passed, but she mightn't appreciate him being wet. Then Clyde jumped up, pushing him a step backwards. The chance blew into the wind. Patting the dog was safe. No woman had ever made him so nervous. On the two occasions she'd been to the house, Sheila accompanied her. There was no sign of the older lady up on the balcony.

They'd been on three more dates, each time preferring to go out of town to ensure a quiet evening. Last week it was just coffee and a walk along the beach in town. She appeared reserved, comfortable in her own space. Becoming lovers was the next obvious step, perhaps only for normal people. He had no idea how to proceed with this lady. She kept him awake at night.

He passed the net over. 'Take a look.' Despite the water dripping through the bottom, she took it with no qualm. Carmen would never have handled a bag of shellfish. Sue had also taken time to come around to such things.

'What's in it?'

'Lunch. Abalone.' He peeled his arms out of the wetsuit.

'Doesn't look like a delicacy to me.'

'Asians don't agree, some'd give up their second child for this stuff.'

'They still alive?'

'Yep. All the meat's inside the shell.'

She surprised him again by reaching into the bag and holding two shells up. They were stuck together so she simply ripped them apart.

'Wow! They're so heavy, like rocks.' Both shells were much wider than her hands.

'Hard as a cat's head my Grandfather used to say. They're everywhere around here. Good size too, normally we get poachers, haven't seen em' for a while. Come on up, I'll teach you how to cook 'em.' A light drizzle swept over as they headed to the house.

'Watched you from the deck through the binoculars. You were under quite a long time.'

The binoculars were in the kitchen. She'd felt comfortable enough to open the door. 'Trying to get some training in, Nat and I are heading off to Hawaii after Christmas.'

'Really, I've seen those big waves on telly. But why go there when it's Christmas?'

'Gets too packed in town. Best waves round then are in Hawaii, anyway.' Suddenly he felt guilty about not telling her earlier. Was this a sign she wanted to become a part of his life? He quelled his excitement.

—

After lunch the rain had cleared. While cleaning up in the kitchen Lucas called out through the window, suggesting a walk along the beach into town. The tide was low.'

No answer came from the deck.

'Hey Isabelle, do—?'

'Lucas?' Her voice quavered.

'Lucas. Can you come out ... please?'

Through the window he saw her long legs huddled up at her chest. Hands covered her face.

A Snake? Too cold, he thought and ventured out to take a look. He'd never seen a snake on the deck.

She pointed up. The bird was perched on the gutter at the far end.

'Don't move, you'll be fine.' He went back inside and grabbed one of Clyde's chicken necks, then tossed it onto the roof. Isabelle peeked between her fingers. He sat down and placed a reassuring arm around her. 'It's okay. Watch.'

The bird hopped about on the roof, scratching, scraping, then reappeared on the guttering with the neck in its beak. With an effortless flap it soared out and circled the beach before retreating to its hollow up in the Bluff.

Isabelle held her mouth wide open. 'What the hell?'

'Sorry. That's one of the peregrines, the female. Didn't expect her to come down.' He pulled his arm back, then wished he hadn't. 'She's more inquisitive than the male.'

'You didn't tell me that thing came down onto the roof. Imagine if Sheila was here. Must have been there for about a minute, just staring at me through those black eyes. And that hooked beak. Angry looking thing, now that it's gone. Guess it was quite thrilling, really.' She was so close, warm breath pampered his cheek. The top of his knee began twitching and stammering again, he curled his toes into the deck, tried to blanket his anxiety with a chuckle.

'That colour around the eyes,' she said. 'Scary yellow, kind of brown underneath too, like a hawk.'

'Yeah, they're a handsome bird. Pretty rare in the wild nowadays. Might've wanted some abalone, probably checking you out as well.'

'Checking me out?'

'Why not, it's breeding season. This is her hunting ground. She sees everyone and everything.'

'Oh my God Lucas, that's the scariest bird I've ever seen and you've just made it even scarier. Good on ya.'

The muscle stopped twitching, he swung his knee a little closer, her shoulders angled away ever so subtly, her head dropped.

Down like a shutter.

He'd seen it before, last week on the beach. On that occasion he also moved a little closer – same thing. In a profound manner Isabelle shied away into her own space.

Was there a troubled person within?

Eyes darted up at him, then lowered.

Unconvinced. Unsure.

Another Carmen situation, perhaps, he'd failed dismally in that relationship too.

Has Isabelle decided she can't move forward with him?

Then why did she come out today? He moved his leg away, just a little. All he could do was offer conversation.

'Used to be another pair living up in the same hollow when I was a kid. One day Nat and I were so bored we tied a bunch of knots in a rope and carried a big star picket and a sledgehammer up the track on the back slope. We wanted to check their nest out. Dad heard us belting the stake into the top of the cliff, man he kicked our arses all the way back to the house. Lucky huh, we could have brought the whole section down with us on it.'

'I could have told you that. Thing would have ripped you to shreds too with those claws.'

He shrugged. 'Eleven years old and bulletproof, I guess. Seen Jurassic Park?'

'Yeah.'

'Remember the scene where the hunter gets trapped by the two raptors?'

'Love that bit.'

'Peregrines are raptors too. One will split up a flock of birds and the other will swoop down and pick off a stray. Fastest animal on earth, three hundred k's an hour, apparently. Notice there's no seagulls around here?'

'Now that you mention it. What about the magpies that live on your boat?'

'For some reason maggies aren't too concerned. Pretty tough birds themselves.'

'What else do they feed on?'

'Galahs mainly.'

'Where's Dimi?'

'Inside with Clyde.'

'Good. Keep that door closed please.'

'They don't hunt dogs.'

'You sure?'

'Hundred per cent.' He moved a little closer again.

'Um. Did you say we could go for a walk?'

He sighed. 'Sounds good, but I'll show you the reef first. Follow me.'

———

He led her through the scrub to the side of the Bluff and showed her the steps his grandfather had carved to reach the top.

'You don't expect me to climb those I hope.'

'Course not. That's the way we used to go up. There's another track that leads up through the bush. Come on.'

They found the track and reached the top. She held Dimi tight, wouldn't go closer than two metres from the edge. The wind had eased, a shroud of mist hovered out to sea. As if on cue a rainbow appeared ending somewhere on the beach in St Claire.

She touched his arm lightly, clearly more comfortable and confident away from the house.

'It's beautiful Lucas. I can almost see the top end of Fishhook Bay and the outline of the next point.'

She looked perfect. Too perfect. The thought troubled him. A gust smeared her eyes with hair, she flicked it away.

'Take a look behind,' he said, 'you can see the whole valley was probably once an old riverbed. He pointed out to sea, toward the east. 'That's the reef, the dark patch straight out from the other cliff over there.'

'Looks like it goes a long way out,' she said. 'Those other patches, are they reefs too?'

'Yeah, but we only surf the big reef. Holds the best wave.'

'Sheila told me. Why aren't there waves out there now?'

'Needs a big groundswell to break. Ten foot or more.'

'Surfing huh. That all you guys do down here?'

'Pretty much, when the weather warms up I'll take you swimming out to the rock pools. Plenty of abs and crays out there, and when sunlight hits these cliffs they take on an amazing transformation of different shades only visible from the water.'

'Sounds cool, I'm in.' She beamed a smile, eyes shone with the prospect of adventure.

'Nat and I had our first cigarettes up here. Got so dizzy we had to grab hold of the bushes so we didn't fall off.'

'I could imagine.'

The hand touched his arm again, this time a little firmer.

'Isn't that falcon under that ledge?'

'That's where the nest is. The bird's up there out over the ocean.'

Her gaze followed his finger. 'I see it. How'd you know it's up there?'

'We're near the nest, time to leave if don't wanna get swooped.'

Her fingers now pressed on his forearm. 'You said they attack in pairs. Where's the other one?'

'That's only when they're hunting. Let's go.'

They made their way back down beneath the Bluff, following the narrow beach and the curved arc of sandstone wall toward the Yellow Rock.

About half way along he felt a light tug on his fingers. 'Lucas, kneel next to me for a second. Come on.'

He knelt beside her, excited, she moved her hands to her own knees. He shook off the disappointment.

'Close your eyes. Listen.'

'To what?'

'Shhhh. Just listen.'

He listened, though he had no idea what he was listening to other than waves.

'That hissing, tingling sound of water soaking back through the sand,' she said, 'I've not heard that before on any beach.'

'Happens on every beach.'

'Probably does but I only noticed it when I came to your house the first time. This is a place of nothing, only waves and wind. Everywhere else there's other noises, but here, there's only water seeping through sand forever.'

'Lived here all my life, never thought about it like that.'

She smiled proudly. 'There you go, taught you something.'

'Guess so.'

She stared up at the towering wall. 'Those dark stains. Hard to believe waves reach that high.'

'Higher sometimes, seven, eight metres.'

'Is it an optical illusion or does the face overhang slightly?'

'Yeah it does, but, never seen any sections fall along here. Don't yell.'

'What's that supposed to mean?'

'Just kidding.'

They walked some more and nearly reached the Yellow Rock when Clyde crashed into the water after a gull. Little Dimi followed and immediately got sucked into a sweep.

'Lucas,' Isabelle yelled, but he'd sensed the danger and ran through the water to the edge of the channel where he fished Dimi out by the collar. The terrified dog let out a yelp of surprise, twisted his little body and latched onto Lucas's finger.

He cried in pain, wrenched his hand away and released the collar. The dog landed several feet away in the shallows. Dimi rolled to his feet and took off along the beach, his frantic yelping echoed under the cliff. Clyde took up the chase.

'Dimi! Dimi!' Isabelle cried. Her dog tore along the base of the Bluff. Clyde had almost caught him when he disappeared beneath a ledge under the wall where sand had washed away. Clyde began to dig, flicking up sand. Isabelle ran up, pushing him away. 'Clyde shoo.'

Lucas trudged up the beach.

'Hurry up, will you.' She patted the sand trying to coerce her dog out. 'Come on, he's stuck.'

Lucas wiped the bloodied finger on his shorts and knelt beside her.

She stuck her arm in the crevice, then sat back up. 'Can't reach him … you try.'

'No way, he just bit me.'

'Well I'm sorry about that, but it's your fault he's in there.'

'What?'

'You chucked him.'

'I saved his life.'

'And you chucked him.'

'You're kidding me, right?' He held back on telling her how vicious he thought her little dog was. 'He would've been dragged out to sea in seconds.'

'Well thank you, but you shouldn't have thrown him.' Her look was mixed with a cross attitude and a half relenting smile. 'Let's not argue. How's your finger?'

'It'll be fine, get a shot later on.'

'I'll come to the hospital with you, but let's dig him out first. Go to the house, get a shovel … or something.'

'There's no way I can dig him out. It'll take half an hour.' He didn't want to mention the tide was turning faster than his fluctuating emotions. This beach would be underwater by the time he got back. Drowning her dog would not enhance the relationship prospects. 'Plus, if you have a look where Clyde dug, it's all rock under there.'

Isabelle began to scrape sand back, then stared at her nails. 'You're right, still, we got to do something.' Dimi whined again. 'Come on Dimi, come on,' she called, twisting her head, peering in. 'We'll just have to call the fire brigade.'

'What will they do?' Wisdom surfaced, he held in laughter.

'They'll work out a way to get him out, you watch.'

'You really are a city girl.'

'Lucas, it's an emergency.'

'They're volunteers, I'm one of them. It'll take too long to get organised.' His mates wouldn't let him live it down either and he didn't want to mention the tide. But she read his mind again.

'And the tide Lucas … shit! This beach gets underwater so quick.' She pulled her phone from her pocket.

'Let's think this through. Might have an idea.'

'Oh, and what's that?'

'He's just terrified, but he knows you won't leave. This might sound ridiculous, but if we walk off, I'll bet instincts will kick in when he sees his meal ticket leaving without him. You watch. He'll follow.'

'You're right. That's so ridiculous, thought you were an architect, not an idiot.' She held the phone up threatening to call.

'Don't call me an idiot, just trying to help.'

Lips flattened. 'Sorry.'

'It's okay. Let's just try. You people from the city always expect others to get you out of trouble.'

'In the city we rely on each other. It's called society, Lucas.'

'Down here we just work things out. Think like a dog. He's comfortable under there. Once you leave, bet he'll come running.'

'That's crazy. I'm not leaving him, no way.'

'Fine.' He rolled over on his back, made a pillow out of the sand, pulled his sunnies down and placed his hands behind his head. 'Try all you want, it won't work. I'll stick my left … my left foot on it.'

'Don't be gross. I know what you're thinking.'

He couldn't resist grinning. 'Seriously, if the dog got in there, he'll get out. We'll wait behind the Yellow Rock. If it doesn't work, we just have to come back.' The Yellow rock guarded the end of the narrow beach. He wondered if she'd climb it or wade through the surf to get around.

She leaned back on her haunches. 'Your shorts are wet. I'll wash the blood out for you later on.'

'Don't worry.'

123

'Hey … you really think it'll work?' She spoke quietly as if Dimi could comprehend their discussion.

'Nothing to lose?'

'Okay. You're on.' She slapped him on the chest, playfully hard and took off down the beach like an athlete, her dress clinging to pounding legs. He couldn't catch her. Long limbs scampered up the side of the Yellow Rock before he even reached the bottom. Lucas finally made the top and laid down beside her, searching for breath. The light easterly blew in his face, refreshing him as they both peered back down the beach.

'This better work.'

'Think like a dog. It'll work.' It had to, Lucas thought.

Still puffing from the sprint, she placed a steadying hand on his back.

Was this some sort of a test?

Emotional hoops.

Experience told him if he reached out to her, she'd only pull away.

Then there were times when she touched him, like now.

She tapped him lightly.

'Listen, I'm sorry. Didn't mean to call you an idiot.'

'I know.'

'I feel bad. You ok?'

'Handled worse.'

'Can you see?'

'Not yet.' The thigh twitched. He needed a change of thinking. 'Where'd you get a name like Dimi from?'

'Oh, it's hilarious. Bought him at two weeks old, but didn't get him till seven weeks. I remember being so excited. Couldn't settle on a name. So in the car on the way home we had our first meal together, dim sims, and with his little white coat, cute little pushed-in burnt face, his fury butt. He so looks like a dim sim on legs.'

He laughed. 'Makes sense.'

'How'd your dog get his name?'

'From a Clint Eastwood movie. He had this pet orangutan named Clyde who followed him around everywhere. Clyde did the same thing when he first came to the house.'

'What do you mean, *when* he first came to the house?'

'Just like I said, got home from surfing one day and found him lying on the doorstep, covered in gravel rash. Vet reckons he jumped from a vehicle, probably after a rabbit. He took him away and said he'd take him to the pound if he couldn't find the owner. So I helped him load the dog into his van, but as I watched them drive off I knew the dog was sad to leave because I felt sad too. Dogs make that connection. Like they know they've only got one chance, and he had the intelligence to find the only house along this side of town for miles. So I went down later on in the afternoon, paid the bill and brought him home. Put a few signs up around town, no one's come to claim him. That was a bit over a year ago. Be hard to let him go now.'

'That's sweet, Lucas. So he's a rescue?'

'Literally. Loves it here, has a strong sense of appreciation. I can tell he's happy because he snores.'

'What? That's not why dogs snore, come on—'

'It's true.'

'Who would know that?'

'I do, and you know what else? I've always thought he came for a reason.'

'Are you nuts, a reason?'

'Yeah.' He shrugged. 'Got no idea why, just what I've always thought.'

'Sounds silly.'

'That's coming from someone who named her dog after a dim sim.'

Eyes lit up, she giggled. 'You win.'

Lucas saw movement. 'Hey look.' Dimi stood beneath shadow of the cliff sniffing the sand. He headed the wrong way, then picked up their scent and began running.

'Get your head down.' He reached out to her shoulder without realising she had moved forward. Her shoulder felt round and soft, yet firm beneath her jumper and when he looked, the offending hand fondled her left breast. He retrieved it immediately. They stared at each other for a long second.

'It's okay,' she whispered, crawling even closer until she stretched over the rock right beside him. 'He's heading this way.' Dimi sprinted up the beach.

'Dimi!' she called with joy, 'Dimi!' The dog leapt up the side of the Yellow Rock into her arms. Lucas received a cherished smile.

'You did it,' she said, kissing her dog. Dimi's ears pricked when he heard barking and wriggled loose, then climbed down onto the beach to join Clyde in chasing more gulls.

'You were right.'

'Normally am.' Then he realised it sounded rather silly.

She didn't seem to care. Foggy blue eyes mesmerised him, then flickered with uncertainty. Seeking trust, perhaps.

This lady could have any man she desired from any corner of the world, yet here she was, on this lonely beach. Why?

'I'll try and remember, you're always right.'

His shoulders slumped. 'Didn't quite mean it like that. What I meant to say was—'

But Isabelle reached out and placed a delicate finger on his lips. 'I'm listening, Lucas. I trust you. You deserve to know that. But there are things—' She paused, her struggle, evident. 'My past—'

The moment arrived like a tidal wave.

'I'm not strong enough yet.' She paused again, lips trembled and he let her be until she was ready to speak. 'I'm scared because I don't know how you'll react. I … I think about you every day. If you want to walk away now I'll understand, because there's a very strong part of me that tells me to walk away from you. Before it's too late. I'm determined not to let that part of me win … but I need time.'

'I can't say I understand.'

'I don't expect you to. I'm just not good at this.' Tears formed, she bravely wiped them away.

A current of wild, confusing emotions pulsated through him. His gut tightened; still he took her hand and ran his thumb over her knuckles. She didn't pull away. 'Can you do something for me?'

She paused before saying, 'Anything, Luke.'

Luke? She'd never called him Luke before.

'I don't know what this is about but I just want you to get stronger each day. Hey, I remember one time when I was a boy, complaining to my mum about the holes in my shoes. My grandfather heard me whinging. Know what he said?'

'No idea.'

'Don't complain about your shoes, son. I've marched alongside men with no feet.'

She nodded gently. 'That's so beautiful Luke … in a tragic kind of way. He must have been an amazing man.'

'After my family died he taught me how we deal with life is how we measure ourselves. If it takes a hundred days or a thousand, he taught me to be stronger than the day before. Of course it's not always true, but seeds can't grow unless you sow them. I guess what I'm asking is, can you try?'

She pressed her lips together, then replied softly, 'Yeah … it's a deal.'

'Will you come for Christmas?'

'I have nowhere else to go.' Her neck straightened, long. 'There's nowhere else I want to be, Luke.'

It was a strange comment in part. He'd asked about her family once at dinner. They still lived in Sydney and rarely spoke to her, and she'd also diverted the conversation quickly to another topic.

Over-used instincts told him enough for now. He began to question just how little he knew about her.

'And thank you for saving my dog. Next time I'll listen.'

'He's fine. I guess.'

He heard the word, 'Coffee.'

The other words barely registered.

'Luke. Let's go to Tom's.'

He felt a light tug on his arm. 'Huh. We don't have leads for the dogs.'

'Our old chestnut, hey.'

———

From the cliff top overlooking the township their dogs appeared down on the beach. But there was no sign of Izy or the man.

Earlier she'd led him along the Great Ocean Road in her red Hyundai, the same car registered in Perth. She had disappeared around a bend as if into thin air. Three treacherous U-turns later he found the driveway. Never would he have guessed there'd be a house along that side of the road, until he saw the letterbox. He parked in the scrub, hiked toward the ocean and found the house. They ate lunch and walked toward the town beneath the cliff. The beach was too narrow. If he followed he'd be seen, so he found the track high above the ocean assuming it also led into St Claire. Now he waited.

Finally Izy and the man appeared from under the cliff.

Who was this man?

A lover?

Ridiculous.

Too short, he dressed like a bum, green board shorts, shabby surf wear tee shirt, untidy shoulder length hair. They strolled apart along the beach without holding hands or showing any signs of affection. Carlo followed the track down to the beach.

The incline was a lot less subtle than the steep slope he climbed back at the house. Three weeks had passed since his altercation with the bikers, and although his insides ached with cramp after the long drive, the walk had stretched him out nicely. Through the gaps in the foreshore trees he saw them wandering over the ocean road to a coffee shop.

Carlo had no plan, but once she heard his voice she would surely accept him. He would take her from this lonely town, back to the life she knows.

Then who was this man?

Why was Izy living in this windblown arsehole end of the earth?

Was he just a friend, perhaps a relative she hadn't previously spoken of?

They left the coffee shop soon after, returning along the cliff top track. He kept his distance back in the scrub. When he emerged overlooking the house, her car was gone. Only a Porsche and a Nissan four-wheel drive remained.

Later in the afternoon she walked to work in her uniform. Through the car window he could see her now, collecting empty glasses in the beer garden.

The clock on the dash showed five past five.

He was only a few minutes late for the interview so he drove up hill to the back of town, turning onto Tower Road. He found the address, cruised past. The gravel road ended at a gate next to the town's water basin. Beyond, a bush track continued into the surrounding forest. He returned to the address. A shaded driveway led him down to the main house where a silver-haired old man appeared wearing blue overalls. Carlo got out.

The man glanced at his watch. 'You must be Corelli. Les.'

They shook hands. 'Paul. Sorry. Bit late.'

Les looked him up and down. 'That's orright. There's the shack.' He nodded toward a small timber building further down the property. 'Follow me. What ya do for a crust?'

'Systems analyst in the meat industry, back in the Wimmera.'

'Computers ya reckon. Know as much about computers as I did Marg's meno fuck'n pause issues or whatever, but got over that no problem.' He chuckled at the memory. 'You'll meet Marg. What ya doing down this way?'

'Just split with the missus. Looking to get a place along the coast. Be good to spend a bit of time down here first before buying. Do some fishing, ya know.'

'Fishin's good off the rock wall down the pier. Just be careful, guys get washed off, end up as bait 'emselves.' He unlocked the shack.

'This is it. Coming onto holiday season could get three times what I'm askin' through January, but if ya serious, two hundred a week. Cash. Me brother built it years ago then kicked the bucket. His kids don't come down, sick of rentin' it out to fuck'n junkies and bong heads. Couldn't get rid of the ants last time.'

Carlo glanced around. The room smelt stale but the furniture appeared almost new.

"One bedroom, bathroom, kitchen, all ya need for two hundred.'

'It's fine, Les. Won't need it till after New Year's, but I'm happy to pay you from now.'

'Orright, I'll fumigate it first. You got kids? Don't want kids runnin' around.'

'No kids, mate.'

'Good. And hey, keep it under ya hat. Don't have a permit for this joint. Council's giving me a hard time, need a permit to take a shit nowadays.' He opened the fridge, the light shone on rows of stubbies. Les didn't offer a beer, he simply handed one to Carlo and cracked another.

They sat on the porch and made an agreement. Carlo paid three months in advance.

The property was surrounded by rainforest and even though it was December, the air was thick of evening chill. Les twisted the top off his fourth beer. Carlo opened his second when he threw Les a bone.

'Get down the pub much, Les?'

'Just about live there in winter. Don't get down much in summer, too many jacks. Marg made me walk home couple of weeks ago. Dinner got cold.'

Carlo grinned. 'Was down here the other day. Got talking to a very pretty woman behind the bar, tall, dark hair. What can ya tell me Les, didn't see any rings, she single or what?'

'Single all right. That'd be Isabelle.'

'Isabelle, that's the one.'

'Tap that thing you'd be a legend round 'ere, mate. Some piece of arse, 'cept frigid as fuck'n Eskimo tits, so the boys reckon. Won't have nuthin' to do with any of 'em. Rumour is she's a lemon. What a God damn waste. Can't get me head round it.'

Carlo tensed his fist and released it, letting out a pseudo chuckle.

Isabelle was single. He could go and see his mother, but who was the man?

He changed the subject to fishing.

————

Just after ten the pub closed and she walked home, alone. Carlo followed on foot through the dead town, the man's car was nowhere in sight.

Would he come tonight?

He went back to the Landcruiser and found a park up in the bush past the hospital within walking distance of her home.

On the half hour he strolled past.

Each time he returned to the car only to be haunted by noises, forcing him to go back and check.

The pounding ocean rolling up the hill could disguise a car. Each crashing wave sounded like a car, even the gusts in the treetops mimicked cars.

Each car travelling east or west along the ocean road sounded like a Porsche or a four-wheel drive turning up her street. But as the early morning hours progressed he became more confident.

Izy slept alone.

At three thirty he laid the seat back and rested his eyes. Thumping on his window woke him. Carlo leapt up. Pain stabbed his back. First instinct was to reach for the gun in the glove box. He chose his second instinct – to see who was making the noise. Morning light pierced the trees and through the moisture on the window, he saw a figure.

A cop? Only a country cop.

More tapping on the glass. He turned the ignition on and pushed the window button down, relieved to see only a parking inspector with a German shepherd tethered on a short leash. Bird songs filled the air.

'Good morning sir, are you aware it is illegal to sleep in your vehicle along the coast.'

What? He thought. Illegal to sleep in a car?

Carlo rubbed his eyes. 'No. Sorry. Ahhh, I'm travelling through. Got tired. Pulled over maybe an hour ago for a quick nap. What's the time?'

'Ten past seven sir, bonnet's stone cold.'

'Must have overslept.' He read the nametag. *DUBERLY.* 'I'm sorry Officer Dooberly, had no idea.'

The man's eyes narrowed, they were small and set too far apart, housed beneath sharp overhanging brows. 'It's pronounced Dub … Duberly.' He flicked his moustache with his forefinger.

Carlo gave a friendly smile. He let the seat up, grimacing as his back tensed. 'Crook back.'

'Sir, I'm not going to book you but please be aware. It's getting on for Christmas, we're mainly concerned with trouble makers, surfers and the like sleeping in cars, making a mess.' Carlo couldn't believe this idiot's job was to wake people up. Good way to get shot. 'No problem, thank you officer.' He started the Landcruiser. Nadine would be asking serious questions, he had planned on being half way home by now. There would be a hundred missed calls when he turned the phone on.

'Drive safe, sir,' the officer said.

10

South of Griffith, New South Wales

The cattle grate rumbled as Carlo drove through the gates beneath the familiar wooden archway with

PARADISO DEL RIVERINA,

carved into the face. He was pleased to notice the rapid growth of the lemon-scented gums lining the drive all the way to the house. Hard work was invested in those trees. As a boy he'd helped his father nurse the saplings through winter frosts. They branched the driveway now. Cattle lapped up their shade on the other side of the fence.

To his left in the front corner of the paddock, an old hay shelter stood from the time before his family purchased the land. Lean smoke drifted from the open driver side window of a silver Mercedes, parked beneath. Another car, also containing Marco Sabina's men had tailed him from the Victorian border.

The house had been extended. A new wing stretched eastward. Roof tiles had not yet faded under the fierce Riverina sun. In the distance a lone figure stood on the front porch.

Papà.

Nausea swam in his stomach.

He passed the row of open garages. Leaves and bark tossed about on the hot winds had settled in clusters behind the wheels of cars crammed side by side.

Garages were full. Everyone's here.

Carlo drove around the loop and pulled up in front of the steps. Franco stood, rigid, face hard and stern, hair still thick and dark. Sideburns full and grey. Long, powerful limbs hung by his side from decades of toil. Franco was a worker. Each day he would arrive home from the abattoirs, eat dinner and work on the farm until dusk. Carlo often helped, avoiding homework when he could.

Palms became moist. He wiped his jeans.

The front door opened. Marco Sabina appeared holding the door for a bandy legged old woman wearing a short sleeved black dress.

Carlo barely recognised his mother.

Tears surfaced. His throat, parched.

Despite her hunched back, she managed the steps with Marco supporting one arm. Carlo got out of the car.

She took a long, sorrowful look at his face then buried herself in his chest, wrapping him in her arms.

'Carlo, Carlo.' She repeated over and over. He nestled his face in her hair, drawing in the aroma of his childhood.

'Mamma.

'I love you, Mamma.'

She had accepted him. For the first time in eight years he fully regretted his actions. Joy, sadness, immense guilt flowed in merging torrents of tears as they held each other. Nails scratched through his shirt. She had strength.

'*M'a scusari Mamma* … I'm sorry … I'm so sorry.' Then he remembered Nicky's words, "*She doesn't believe you did it*". Yet he felt no consolation, only an even greater sadness. '*M'a scusari Mamma.*' Fingers found ribs where there was once ample flesh, flushing him with more self-condemnation.

'Merry Christmas, Mamma.' The lump in his throat shuddered. He caressed her back.

'How are you feeling?'

'Good, my Carlo. Good. Much much better now. Merry Christmas. Oh my darling, I can't believe it. You are back to me.' Loving hands touched his face and though her pallid cheeks bore only a tinge of rose, eyes were moist and rich with joy, not torn by worry or disbelief that this *was* her son. He glanced around. Franco had disappeared, the rest of the family huddled beneath the verandah, watching. Nicky and that pig of a wife, Cristina. Angela's hand threaded the arm of a tall, strapping young guy, the only man dressed in a suit and tie. Marco and his wife stood next to Jimmy and Donna Riggs.

Strong fingers pressed into his shoulder. *Papà.*

'*Buon Natale, figghiu miu.*' (Merry Christmas, my son). He touched his father's cheeks, felt the leathery skin. Fingertips dug into his back as they hugged.

'Papà, Merry Christmas,' Carlo whispered, weeping openly.

His mother turned to the family. '*È arrí ccu nuantri.*' (He is with us again).

Cheering and laughter rose. Angela ran down the steps. 'Is it you Carlo, is it really you?'

Angela, now a woman, so beautiful, just like Nicky said.

'Angela.'

When she heard his voice she squealed and jumped up, he lifted his kid sister off the ground. Arms flung around his neck. She kissed him over and over, grabbing at his cheeks. 'I can't believe it. Merry Christmas, Carlo.' Eyes sparkled like her diamond earrings. 'I have someone special for you to meet.'

'Heard you're getting married. Congratulations.'

'Thank you Carlo, you will like him, promise me.'

'Give me a look at you,' he said. 'You're much too pretty to get married.'

She slapped him on the chest and spoke softly. 'I'm no longer sixteen. We're in love. You *will* be kind to him. Promise me.'

'Naturally. If he's not like that Priarto boy, then I promise.'

The Priarto boy was her first boyfriend. But his mother had brought Angela up proper and the boy broke her heart by screwing a school friend. Carlo was living in Sydney when his mother called. Angela wouldn't come out of her room, refusing to eat. Carlo returned home and after spending the night sleeping on the couch in Angela's room, she eventually opened up to him the next morning.

That day he took Marco into Griffith and found the boy's car parked at a pool hall in Banna Avenue. Marco locked the door so no-one could leave, Carlo snapped both the kid's legs. The matter ended when the boy's father, a local grower visited Franco that night and apologised for his son's behaviour.

'Come, Carlo.' She led him by the hand.

'Daniel.' She motioned to the young man who smiled and stepped forward.

'Carlo. Meet my fiancé, Daniel.'

They shook hands. 'Merry Christmas, Daniel.'

'Nice to meet you, sir. Merry Christmas.'

Carlo detected an air of confidence. He liked the cut of the lad, good square shoulders. Nicky's words rang again. *"I'm grooming him."*

'Sir?' Marco bellowed, with a cheery laugh.

'I know you're not familiar with respect,' Carlo replied. 'I can teach this young buck a—'

Angela lashed out, striking him with an open palm across the shoulder. 'I warned you.'

He chuckled without letting go of the man's hand. 'How old are you Daniel?'

'Twenty-six, sir.'

'Call me Carlo.' He nodded toward his father, chatting with Jimmy on the steps. 'You call him sir.'

'Yes … Carlo.'

Carlo still hadn't let go of the hand. He gave it a firm squeeze, this time nodding toward Angela who was now helping her mother up the stairs. 'See that smile. You're main purpose in life is to make sure that smile is permanent, Daniel.'

'I will always take great care of her.' Daniel's shoulders stiffened back.' You can be sure—'

'Damn right I can be sure.'

Carlo gave the hand another press. Eyes danced left then right. The first sign of nervousness, leaving no doubt Daniel knew the fate of the Priarto boy. Carlo released the hand.

'And this man here ... don't call him sir, either. Come here you old Bull.'

Laughing, he drove his hand into Marco's. Carlo tried to wrap the palm early, the Bull was too quick, a crushing handshake locked on. Marco's grin was just as menacing.

'Merry Christmas, Piccolo, if it is you?' Marco let out a mild chuckle. 'I know it's you. You're still slow, eh.' They hugged, slapping backs.

'That boot maker of yours still in town?' Carlo said.

'Piccolo, it's Christmas day. Maybe the day after tomorrow we'll get you new boots, uh. Let me look at you. Been working out?' Marco stood four inches shorter than Carlo, a chest like a wine barrel. Carlo remembered too well the floggings Marco handed out in the back stable they'd converted into a boxing ring. Marco stepped back, eyed him up and down and shot out a tap to Carlo's ribs. He winced at the bolt of pain. The Bull gave a look of surprise. 'Piccolo, what's this?'

'Don't,' Carlo whispered, glancing around nervously. Everyone was talking and laughing. No one noticed. He went to touch Carlo's side again, but he was ready and blocked the arm away.

'We have some talking to do later on, eh.'

'Hit the side of the pool at the house where I'm staying.'

Marco crossed his arms, gave a sideways glance. 'I know you too well, Pazzu.'

'Carlo?' Marco's wife, Louisa greeted him with a kiss on the cheek. Carlo gave her a hug, happy to be away from her husband's suspicious gaze. He moved quickly to exchange greetings with Jimmy and Donna, then Nicky and Cristina. Her kiss, icy as a Tasman Sea breeze. Carlo wondered if Nicky still kept his mistress in Sydney, she was much younger, far more attractive. He should be rid of this woman by now.

Someone grabbed his hand. 'Come on, I've got a surprise for you,' Angela said, leading him through the front door.

Inside the grand entry, a Christmas tree almost reached the second storey ceiling decorated with flashing lights and tinsel, glass baubles the size of basketballs with boxes of presents overflowing around the bottom. His eyes spiralled up the marble staircase. Wire stays attached to the landing supported the tree.

'How the hell did you get that in here?'

'We had to take the patio doors out, Marco helped me,' she said, grinning with pride. 'I even bought presents for you to give out.'

'You're quite the organiser. Papà let you put that on his floor?'

'He's mellowed. Things have changed around here.' She gave him a slightly defeated look. Carlo's concern grew.

'How's Mamma going, really?'

'She's doing well. The doctor says if she continues to improve he'll take her off the medication soon.'

'Okay. Good.' Nostalgia overtook him. He longed to be the kid ready to explore the old, along with the new, to feel the cooler night air draw through his bedroom window. He poked his head in the dining room, Anita was lighting candles on the table. A fondness swept through him. She disappeared into the kitchen and as the family mingled in through the entry, Carlo followed her.

She was facing the bench carving up pork. He placed a hand on her hip. 'Hello, Anita.'

She gasped and spun with the knife in her hand, forcing him to shy away from the point. Her mouth froze wide open in shock, then a squeal followed, her smile broke out, laughing the same sexually adventurous laugh from all those years ago. 'Carlo?'

She had recognised his voice.

'Carlo, is that you? I … I've heard—'

'It's me, Anita.'

She reached up, wrapping her hands around his neck, planting a voluptuous kiss, lips still full, succulent.

'Your face? What have you done?'

'It's a long story. But it's me.'

'I can't believe it. I miss you,' she whispered. To his knowledge, only Jimmy and Nicky knew of the affair. 'Happy Christmas darling, I never expected to see you back here. I couldn't ask any questions. What happened—?' Then her eyes widened, 'I should have known. Your mother asked me to make pea soup, your favourite. It's on the stovetop.'

He glanced at the pot as the kitchen door swung open. His mother's smile was strong and radiant. 'He is back, Anita. What do you think, eh?' She raised her hands in triumph. As well as an employee, Anita was a devoted and loving friend of his mother. Whenever his parents travelled Anita went along. She lived in her own quarters with an ensuite and a living room Carlo used to sneak into.

'I know, I know. What a Christmas present, huh.' Anita's face glowed. 'Go, sit down, I'll bring the meat out.'

'Everyone is getting ready Carlo, come on,' his mother said leading him by the hand.

Children's screams and pitched voices echoed through the dining room. Cristina and Donna sat them all at the far end of the table where they chattered noisily, comparing toys, showing little interest when Franco introduced their visiting distant cousin from Queensland. Marco's eldest son Lou, a strapping lad portrayed an inquisitive expression. Marco would handle any questions. Carlo sat next to Daniel. Nicky sat opposite and behind him, Carlo noticed the family photos set out on the antique wall unit in between the statues of Mary and Christ nailed to the cross. He studied himself, the old self. How would Mamma cope with new photos? Where will they be placed? Anita appeared, positioning the meat amongst the steaming pasta and vegetables before taking her seat beside Carlo's mother.

Anita was the only other person at the table without a partner. Thoughts turned to Izy. He'd been down the coast on two further occasions. Both times she slept alone.

Faithful Izy will take her seat next year.

——

'You will stay here on the farm for two weeks with your mother,' Franco said from behind the desk in his office. 'That's all I'm willing to risk.'

'What about after that?'

'I am sending you back to Melbourne.'

Carlo was so surprised he had to hold back from glancing over at Jimmy, who was leaning against the windowsill to his right. Marco stood at the door behind them. Nicky was seated next to Carlo.

'Why Melbourne?'

Franco moved around the desk and stabbed his finger at Carlo, his demeanour remained calm and even as always. 'If I had my way you would not even be in this country. What do you want? You want me to allow you to go back to Sydney? Is that it? Do I have to explain what happens if this goes wrong?' Your brother wants to send you to Queensland. Maybe he's right, but Benny says he should keep you in Melbourne.'

'When can I visit Mamma?'

'Anytime. But you are not permitted to go into Griffith or visit anyone in the Riverina, or anyone else who was a part of your old life. Your mother is the only reason you are to return to New South Wales. She has improved so much, we are travelling to Sicily in February. Her cousin Maria is sick. This will be the last time they see each other.'

'She's well enough to travel?'

'The doctor says yes.'

'What are your long term plans for me?'

'When things settle down Nicky will take you up north. You will live on one of our cattle stations. There will be opportunities to work your way back into the business. Of course there is a position for you, but you have to work hard first.'

'Yes Papà.'

Banished again. He thought of Izy. This cannot work. How would he get the chance to approach her, or even to keep an eye on her?

'Good.' His father returned to his seat behind the desk.

'You will have no contact with anyone except for me,' Nicky said.

But Carlo ignored him, levelling eyes at his father. 'Why did you not act?'

Franco looked up, astonished. 'What did you say to me?'

'You know what they did to me. What they tried to do to us. I am your son.'

Franco's eyes narrowed. 'Are you telling me it was not your fault?'

'I'm telling—'

'No Carlo, you're telling me it was not your fault. Nothing ever is. It was your own business. *Dita sporche Carlo*, I always warned you.' Franco pointed at Marco without taking his spearing gaze off Carlo. 'Dirty fingers. Marco warned you too. For once you are going to learn to take ownership.

Nobody else is to blame.' Franco turned to Jimmy. 'Why didn't I act, Jimmy?'

Jimmy folded his arms. 'You're safe, Carlo. You're alive. The family is intact, your mother is improving, business is good. L'ombrello is performing better than any other super fund in the country. Everything else is under control. It's not about you, mate. It's business. Always business.'

'Thank you, Jimmy.' Franco turned back to Carlo. 'Do you understand what you are to do?'

Carlo glanced at Nicky, then at Jimmy. The old firm was solid without him. 'Yes, Papà.'

'Good. There will be no further talk of this. There is peace. I want no disruptions. Leave us.'

————

Mid-afternoon, Carlo found a quiet moment and ventured out behind the house to the stables. He wandered slowly taking it all in, relieved to be sent back to Melbourne, closer to Izy, closer to rebuilding their old lives.

Perhaps Benny might be able to have Nadine return while he worked out his plans. Yesterday she delivered him to the home of Eddy Mollica, a long-time family associate who owned olive groves on the Murray River. There were no hugs or kisses when he asked if she would miss him. Instead Nadine replied she'd miss the leather seats in the Landcruiser more. He'd become accustomed to her humorous barbs. *"It's been fun,"* she'd said before slapping his butt and driving off in a hire car. He was a little sad to see the last of her.

Perhaps it's better she was gone for good.

The wind had died, horse flies lingered. The stench of stables wafted in the shimmering, rising heat. He was home. A head poked over the stable door. 'Alfie?' The horse let out a quiet nicker and shook its head rapidly.

Carlo stroked his horse's nose, delighted to see him still alive. He spoke low. 'You remember me, Alfie? How is it you still know me?' The horse nuzzled his shoulder.

'I've been taking good care of him for you,' Angela said from behind.

'Thank you, he looks in excellent condition.'

'Ride him when I can. Let's ride later on.'

'Sure. I'd like to see the river at sunset. How's Remy?'

'Oh, he's beautiful, Carlo. Come take a look.'

Angela led him toward the stable. 'Remy, I have someone for you to meet.'

He chuckled at his sister's exuberance, the horse appeared at the stable door. 'You remember him Remy, I know you do.' She opened the door.

Remy stood at seventeen hands. A magnificent bay of Beduino bloodline Carlo imported as a gift from Mexico to help her through dark, sweet sixteen moods. Long days spent in her room quickly became distant memories. His mother had commented at the time, *"It's like getting my daughter back."*

She grabbed a currycomb and with her back to Carlo, began grooming the horse with long, sweeping strokes. 'How long are you staying?'

'Back for good.'

'Mamma needs you here. I'm not going to discuss what happened Carlo, but what you did to Mamma, you nearly killed her.'

Her authoritative tone stunned him for an instant. His kid sister had really grown up.

A Caruso, after all.

Perhaps more like her father than her mother.

'What you did was unforgiveable.'

Wo, he thought. She spoke like Franco, so calm, so measured. Carlo realised he had missed more than just eight years of her life. 'Don't you speak to me like that.'

She spun on her heel. 'Who the fuck do you think you are? You're lucky you have this family. You have no idea what you put us through.'

'Don't you dare treat me like some outcast.'

'Shut the fuck up, Carlo, just shut the fuck up! I've waited a long time for this. I know about your business in Sydney. Why did you think you could get away with it?'

He glared at her in disbelief, then out of the corner of his eye he saw Jimmy approaching with beers in each hand. 'We'll talk about this when we ride later on,' and he left the stable.

'Yes we will.'

He glanced back. She wasn't even looking at him while she stroked the horse, so he attempted to walk off again.

'Hey,' she called.

'What now?' He turned and faced her.

'Thanks for being kind to him. I love him.'

He studied her, standing on her toes combing the top of Remy's back.

Able to move on easily, so much like Papà.

Jimmy passed over the beer. 'Cheers.'

'Cheers.'

They tapped beers. Carlo led Jimmy away toward Alfie's stable.

'He still knows me, how about that,' Carlo said, scratching Alfie's nose.

'In many ways animals are smarter than us.'

'That's for sure. Don't have to put up with any of the bullshit. Thanks for the support in there.'

'You *did* get my support,' Jimmy said.

Carlo grinned. 'Got something for me?'

Jimmy handed over an envelope.

'Thanks mate.' Carlo slipped it in the rear pocket of his jeans.

'Hey listen, Carlo. I've never let you down, but what the hell are you doing crossing paths with these guys? You're back in the country for one minute.'

'It's personal. All you need to know is how much I appreciate this.' Behind Alfie he saw his old stock whip coiled on a nail at the rear of the stable. He unlatched the door, wandered over and lifted the whip.

'Personal?' Jimmy replied. 'That attitude got you into all this trouble. Fuck'n bikers? Let Nicky take care of it, whatever it is.'

With the whip in his hand, Carlo's mood brightened. 'I handle my own business. You know better than anyone.'

'And you know what happens to me if Nicky and Franco find out I gave you that information?'

'The only way they're going to find out is if you tell them. And you're not going to do that.'

'I feel like for the first time in my life I've been disloyal to your father.'

'Nobody lives forever Jimmy. Start thinking about your loyalty to me. You mean too much to this family. Nothing will come of this.'

'Yeah, what about the girl?'

Carlo felt his anger rise but kept his temper in check, clasping a hand on his friend's shoulder. 'You're like a brother to me, but you're worrying about matters that don't concern you.' He tightened his fingers but Jimmy didn't flinch. He'd always known he could push Carlo further than any other man.

He left the stable. Jimmy followed.

'Carlo—'

Carlo put his index finger to his lips and motioned toward Remy's door.

They walked clear of the stables, out of his sister's earshot. Two light aircraft tails stuck out of the hanger behind the stables. Nicky and Marco were both competent fliers.

'There's not a day when I don't think about her.'

'You can't possibly mean that. Let it go.'

'Could you let Donna go?'

'That's different.'

'Different? What right do you have to tell me your situation is different than mine? No man has that right.'

'What the fuck's going through your head? She'll go to the cops again. Besides, you heard your father. He'll send you to Queensland.'

'I can't go and live up the back of shit creek without her. Set up an account.'

'You know I'd have to speak with Ricky.'

'Use your own funds.'

Jimmy gave a relenting sigh. 'Haven't closed the overseas account yet.'

'Good.'

'Shit Carlo. This is trouble. I can feel it in my bones. She's probably got a life down there. It's all over, mate.'

'Know what? Coming here today makes me more determined than ever. Even my little sister's getting married.'

'Determined? You're determined to get yourself killed, that's all you'll achieve. Let it go, Carlo. Nicky 'll look after you, he'll get another girl.'

'No one looks after me. You know that.'

Jimmy could be right, although Carlo didn't want to tell him. Instead he placed an arm around his neck, reeling him in. 'Merry Christmas, buddy.'

'You too. Glad to have you back home, mate.'

In the distance a shadowy line of river reds showed where Murrumbidgee River slipped through the countryside. Carlo sculled the rest of his beer and tossed the empty can in the air. He watched it rise and fall toward the ground and cracked the whip. A puff of dirt flew as the tail lashed, sending the can straight up into the air again. 'Still got it, Jimmy.' The can fell. He took a step forward and thought of Blackbeard. He cracked the whip once more and missed. The can hit the dirt.

———

Lucas reached the study just as the ringing stopped. A missed a call from Nat. They were due to fly out to Hawaii in two days. Nat had come out and spent Christmas day with them, but he'd left over an hour ago.

Lucas picked up the phone to call him back when the words *DO YOUR WORK* glided across the otherwise vacant computer screen.

For no particular reason he pressed the space button.

The inbox appeared, eleven unread messages. He deleted three spams, the fourth was from Carmen dated the twenty-third of December with an attachment titled, IZY.

Fingers hovered over the delete button. In the subject box was written,

'Has she told you yet?' He opened it and read.

'Dear Lucas,

I hope you're well.
I know you won't answer my calls or emails but you must read this.

He clicked on the attachment, a picture appeared. She was much younger. Cheeks were square, expertly shadow-lined and hollowed like they were chiselled thin.

'IZY?'

He glanced back at Carmen's words.

I came to see you a week ago. You weren't home, I found you in St Claire. You walked right past me. I was sitting on the steps of the Lifesaving Club and I saw her with you. She is so beautiful. I left, sad, lonelier than I

have ever felt in my life, yet happy for you. But her face haunted me to the point where I couldn't sleep.

Then it came to me. Earlier in the year Connie and I went to the pub while you and Horry were surfing. She was the barmaid. At the time I thought I knew her face, though I couldn't place it.

Then when I saw her with you, the recollection came on much stronger so I Googled her. Isabelle Kelly is a former model known as Izy, a very infamous model from Sydney.

I know it's true because I came back down and saw her in the hotel. I should have come to see you then, but I didn't want to interfere. Now I'm interfering. I'm sorry. I know what you'll think of me, but I'm concerned for you.

She appeared on the cover of every magazine...'

He opened his explorer, typed in IZY.

Izy ... do you mean Isabelle Kelly? He clicked.

Isabelle Kelly. Model known as Izy... Google profile...

Links to Wikipedia pages, web addresses.

He clicked the images tab. More photos loaded up, coloured and black and white, all professional, row after row, each shot portraying different hairstyles, varying colours and tones. Beneath it all was Isabelle. Fine, delicate, provocative, and so different. He clicked on *more...*

The download speed, slower than life. A link to a Wikipedia page popped up but his eyes scanned ahead, driven by the fear of unknown knowledge a fingertip away.

A link to the Sydney Morning Herald.

Izy questioned over Murders...

His chest tightened.

Model Isabelle Kelly arrested in relation to the murders of Sydney Detectives Craig Welham and Sam Benson...

In a state of semi- denial he searched for the name.

Carlo Caruso, wanted for the murders of Sydney Detectives...

Fully aware of the name, truth sharpened his mind, it sent nerves tingling across his scalp.

Crimes of the century... Carlo Caruso. Australian Mafia stories. Two million dollar reward... The Fox http://google profiles.

He recalled how the media had dubbed Caruso The Fox after all the supposed sightings around the world. Laughter rose from the deck. Through the sliding door this lady chatted with Steve, sipping red. Since eight that morning they'd prepped and cooked Christmas lunch, laughed and toasted with Steve and Horry, their families too. Patto, Thumbtack, Tom and Sheila had joined them at various stages. Even Reno and Stella came out for an afternoon drink. The house hummed with life. They'd eaten leftovers for dinner on the deck while a majestic Christmas day sunset sank beneath the orange Bluff.

Fingers interlocked, blood rose in clenched knuckles, a mind buried in thought, studying a photo he knew too well.

The Benson Boy.

More innocence seemed lost forever when an entire country woke to the news this boy had been playing the nation's favourite pastime, backyard cricket with his dad hours before the two officers were gunned down by Caruso.

The image of the little boy standing tall, supporting his mum as she knelt weeping by his dad's graveside was the media's favourite *go to* shot of the crime.

His hand fumbled onto a pencil and paper, he scratched the word *RESOLVE* between two lines.

Air moved behind. Her reflection filled the screen. He spun and saw crumpled lips, tears already streaming down her shattered face.

'I'm sorry Lucas ... I ... I—'

She turned and fled.

———

Lucas followed the taillights in the distance, keeping back, giving her space through the tight bends. He thought about letting her go, yet couldn't stand leaving her alone for another Christmas, a lifetime of Christmases, perhaps gone. She turned up her street. When he pulled up at the house the door was shut. Lights were off.

He knocked.

'Isabelle.

'Isabelle.'

A faint noise. A creak. Weight pressed against the door.

'Isabelle ... please?'

The door finally opened. She clutched her dog, face distraught.

'I want you to go.'

'You know I can't do that. I'm in love with you.'

'After what you've just read? How could you—?'

'More than you can believe.'

After an extended moment she turned away and walked to the couch, still cradling Dimi.

Lucas closed the door and sat next to her.

'I told you I'm not good at this, now you know why. I've never felt like this about anyone, Luke.'

'So you didn't love him?'

'No.' She put the dog on the floor, it trotted off down the passage. 'It was just the physical infatuation of a young, naive girl who's long gone. I can't talk to her ... only live with her.'

He placed an arm around her, pulled her in, she didn't resist.

'I wanted so much to tell you before Christmas. Didn't want to ruin today, or your holiday. Now I've probably ruined everything. In my mind there was always an excuse.' She pursed her lips, wiped away tears, took a deep, quaking breath. 'Carlo and I lived together for two years.'

He lifted her chin. 'Not now.'

Her lips froze then parted and they kissed and gently butted foreheads, he kissed her again and again, unable to stop.

'When can I tell you, Luke?' Her breath, hot. 'I've been practising in the mirror. I have so much to tell.'

'After.'

She let out a small moan. They kissed, long. Her blue eyes wore conviction. 'I didn't want you to come ... look at you, Luke. I love you so much. Can you excuse me?'

Before he could find words she stood and disappeared down the passage. Minutes later bare feet padded back down the hallway in a nighty, ghosting in colour from white to pink; long, but it still hung above her knees, wavering, inviting, clinging to the naked darkness below her waist. She carried Dimi's bed with Dimi in it and placed it on the living room floor. The dog relaxed and curled up again, he'd had a long day.

'Ummm ... he normally sleeps in my room.' Her face had been freshened, gone were the blotches, tears and caution, replaced by the perfect smile. A hand stretched out, she nodded gently. 'I deserve you, Luke.'

11

'I was a child model. By fifteen I'd signed with the largest agency in the country. My family were Adventists. Dad was a pastor and my mother – who also managed me – desperately tried to keep me in the church. Had enough of religion by then. My mind was expanding. I wouldn't listen. Within two years I hired my own manager.

'I remember myself at that age, couldn't be told anything,' Lucas said.

'Religion taught me to look one way. Modelling, the career my mother pushed me into showed me many other roads. Guess I must have been a sitting duck for a parasite like Carlo Caruso. Nine years older, rich and very handsome.

'We met at a party, moved in together not long after I turned eighteen. Pretty much destroyed any relationship with my parents.

'It was easy to be with Carlo – all things aside – I have to say it was an exciting time. He owned a penthouse overlooking Sydney Harbour, life was surreal, the world just moved about below us. We had our separate careers. He told me he worked for his family in the meat business. Turned out to be the leader of an international drug ring, I had no idea.'

'How could he hide all that from you?'

'Never saw him do drugs, simple as that. You wouldn't believe some of the parties we went to. Bowls full of cocaine – on tap, as they used to say – yet he never touched it, not in front of me anyway. Carlo was a fitness fanatic, spent hours at a time in the gym.'

'What about you?'

'Tried coke a few times, didn't like how I felt the next morning, saw what it did to other models so I didn't touch it again.'

'I'm glad you're truthful about that.'

'I'm an honest person, Luke. I'll never lie to you. There are some things I can't tell you about the investigation, but you're … you're my best friend, now this.'

'I'm sorry. I didn't mean to—'

'It's okay. I want you to speak your mind.' Light breath pampered his skin, she twirled fingers through the hairs on his chest. 'Everything has manifested to this moment right now, I realise it's a lot for you to absorb.

'The first inkling I had was on a working trip to Los Angeles. Carlo surprised me by turning up on the second last day, totally unannounced. I was happy to see him, though I remember how weird it felt. Said he had business in America, yet I found it strange he hadn't told me beforehand.

'When we returned to Sydney I was called in for a briefing. Three ex-models ran the agency, they questioned me about the trip, which seemed okay. Then they asked about a man named Kurt Stein. I denied knowing him, as I honestly had no idea who my bosses were talking about. Then they informed me Stein had attended a function on our last night in L.A. and was found in a garden bed, beaten almost to death. He told police the man who assaulted him was with me at the party.

'Then I clicked. I'd been talking to a photographer named Kurt. We had a drink, he seemed a nice man but I didn't know his last name. It made me look like a liar. Their questions led to Carlo, was he ever violent toward me, toward anyone I knew. I said of course not. I became so confused. I didn't believe Carlo bashed that man. Not my boyfriend, no way. I got defensive.

'They asked about his business and also of his father. I told them everything I knew. I'd only met his father twice. They live on a farm near Griffith. Their house is … well, it's a mansion on thousands of acres. Carlo had an office in Sydney, that's all I saw of his work. Afterwards I realised how little I actually knew about him.

'I enjoyed a good relationship with my bosses and had nothing to hide. But despite saying they were concerned about my welfare, I knew they weren't telling me everything. I was scheduled to return to L.A. the next month. The trip got cancelled. I was devastated. These ladies ran a business in a tough industry. They knew a lot of important people and I found myself questioning how they could be wrong.'

'Did they somehow know this guy was a drug dealer?'

'Who knows? But I believe they knew a lot more than they were letting on, and I also think they unwittingly put my life in danger. A part of me was so angry, another part of me knew sometimes we find ourselves in a position to say something, then better judgment or legalities prevent us. Things work very differently in high circles.'

'What do you mean by that?'

'Exactly what I said. If you haven't been there, it's hard to explain. Information gets passed around. In the weeks leading up to the murders Carlo spent most of the time away. The few times we were together he seemed distant, aloof. I told myself if he was having an affair, I could handle that. I had no idea he was setting up a large importation of cocaine.

'I began to see through the flowers and gifts and crap. Carlo had arms the size of my thighs, I began to see a man I didn't know, a man who could easily have beaten that poor photographer to a pulp ... and he did, in a jealous rage. Not that he had anything to be jealous about. I never cheated.

'I also remember being scared of the real answers. Couldn't confront him. When you're in denial, fear and cowardice seem to run strikingly parallel and I didn't have the courage.

'Funny thing is, in all our time together we never argued. Until one night at dinner. He must've sensed something was wrong because he told me if I ever left, he would find me and kill me and any man with me.'

'He threatened to kill you! Why didn't you leave then?'

'Fear. I saw the killer in his eyes. I didn't know what to do. I wasn't speaking to my family, felt I didn't have the support of the agency and Carlo and my manager knew each other well. Turns out he was also involved and went to jail. I felt so alone. The next day after that dinner I made a call to the police but hung up. That was four days before the murders. When they checked my phone records after the arrest, that phone call did not go well for me. They accused me of holding back information.

'I wanted to leave, but couldn't work out how. Often I think about the consequences. Then the murders happened. You probably look at me differently to the girl you just made love to.'

'No, I don't. You're the same person I'm in love with.'

'Thanks,' she still sounded despondent. 'Just needed to hear it I s'pose. It must've been a tremendous shock what you read earlier. Believe me. I know. He lived a double life. When the police arrested me, that's the first I knew about his involvement in either drugs or those murders.'

'Didn't he use some sort of machine gun?'

'Yes. It was horrible. I'd heard about the shootings on the news. Two officers machine gunned, felt like our city had changed forever. Went to bed around midnight, they raided our apartment at four am. Carlo had disappeared, they led me out in handcuffs with only a jacket to cover me. Could've taken me through a back door but reporters had been tipped off. My trial by media had begun. I became public enemy number two. The Police held me for questioning, then released me back into the custody of my parents. No one has seen Carlo since and the media came after me instead. Camped in our street. Even neighbours were doing interviews.

'Funny thing is, Carlo's father is supposed to be a very powerful Mafia figure, yet the media don't go near him. I was an easy target, the model with the world at her feet. They're the professionals at all that tall poppy crap.'

Lucas racked his memory. 'I remember some story about a priest or a pastor assaulting a media crew. Must have been your dad?'

'Yeah. They couldn't get to me so they hassled Dad for an interview outside the church. Dad's a big man and very kind, but he lost it. He'd just delivered a sermon when they approached him at the church gates. They think they have a right because they're the media. They take footage of you leaving your driveway with the window wound up, then say they have a story. I don't get it. The paper ended up dropping the charges, but even still, I knew I couldn't stay in Sydney. So did Dad. When he came home from the police station that day, Mum and I had a huge fight. The devil incarnate she called me. Dad told me my only choice was to go to the U.S. to live with members of the church. It was insane. No way was I becoming some zealot's fourth wife in a religious boot camp in the bloody Bible belt. I got out of there. Just grabbed my purse and Dad's car keys and drove to the train station. Hardest thing I'd ever done.'

'Why? You'd left home once already.'

'Wasn't that. I'd never driven a car before. If I wanted to go somewhere either Carlo would drive or the agency would send a car. That's the kind of sheltered life I led. Don't worry, Dad found the car easily enough, the one parked sideways with the keys above the visor like I'd seen him do. I caught a train to the airport and the next plane to Perth with only the clothes I wore. It's not that I don't love my parents or didn't appreciate anything they did for me, we're just vastly different people. I was well adjusted for my age, fiercely independent. Going back there felt like going back in time. How can I explain it? The walls closed in. My skin crawled like someone was running fingernails down my soul. My older sister's marriage had failed, leaving her to raise her two boys on her own. She'd come over to see me just to make herself feel better, I knew what was going on. We were never that close and she was jealous of my career. I do miss my nephews though. They were cute, but too young to remember me and that's probably best for them.'

Lucas thought of his past life with Sue, his parents, the intense emotions, disbelief, the vast depths of depression.

The blur of the funerals.

He stroked her cheek. Somehow he understood.

Was there an obligation to like your own family?

She continued, 'Perth liberated me. As the American's say, I became a regular. My sense of pride returned, did a lot of soul searching. I was away from all the influences in my life and able to self-analyse. The only wrong decision I had made was being with him. The agency released me. Nobody knew me or recognised me. I changed my hair, dropped the make-up and used my middle name Anne, got a job, bought clothes off a rack for the first time in years, got my licence and bought my apartment which I still own.'

'I would've thought the police wouldn't let you go.'

'I rang a police officer as soon as I landed. He's a very special man to me, Luke. His name is Inspector John Ingliss. He was in charge of the two officers killed. Someday I want you to meet him and his wife.'

'Why? I would've thought this would be all behind you?'

'It is behind me. Umm … I hope you don't mind, I rang him and told him all about you.'

'I guess not, but why would you do that?'

'I was so excited about you, just had to tell someone. Conversations are difficult with my parents. They visited me once in Perth. We have little in common. John is the only person I wanted to ring.

'You remember the day when Dimi got stuck under the cliff. I came home from work that night and rang him – even though it was late – I just had to tell someone about you, how coming here is the best thing to ever happen to me. We talked for an hour about your beach house, your dog and how we met. How it's the coldest, most drizzly, windy place I've ever been to, also how beautiful and rugged it is and how you all treat me as a normal person. I also told him I was almost ready for you.'

'What'd he say to that?'

'He was stoked for me, as you guys would say.' She tapped him on the chest. 'He said I deserved you. Told me not to let you go. Not that I wanted to, I just needed a lot of assurance because there were times when, as you and I got close, all I could think of was running. Leaving this town forever, not involving you in any of this. He made me stay. Said I have a right to happiness.'

It was a heartfelt reply and he kissed her forehead. 'If he means that much to you, sure I'd like to meet him one day.'

'You speak of your grandfather and how he got you through losing your family, well, John Ingliss is the person who got me through.

'When I first met him I was a wreck, accused of being an accessory, told I'd be going to jail if I held back on anything. I couldn't blame them after what Carlo did. I just couldn't help them. Then John Ingliss stepped in. He'd watched my interviews, watched me go through this gruelling process. He was head of the investigation. At first I didn't trust him, you know, the good cop bad cop thing, but he quickly won me over. When my father got into trouble he worked hard to get the charges dropped. He'd also come out to the family home and talked to me one on one. They're not supposed to do that, you know. I placed my trust in him.

'We spent lots of time together discussing Carlo and the events leading up to the murders. His approach freed up my mind, I was able to help.

'So no one's heard of this guy since?'

'No.'

'What about this officer, what does he think happened to him?'

'There's been reports, mainly from overseas. John chases every sighting. Nothing's ever come of them. He's very thorough but believes it's highly unlikely Carlo's alive. Apparently he crossed a lot of people in the Mafia. John told me if they killed him, it most probably happened in the weeks after the murders.'

'There's no proof, is there?'

'Not officially … but—'

'But what?'

Isabelle sighed. 'You asked me once why I left Perth. The real reason was because of the media. The same reporter who my father assaulted fronted me at a café one day. I was having coffee with a friend. The guy just walks up and says he's doing a story. Would I like to comment? I couldn't believe it. I told him to piss off and that's what he wrote in the article. It became a big story in Perth. Rumours soon spread that Carlo lived in W.A. and we were still together. It was all my fault.'

'How can that be your fault?'

'Because I lied, that journo did his research, too. You see, I worked in a bar and a different man would hit on me every night. After what I'd been through, I just wasn't interested so in an effort to get rid of them, I started saying I had a partner working in a mine up north. Once the media story came out, these men I'd burnt off found out who I was and put two and two together. All hell broke loose and next minute I'm being questioned all over again. The police went through mining employment records looking for Carlo. Cost me my job too.'

'I can see how that would happen, but how do you know he's dead?'

'Carlo's associates have the ability to gather information on just about anyone. The only positive thing about the media finding me is that Carlo didn't. That's why I believe he's dead. When we were together he'd always ring me, wanting to know where I was all the time. I thought it was just attention. John Ingliss explained it was far different. There was an evil, possessive side to him. He believes if Carlo is alive he'd have come looking for me by now.'

'Why didn't you just change your name through deed poll or use witness protection?'

'John didn't trust either one. Carlo's family have contacts throughout every business sector, even government. There's always a record somewhere. He and my lawyer set me up so I virtually didn't exist. The structure they used was good enough for a while but in the end the reporter found me, and Carlo didn't. I'm more scared of the media now. That's why I gave up my childcare course. Could you imagine a parent finding out who I am?'

'But you're using your real name here?'

She gave a wan smile. 'It's the first step in trying to obtain some sort of a normal existence. Since the day I began modelling I've always been known as Izy. I don't want to be Izy or Anne or whatever. I want to be me, Isabelle. I think it's a nice name and I'm being me for the first time in my life. I'm determined not to become a victim and I'm happy within myself. You've changed me too, Luke. I want you to know you're not getting involved with a broken person. I'm not damaged anymore. You've made me stronger. You became my friend first. I didn't want to tell anyone about what I've been through, but meeting you is fate at her delightful best. It's been hard for me and now that you know, I feel so ... so light.'

'All that matters to me is you stayed.'

'Know what? Leaving wasn't really an option.' She paused. 'I've learnt to block his face by concentrating on something in front of me, most times it's you I concentrate on. I've been able to train myself almost to the point where I can forget what he looks like. Sometimes I have these nightmares though, I see him.'

'Maybe I don't let you sleep alone tonight.' A yawn happened he couldn't control, her perfect smile spread.

'What a nice Christmas present, I'd like that.' She kissed his chest. 'When I first drove into this town I felt it drawing me in.'

'St Claire does that, even to me. My grandfather once told me every decision revolves around chance, each second, every minute is a new opportunity in time. Like a wave, he said. Anyone can come along and ride the next one. It's up to you and you took your chance. Even gave me a second chance, remember?'

'Glad I did. Sounds like he was an intelligent man. There's a lot of him in you.' A serious look washed over her. 'How do you feel about all this … us… now that you know?'

'How do I feel?' He heaved and rolled her on top of him, smothered her in kisses. He wanted to tell her how happy she made him feel; then he thought of Sue. She would approve.

Isabelle giggled her wicked laugh. 'That's how you feel, huh?' She moved slowly onto him.

'Come to Hawaii with me?'

'I can't, Luke. I have to work. Why don't you cancel? Stay here with me … don't want some hula girl stealing you.'

He smiled up at her. 'Ohhhhh, trust me. I'm not that guy. I want to spend every moment I can with you before I go, but I can't stay here either. The accident happened on the twelfth of January. I can't be near this place.'

'Oh Luke …'

12

Surfers peppered the water. Crowds suffocated the beach. St Claire's main road crawled with tourists. They huddled in the beer garden, spilling out onto the footpath in front of the café where Izy often drank coffee.

Carlo mingled in well. Just another face shaded by another sun hat beneath the foreshore trees, reading a book. The sun warmed his face, although each day the sea breeze lowered the afternoon temperature along this coast. After years on the run he struggled to concentrate, only able to read a page at a time before lifting his eyes. And that's how he noticed Maddigan's car. The Porsche's low profile, it hadn't moved from the house for over a week.

Maddigan and another man parked in front of the hotel where Izy worked, forcing him to look up constantly. Annoyingly, he found himself reading the same lines over and over.

Izy left the pub an hour ago. Carlo had driven up her street twice since.

Twenty minutes later Maddigan strolled out of the pub and drove off. Carlo closed the book and headed for the Landcruiser. He followed up Roy Street, into Izy's street, cruising past just in time to see her long arms wrapped around Maddigan on the porch.

———

'Hmmm.' Isabelle smacked her lips when they stopped kissing. 'You taste nice. Like beer.'

'Horry drove from the airport. Wanted to surprise you so we called into the pub thinking you might be there. He made me have a beer.'

'Oh, I love that. Horry made you, huh. I'm so glad you're back, Luke.'

He heard an excited whine but before he could grab the door, Clyde ripped a hole in the fly wire.

'Oh Clyde. No!' Isabelle said.

'Don't panic. That's easy fixed. Few tacks. Bit of fly wire.' Lucas reached behind her and opened the door. Clyde jumped up, his bulk almost pushing Lucas off the porch. 'Sorry boy, you have to learn to come second from now on. Knew he'd be here.'

'Did you even read my emails? He slept here nearly every night while you were away. Think he went a bit ratty out there on his own the first few days.'

'He's got abandonment issues.'

'He missed you. I missed you, Luke. I love you and if you go away again—'

'You're coming next year.'

Clyde scratched him as if he understood. 'You're not,' he said, laughing. 'Bet he's been sleeping in my spot.'

'He's teaching Dimi bad habits. They're so in the lounge tonight.'

'Promise?' he said, backing her up against the front wall.

'You bet.' She grinned and bit his lip gently. Her eyes lit up. 'Guess what I did while you were away.'

'Oh great. The guess what I did question. How am I ever going to—?'

'Threw all my heels in the Salvo bin.'

'How would anyone ever guess that?'

She giggled. 'You'd have no idea what they cost but they're worth nothing to me anymore.'

He ran his hands up the inside of the back of her top. 'That's nice. Let's go in.'

'Don't get any big ideas. I'm on my break. You can walk me back down in a minute.'

———

Carlo pulled the punch at the last second but still cracked the panelling on the dashboard. The glove box jolted open. The butt of the gun appeared as if with intent. It had taken all his efforts to quell his fuming rage, somehow he managed to keep driving. He reached over and slammed the glove box shut, then drove back to the beach and parked.

The festering wound of humanity swarmed by. Spoilt shits of kids who want and want, scream till they get, were towed between beaches and ice cream shops and cafés by pear shaped bodies, too embarrassing for the water, too unfit to do anything other than just see the attractions, visit relatives and so called friends who'd probably retired on the coast to get away from them and their chips and their biscuits and soft drinks and cakes they'd feast on as snacks before time came to devour the next meal.

Maddigan *is* sleeping with her.

Fires of anger flared, hot flushes rose fuelled by a boiling hatred for Maddigan, hatred for this circumstance, hatred for what Izy had done to him. Leaning the seat back he closed his eyes. Sweat trickled from the heat of the direct afternoon sun magnified by the windscreen.

Don't go back, he warned himself.

Pain throbbed in his temples. Each beat tightened like a vice, he rubbed them to no avail.

Go back. Kill them both.

No, another voice warned.

How many other men you dirty tainted bitch. Both must be killed. End this now.

Nicky would bury that pig of a wife in a lonely paddock if she ever strayed.

What would Papa do? Unthinkable. They're from a different time.

Marco's not. Louisa would pay the ultimate price. Not Izy.

Maddigan must die instead.

From his pocket he retrieved the piece of paper from Maddigan's study, staring at the written word, RESOLVE.

The word held strength, firmness. Finality.

Franco would resolve.

Blood seeped through the skin of his knuckle. Clammy hands gripped the wheel. He closed his eyes processing the word, questioning why he didn't resolve all those years ago.

His father always taught him to keep a calm centre, to little avail. Now he had to learn. He had to change for Izy.

Carlo pictured Maddigan's dead wife; photos littered the home.

Some men hang on.

Many chances had gone by in the last week to approach her. Instead he filled his head with excuses.

Cowardice excuses.

Grief must be her way forward. Grief will provide opportunity. Maddigan's death must be an accident.

When? How? This town was choking with witnesses, plenty of extra cops. Through the windscreen the great tar snake slithered parallel with the sea from east to west, isolating St Claire. Roadblocks could easily be set up. Only one other road led out of town, the dirt road heading north up into the rainforest.

The tee shirt tightened around his neck. He needed air. A family were spilling over the table he'd occupied before. They'd unpacked a hamper and were arguing and ripping up and gorging on a cold chicken, so he grabbed the book and found another bench closer to the foot of the pier. Minutes passed. He opened the book in an effort to look normal, but now he couldn't even concentrate on a sentence.

A dog growled.

He lifted his eyes.

'Shit!'

The Ridgeback-cross stood in front of him. Hackles raised. It knew his scent.

'Clyde,' a man called, followed by a sharp whistle.

The dog's ears pricked.

So did Carlo's. He turned cautiously. The dog gave a last snarl and trotted down to the pier with its tail high. Izy was dressed for work holding Maddigan's hand, chatting to a large guy outside the fish shop. They must have passed rather close. Maddigan kissed her and walked off with the other man along the pier. Izy headed up the slope toward the pub, toward him. The car was only a short distance away but he would be walking right in front of her, and he'd left the hat in the car.

He moved fast in the opposite direction along the crowded beach toward the lifesaving club. It was all he could do to get out of her path.

'Hey!'

He kept walking.

'HEY!' A venomous, piercing disdain hung in her voice.

Heavy panting came from behind. Close.

Don't turn around.

A high pitched shrill filled the wind again and again. Someone yelled. 'Is that lady all right?'

'Help her.'

'CARLO!' She shrieked. 'CARLO!'

'Someone drowning?' another called.

'CARLO!'

He had to turn.

Face her. Show her.

He spun around. She knelt in the sand, staring up, her mouth, agape. He couldn't speak, she'd recognise his voice.

Questioning glances crowded around.

'Something wrong, mate?

'Hey, d'ya do something to that woman?' asked a slob of a man in board shorts.

Carlo shrugged, acting dismayed. Izy held her hands over her chest. Wide eyes locked on his face.

'I ... I'm sorry,' she said between stalled breaths. 'I ... I thought ... you were someone ... someone—'

She mouthed the word *"else"*, closed her eyes, hung her head and slumped onto the sand.

———

Carlo overshot the driveway. The Landcruiser skidded. Wheels tottered and jittered over the corrugations. A plume of dust drifted over the car. Caught in helpless anger, he'd driven too fast. He reversed, drove in past the main house and pulled up in the shade in front of the shack. No longer could he trust himself with the gun in the car, so he wrapped the Glock inside a jumper and carried it under his arm toward the shack. A voice called out, 'Corelli. What the hell ya doing driving like that?'

The gun slipped, bouncing end over end on the dirt. Old Les was somewhere behind. Despite the surprise, Carlo kept his wits and dropped the jumper over the gun. He picked them both up and turned. Les stood at the woodpile over at the house, a wood splitter rested over his shoulder.

'Sorry Les.'

Les cupped a hand to his ear. 'What'd ya say?'

'Sorry,' he called louder. 'Be over in a minute.' Les was as deaf as a post.

A newspaper lay folded on the doorstep. The headline screamed,

THUGS ASSAULT BI-LAWS OFFICER.

Inside the shack he tossed the paper and stuffed the Glock down the back of the couch. Locked in a state of mistrust he even thought of burying it in the bush, but Les's mangy dog was always snooping around. He plugged his phone in. Messages buzzed through with each seep of charge. All blocked numbers.

Nicky, no doubt.

His mother's health had improved dramatically since his return, though he'd have to call in soon. He slumped on the couch, contemplating. If he went back down to the beach he could be recognised as *that man*. Tomorrow it would be *that man* from yesterday.

The chilling scream, he could still hear it.

Her voice filled with hatred.

It all happened so fast. He'd been able to walk away past the lifesavers hurrying up the beach, their concerned hands steadying her. Out on the pier Maddigan appeared oblivious to the goings on.

Jimmy was right, this was a mistake to come here. His anger had almost brought him to unwanted attention, but there was a positive. He'd been able to keep control and drive away from her house. Today, he'd made that first step.

Change had to be made for Izy.

For the family.

Change was in the wind.

He made a quick salad, alone with his thoughts and the chirping birds in the trees outside. Eating well made him function better.

Les was splitting wood, Carlo approached.

'Listen here, Corelli. Kids next-door ride their bikes up and down that road. You'll hit one of 'em, driving like that.'

'Sorry, Les, golf ball rolled under me foot.'

'Golf ball, ya reckon. Just be careful then.'

'Sure. Hey, got another axe?'

'Nah, mate, if ya want some wood just take it off the pile.'

'Was going to help,' Carlo said, 'you'll give yourself a heart attack in this heat.'

'Job's gotta get done. Nights get chilly in March and Marg's like a boy scout without a cock, you know. Always be prepared.' He pulled a hanky from his overalls and wiped the sweat off. 'Go for your life. This shit's a young man's work anyway.' He handed the splitter to Carlo and placed another log on the block. Carlo raised the axe and the second Les's hand moved away, he split the log clean. One half toppled on Les's foot. He tried not to grin as the old man jumped back, unable to hide his astonishment.

'Give me a bit of time, will ya.' He placed the next log on.

'Sorry, Les.'

Carlo brought the axe down time and again. His insides had healed well, he found himself in rhythm thriving on the hard work. Les replaced the logs on the block at a full arm's length, keeping well back. Soon the pile stood a metre high and even though Les was no longer swinging, the acrid tang of the old man's sweat tinged his nostrils.

'You do all right for an office boy.'

Carlo gave a thin smile, the phone rang in his pocket, he let it ring out.

It rang again, compressing his thoughts.

'You gonna get that?'

Carlo ignored the old man. He was in the zone, swinging freely. Sweat soaked his tee shirt, so he took it off.

'Christ almighty you're fit,' Les said and placed another log on.

Carlo focused on the white bristles on the back of Les's neck, and pictured Maddigan. What would the sound be like? Moist? Dull?

Timing must be perfect.

You were wrong about Izy, old man, Carlo wanted to tell him. I should do you a favour and ensure you don't suffer any of life's illnesses, including life itself, he thought.

Thwack.

Les reeled back. Carlo sensed his fear. The axe handle wielded decisions over life and death. Les wiped more sweat as blows rained down, swift and powerful. Energy built with each generated smooth arc. Wood chopping was therapeutic and he recalled the time he'd beaten a teacher, Mr. Hennenberg, senseless in year ten. When his father read the report, Marco was ordered to take him to the stable where Carlo was belted for six five minute rounds, then made to split and stack logs up to the height of the stable wall before he got any dinner.

Carlo raised the axe. Nerves or fear got the better of Les and his fingers caught a splinter, causing the log to topple on its side. Les wrenched his hand back as Carlo merely lengthened the swing into the backside of the block. Les gasped and stepped away hurriedly, almost falling on the pile. Eyes wide with terror. Carlo syphoned it all up.

Power grew within. A power he hadn't felt for a long time. As a young man in Griffith, he took it upon himself to ensure no one crossed the Caruso family, then carved his own reputation on the criminal world of Sydney. But those days were on hold. Today he placed himself in extreme danger again. Only this time, he'd thought first and felt proud of his newfound ability to drive away and resolve. Just like his father would do.

Change was in the wind.

'What happened to ya hand?' Les asked.

Blood was trickling from his knuckle where he'd punched the dash earlier. He relaxed his grip on the axe handle, like Marco had taught him when handling pistols.

'Must have scraped it on a log.'

Les checked his watch. 'One o'clock, time for a beer.'

'Why not.' Except for the initial interview Carlo had refused all of Les's invitations for a drink, which came at all times in the afternoon. The older man wandered off to the house.

Breeze rustled the empty treetops. The bush fell away down a valley. In the distance skyline met a fade of ocean. Carlo pondered. If his bearings were right, Maddigan's house must be down there somewhere. Almost due south as the crow flies.

Les returned and passed over an open stubby. 'Cheers.' He took a long mouthful. 'See that newspaper I put on ya doorstep.'

'I did. What's that about?'

'Put it there to warn ya, lots of arseholes getting round this time of year. Poor Duberly's just doing his job. Cops got 'em, thank Christ.'

May not have liked getting woken up. Carlo held the thought.

'Want me to get Marg to take a look at that hand?'

'She'll be right.' Carlo picked up his tee shirt and wiped the blood. 'Do you head down into the forest much, Les?'

'Nah, stuff that. Used to bushwalk with the kids years ago. You been down there yet?'

'No. Thought I might do a bit of hiking this afternoon. Are there tracks to the ocean?'

Les finished another swig. 'Yeah. Long walk though. Gotta cross the ocean road of course, and then you can't get down to the beach cause the Bluff runs along there.' He emptied the stubby down his throat.

'The Bluff?'

'Straight line of cliffs heading east from town.'

'That so?' Carlo said, happy to know his bearings were right. Les twisted the top off another beer.

———

After a restless afternoon snooze Carlo drove back down past Izy's house. The Porsche was still in the driveway. Down at the pub, Maddigan and the big fisherman could be seen through the windows. He returned to the shack, this time in a controlled manner. He hadn't taken the gun. Another test of will. Yet he soon found himself brooding again so he decided on walking through the bush and across the Great Ocean Road. He easily found the house. No one was home.

On that lonely beach he took the time to contemplate how vulnerable he'd left himself earlier. This poisonous little town would bring about more wrong decisions. His heart longed for her. Loathing for Maddigan grew with each breath. Maddigan will die, but only when this town quietened down. The worst-case scenario had become apparent. After all the years in Perth, Izy was now in a relationship.

While trekking home through the bush he turned the phone back on and when he'd almost reached the shack, it rang. This time he answered.

Nicky's voice tore down. 'Where are you?'

'Down south.'

'Bullshit. Just spoke to our friend. They checked on you.' Carlo knew he was referring to the Chin.

'Don't worry. I'm fine. Staying elsewhere for a bit.'

'Don't worry, uh. I'm not worried about you. Fran—' Nicky stopped. 'He wants your balls on a leash or he's going to send the Bull down there. I gotta keep lying for you, I'm too busy—'

'Is there a problem?'

'You! You're the fucking problem! You just can't disappear like this! Answer your fucking phone! They leave for overseas in a under a week, you have to visit before she goes. The family doesn't need this crap. She'll get sick again and, well, you gotta do this right or—'

'Listen … you're cutting in and out …' Carlo said. He'd already decided he had to leave tonight and if there were issues with his mother, Nicky would have said so by now. As he spoke he moved the handset toward his leg to make it harder for Nicky to hear. It didn't work.

'Yeah, well I can hear you, no problem,' came the voice in the silent forest. 'You know where you're supposed to be. Get there now.'

'Look … don't have … worry.' He swung the handset so Nicky would hear air rushing, but the reception was good because the phone tower was at the top of the next hill behind the water basin. 'Be … back … a day.'

'Hey … hey …' was all Carlo heard before he turned off the phone and trekked up the last section toward Les's property.

———

Later under the evening twilight, Carlo knocked on Les's door.

'Come in mate,' the old man said and went straight to the fridge. Carlo said hello to Marg, a quiet, homely lady. She returned the gesture and focussed back on the stove.

Les handed over a beer.

'Ta Les, had a long walk before. Cheers.' They clashed stubbies and drank.

'Grab a seat. What'd ya find down there?'

Carlo slid out a chair and seated himself. 'Just like you said, all bush and valleys till you hit the cliffs.' He took another swill. 'Listen Les, have to go away on business, can you hold the shack?' He produced a wad of cash and began counting out notes. 'Here's another four months rent, might return for the odd weekend.'

'Sure Paul, no worries.'

Carlo laid the bills on the table.

Marg swooped. 'Want sumptin' to eat?' she asked, stuffing the cash down her ample breasts. 'There's plenty of roast. Let me chuck more veggies on.'

Les's mouth sprung open, devastated that his beer money had vanished.

'Sounds good, Marg,' Carlo replied, grinning at Les. This had been a long day, one of the worst in his life. Emotional tiredness seemed to be the most draining of all, and he knew he had to leave this town. His father was asking questions. Plus, there was more than one score to settle.

PETER EDWARDS

Part 2
The Murrumbidgee
Meeting

PETER EDWARDS

13

Buchannon,
One hour's drive north of Melbourne
Three weeks later

Greg Rickshaw backed the Harley off and rode up onto the footpath, forcing the queue of stunned pensioners to shuffle forward close as possible to the door of the bank. He cut the bike at the auto teller and hopped off.

'Bright morning,' he said to the lady with an ice- blue rinse at the end of the line. She focussed on the back of the head of the man in front, clutching her purse as though her life was in there.

He slipped his card in the machine and entered his pin. After three days of mournful partying celebrating the life of Tinny – the club's Sergeant-at-Arms – it felt like a hammer was tapping away inside his skull, so he took off his helmet.

'Pension day huh,' the biker said, nodding at the queue. 'Like to babble on for a bit to the tellers, don't they?'

WRONG PIN TRY AGAIN

'Fuck it,' he cursed, copping the woman's sideways glance. He punched the numbers in again.

'Nice hair. But blue ... why blue? Surely you're not on the pull at your age?'

He got no answer of course and focussed back on the screen,

WRONG PIN TRY AGAIN

Panic set in. One chance left before the card got swallowed again, he'd have to stand in line. Cash was a necessity today. He'd blown the last of his speed while cleaning the carby on the bike in the early morning hours. He pressed cancel, wiped his card on his tee shirt, wiped the grime off his fingers and re-slotted the card, pressing each number with precision. The machine soon produced eight hundred dollars.

'Gotta love modern technology,' he said. Despite the thumping in his head he still found a smile, waving cash at the old lady. 'Get with it.'

He fired up the Harley. It ran like a dream now. On Monday it stalled on him at Tinny's funeral in front a crowd of onlookers and TV cameras. Nearly a hundred bikes were held up, prompting a warning of disrespect from his older brother Norman, the president of the Sons of Cain.

Tinny was executed in his own home by a single bullet to back of the head.

Many other clubs sent representatives as a sign of respect and solidarity toward the Sons, more importantly to also show their clubs were not involved. Rickshaw believed none of it. Angels had been holding patch-over discussions with Norman, but Tinny, a brutal enforcer stood in their way. He would never have agreed to join another club. Rickshaw's first duty when he became the new sarge would be to find out which one of them pulled the trigger.

For now though, he had to concentrate on the drive down to Melbourne. It was time to turn the screws on Jeremy Garland, the stockbroker who owed the club forty-five grand. Also, he had to score.

———

An hour later, Rickshaw arrived in Melbourne and pulled up outside the Collins Street building where Garland worked. He walked down two levels to check the car was in its rightful spot and returned to his bike. The broker always left for lunch and sure enough, within half an hour, Garland's Audi appeared at the street-level exit. Rickshaw followed him to Prahran where he met the wife in an outdoor section of a café. He allowed the Garlands a few minutes before he entered, ordering coffee and a custard tart. He sat at the table behind them. A woman occupying the table picked up her coffee and moved.

'Are you just going to ignore me?' the wife asked Garland. She had a tidy rig. Blonde with a bony arse, great tits. They had a Hawthorn mortgage, she didn't work, drove a BMW and the jerk simply didn't have the earn to keep it all flowing. None of that was Rickshaw's problem. He recalled his brother's words. *"Deliver this cash and you'll get the sarge's badge."*

'Everything's fine, honey … really,' Garland replied, but the hapless broker kept glancing over her shoulder. Rickshaw wore his club vest for the occasion. He gave Garland his finest evil grin and bit down on his tart.

'Everything's *not* fine, darling. I went to pay the school fees this morning and my card—'

'Honey please, next week, Wednesday, I'll top it up. Wednesday, okay. I'm sorry.' Garland tried to speak quietly, but Rickshaw leant in behind the wife, listening to every word. A waitress served them coffees and toasted focaccias. 'Been buried in paperwork and dealing with shit all morning, too. Can we just eat?'

'You're pale. It's what, only twenty-five degrees, we're under an umbrella and you're sweating like a pig.'

'Honey?' The pleading Garland stared past her like a bad newsreader. The wife followed his gaze and faced Rickshaw.

Her eyes fell on his beard, he looked down, brushed some custard tart out.

'Morning Mrs. Garland.'

He almost felt the vacuum as she gasped.

'How … how do you—?' She turned on her husband. 'That man knows my name.' She stood, wrenching her bag off the chair.

'I don't know who he is, honey.'

Rickshaw grinned and poked his tongue out, inches from her arse. She spun back and caught him. He prepared himself for a slap. It didn't come.

'You pathetic excuse for a—' She faced her husband. 'What the hell's going on? And then her eyes widened, her head shook slowly. 'No … no no no—'

'Honey … I can explain—'

'No! No fucking way!' She thrust a finger at Rickshaw. 'You can't explain this. Not this time. We will talk … later. I'm eating at the tennis club. Don't even *think* of coming there. When will you be home?'

She got no answer.

Her chin tightened, the bottom jaw was thrust forward, 'Jeremy, I'm speaking—'

'Uh. Six … six … at the latest.'

Rickshaw raised his eyebrows and began to laugh when an uncontrollable tickle rose in his throat. He coughed up a hunk of phlegm, only part way though. Half sat in his throat, half in his mouth forcing him to retch until it moved enough to be able to swallow. As he did this air whistled back through and a pastry crumb got sucked down, also lodging in his throat, causing him to gag and hack at the air until the crumb flew out and he was finally able to recover.

Garland's wife yanked her skirt down and stormed out.

The stockbroker swirled his coffee. Then without looking at Rickshaw, he stood to leave.

'First thing in the morning, Sunshine,' Rickshaw said, as the blood returned to his face. 'Make sure it's all there.'

'What time is—?'

'My fuck'n time. Be ready.'

With his head bowed, Garland straightened his tie and left.

Rickshaw tucked into their focaccias. As he finished and wiped his beard he noticed a man, a big fella in the far corner of the café. The man looked up from his coffee, straight at him.

A familiar face, a cop, maybe? Perhaps they'd come across each other in jail.

He thought about wandering over to enquire, but hadn't slept for three days since Tinny's funeral. Withdrawal symptoms had begun to kick in too, so he left for the clubhouse.

———

Later in the afternoon Carlo relaxed in the shaded park opposite Hagan's Hotel in Buchannon, eating chips dipped in gravy purchased at the truck stop on the highway just before the turnoff. He shared with the same magpies from last week, and the week before. They were fascinating to watch. The most dominant bird was a mother who made sure she and her chick got the bulk of the feed. The chick already showed traits of its mother by screeching and running at older birds that dared to approach. Soon enough a flock of seagulls joined in.

'What are you fellas doing so far from the beach?' They too demanded their share, so the magpies shed their prejudices and banded together to fight off the gulls. The warm, dry northerly bent the treetops, the drifting heat in the air reminded him of Griffith.

He'd grown tired of following Rickshaw and decided to return to Buchannon. He took petrol out to the house, unloaded the gun and fed the dogs. Rickshaw's two buddies,

Squash and Baz both worked on a road crew along the highway. Conveniently all three lived in the one town.

Rickshaw, a creature of habit arrived at the hotel not long after Carlo finished the chips. The fat biker hitched up his black jeans and waddled into the pub for the afternoon.

Carlo read in peace until the clapping of two more choppers rewarded his patience. Engines revved in unison, they parked beside the other bike. Soon after he drove his car up the hill leading out of town and parked at the lookout beside the sign,

PLEASE DO NOT LITTER OUR PRETTY SALLY

Panoramic views over the Happy Valley stretched out below. He reclined the seat, read some more until his eyes shut. Soon, the roar of Harleys climbing the hill toward Rickshaw's farmhouse broke his snooze. He tried to sleep again but thoughts turned to Izy and Maddigan. He'd found it difficult to leave St Claire, even though he'd made up his mind to let Maddigan live until the season quietened down. Driving out of St Claire, emotions ebbed and flowed and they only began to subside properly once he was a couple of hours away from the town. He felt proud of his newfound control, despite the compelling urge to turn back.

Eventually he washed Izy from his mind and dozed off again, waking to the noise of a truck's air brakes. The sun had almost slipped away. The clock on the dash said half past seven.

He drove back past the pub. Rickshaw's green Fairlane was now in the car park. Hunger beckoned. He headed out the other side of town into the countryside keen to explore a winery he passed a week ago. Stones crumpled as he steered up between the rows of vines, parking at a white homestead.

Carlo selected a table at the back of the empty dining room offering full view of the gardens and entry. A short middle-aged waitress, neatly uniformed in a white shirt and a long black skirt over thin ankles, headed toward him. A younger, burgundy-haired waitress met her in the middle of the room. The two ladies spoke briefly before the first waitress headed back to the kitchen, the second lady approached.

Her open neck shirt exposed the insides of freckled breasts. "Sally" was printed on her nametag. Bruce Springsteen's song Red Headed Woman sprung to mind.

One leg was crossed over the other, a pen tapped away on the note pad. She smiled the smile of a thousand women then bit her lip.

'Hi, my name's Sally.'

'As in the Pretty Sally lookout back in Buchannon.'

'That's right,' she beamed, 'I'm named after it and I'll be your waitress for the evening.'

———

Carlo woke and absorbed his surroundings. It took a few seconds to adjust his eyes. Sally lay naked in the bed beside him, dead to the world.

"I'll be your waitress for the evening."

Everything in the room was purple, blood red or mauve. Even the bra she'd chucked on the floor in the mad rush to spread her legs, was purple. She'd found her colour range and when he'd arrived at her house she produced a bottle of the same local red Carlo had enjoyed for dinner.

He checked his phone – quarter past three a.m., plenty of time. The alarm on his phone was set to vibrate at three thirty. He switched it off and dressed, careful to smother the chinking of his belt. With his boots tucked under one arm he snuck out into the entry passage.

As he twisted the front door latch, a noise from behind startled him. He turned to see a fair-headed child in the passage dragging a pillow, wearing Spiderman onesie pyjamas including the feet. Carlo recalled she'd mentioned the kid was three years old. He knelt down.

'What's your name big guy?'

'Jaxon wiv an x.'

'Well Jaxon with an x, go snuggle up with your mummy.'

The child nodded, producing a bewildering smile. Then as he turned, Carlo gently touched his arm.

'You look like you'll grow into a big strong boy. Always remember to look after your mummy. Mums are very special.'

The kid buttoned his lips and gave a manly nod, then toddled over, slipped into the bed, hauling the blanket up beneath his chin. Eyes wide like dinner plates, as Anita often said. Sally rolled half way and looped an arm over her boy without waking.

Carlo gave him a wink and left.

14

Harleys shone under the front porch light. From a distance the square shape of the old Fairlane could be seen down the side of the house. Carlo estimated Rickshaw's land to be ten acres, much smaller than the surrounding farms. On his second pass down the narrow bitumen road, he killed the lights and hid the car behind a row of pines.

With his backpack slung over his shoulder, he crept up a line of saplings inside the boundary of the adjoining neighbour's fence line. A horse whinnied in a rear paddock below a field of stars and a waning moon. The only other sound was George Thorogood's music as he passed alongside Rickshaws house. Using a penlight to dodge the rabbit scratchings, he kept moving until he was adjacent to the shed near the back of the Rickshaw's property.

He climbed through the wire.

A mild northerly brushed off the plains, he approached with the wind at his back. Rickshaw didn't farm; not even a vegetable garden. Carlo slipped easily through long grass to the back corner of the shed. Not a whimper came from the blue heeler crosses, living their sordid lives chained to kennels in the section of yard between the shed and the house.

He rested the backpack against the shed wall and pulled the bacon out. During the day it had turned nicely from the heat in the Landcruiser. A chain scraped across the concrete pad beneath the kennels. One of the dogs stretched out and sniffed the wind, letting off a growl. The other dog appeared, snarling a warning and scratching fleas off pinched ribs. Earlier in the day they wagged their tails in anticipation of a feed. Not a daily event, Carlo guessed.

Of the trio, only Baz had a girlfriend. Carlo wanted to make sure only the three men were in the house, so he crept forward, tossing a slice of bacon at the closest dog. The second dog raced to the length of its chain, barking ferociously. The other turned to protect the food. A vicious fight erupted.

The laundry light came on, then an outside light flooded the small verandah. From behind the shed Carlo watched as the tall, uncouth, long-haired figure of Squash appeared.

'Shut the fuck up ya mongrels,' he yelled in his high-pitched, nasally drawl.

He lit a smoke.

Took a few minutes to scan the yard.

The dogs finally settled.

Squash snivelled then hoiked and spat. After two more long drags he flicked the cigarette toward the kennels and returned inside.

Carlo approached again, hurling another hunk of bacon toward the first dog. The second dog launched into a mad frenzy. The music stopped. Rickshaw bustled out the back door onto the verandah, his obese frame blocking most of the light. Squash followed along with the third man, Baz. Rickshaw outweighed each man by at least fifty kilos, though Baz looked strong from shoulders to hips, easily the most physically imposing of the three. The dogs were now in a state of uproar.

'Axel, Rose! Fuck up!' Rickshaw bellowed. The barking only increased. He spoke to Baz, who disappeared around the side of the house. Squash shone a torch across the yard. When the light passed over the dogs calmed. Baz returned minutes later. Carlo assumed he informed Rickshaw they weren't being raided. Squash switched off the light and the dogs took up their frantic barking again, infuriating Rickshaw.

'Righteo! That's fuck'n it!' He produced a stick from inside the laundry and marched toward the dogs. The closest one fled into its kennel. The other was still barking at Carlo when Rickshaw grabbed hold of its chain, striking it across the back. A sickening yelp followed.

'Enough, Axel.'

The sorry dog bellied down in submission. Rickshaw lashed out again striking its head. Another yelp. Carlo thought of putting a bullet in the man but his plan was to not let off shots outside.

Rickshaw wasn't finished. He reefed the chain in. The dog darted left as the stick missed and rebounded off the concrete pad, jarring Rickshaw's hand. The stick fell and bounced end over end.

'You cunt!' He shook the hand. Axel tried to bolt, winning a short length of chain. Rickshaw retrieved the stick but the dog turned on him and snapped. Then – despite being anchored by the dead weight – Axel pulled, desperate to reach his kennel. The chain was wrenched from Rickshaw's fingers. It locked around his ankle sending him off balance, backside first onto the concrete followed by a dull thud as the back of his skull hit.

Like a beached sea lion after a long swim, he rested, groaning.

Laughter rose from the verandah.

Eventually he lifted himself up on one arm.

'Fuck'n mongrel. Git 'ere!'

He hauled the dog back enough to untangle the ankle. Axel made his final lunge toward the kennel and before fingers were ripped from their sockets, Rickshaw let go.

Baz and Squash were in hysterics.

Rickshaw cast a long sideways glance toward the house, then said to the dog, 'You'll fuck'n keep.' He made a pistol out of his fingers and fired, then rolled over and exploded into a coughing fit, gagging and choking like he was bringing up a wet sock.

The laughter continued. Rickshaw propped himself up, then using the stick as a crutch, staggered toward the verandah. 'So ya reckon that's a good fuck'n laugh Squash?'

Carlo heard the crack as Rickshaw belted his colleague across the shin.

'Fuck you,' Squash cried, stumbling back frantically rubbing his leg. 'Why d'ya do that for?'

'Can't I be in on the laugh?'

Like lightning he moved on Baz and cracked his forearm. A cigarette danced like a firefly through the air. A can clunked on the verandah floor.

'Fuck me!' Baz yelled. 'You're psycho.'

'When d'ya work that one out, Baz?' Another swift blow across the knee saw him leap off the verandah. Carlo figured both men could overpower the larger man, but guessed Rickshaw wielded more than a stick. Squash was still rubbing his shins when Rickshaw clobbered him across the back of the hand, sending him hobbling onto the grass with Baz.

'Lost ya sense of humour, Squash? Had enough?'

Squash held a hand up. 'All right, all right! Sorry, fuck ya!'

'What about you, Baz old mate?'

Baz pointed his finger up at Rickshaw. 'Hit me again 'n I'll—'

Rickshaw whacked the finger. Baz yelled in pain and leapt backwards, dancing on one foot.

A sharp snigger filled the night. 'Ya know Baz … only thing I remember from school is a history lesson bout some U.S. president with a big fuck'n stick. Ya obviously wagged that day.' He chuckled at his own joke. 'Don't have to shoot me dog now.' His mood appeared to have lifted until he launched into another bout of coughing. When he cleared his throat he said, 'Reckon ya had enough, boys?'

Both beaten men remained silent.

'Put the bikes away, gotta piss off to Melbourne soon, visit our favourite little broker. We're taking the car.'

From experience Carlo knew Baz and Squash could pack punches, he also realised Rickshaw controlled their loyalties through the constant flow of free amphetamines.

Like trained chimps they followed him past the corner of the house. Hogs ruptured the night. Within seconds Carlo heard the soft squeal of brakes from inside the shed. He snuck along the back wall, stopping halfway to listen. A fridge door opened, air expunged from cans. They had moved on from violence like professional businessmen would move from one agenda to the next.

———

Voices filtered through the shed's iron cladding. Squash complained about his hand.

'Quit ya winging,' Rickshaw said. 'Say ya had an accident at work. Get compo, spend the arvo with me in the pub. Six hundred bucks plus ya day's pay. Am I a genius or what, Baz?'

Silence followed.

'Should've broken your hand, too.'

'Knee's rooted. Get compo for that,' Baz replied.

'Now that's the spirit, Baz old mate.'

Carlo heard a tinkering noise.

'Hey! Where the fuck did that come from?' Rickshaw said.

'What?' Baz asked.

'That jerry can.'

He'd noticed the extra can. Carlo had been meticulous and bought a petrol container the same size and brand as the other two containers Rickshaw kept in his shed.

'Must be yours,' Squash said.

'Nup. Wasn't there earlier. Fuck! It's full too. Sure yous didn't knock it off from work?'

'Positive. Ya brother must've dropped it off.'

'Must've,' Rickshaw said.

A high-pitched squeak of un-oiled iron sounded right next to Carlo's ear. The door swung open forcing him back, he placed a steadying hand on the shed wall. He hadn't forgotten about the rear door, nor did he expect them to open it, but luck was on his side. He was shielded from view because the door opened toward him. Moments earlier he'd have been on the other side and forced to shoot.

The bag.

He'd left the backpack with the other gun, a 9mm back at the corner of the shed. He eased the Glock from his belt. If they saw the bag it would all go down here behind the shed, not in the house where he wanted these men to know where this was coming from. They'd contaminated his mind for weeks.

Squash stepped out past the elongated light, so close Carlo heard his laboured breathing. He began urinating. The flow was long and constant, he shook himself off, lit a smoke. The side profile of Squash's nose appeared flush with the brow and the bottom lip, like it was pushed in from some type of horrendous accident.

With the weapon aimed Carlo remained as silent as the tobacco on the wind. Rickshaw and Baz meandered through the door.

Baz moved into open ground and also began urinating. 'So all we get's six hundred bucks for touch'n this prick up.'

'Six hundred each,' Rickshaw replied. 'He'll have the cash. Should be a piece of piss, probably won't even have to lay a hand on 'im.'

Carlo poised ready to shoot.

'This broker got any daughters, or what?' Baz asked.

'Yeah he does,' Rickshaw said. 'Two, 'bout twelve years old you depraved fuckwit.'

'Bit young,' Squash said. He kicked his boot into dry dirt, bringing up dust.

Rickshaw glared at him, but let the comment go and the three men wandered aimlessly towards the corner of the shed. Black clothing melted into the night. Carlo lined up the shoulder blades of the unsuspecting Baz, the closest man to the shed wall where the backpack rested.

A headshot would be clean, he backed his accuracy, although there was safety in putting two slugs in the man's back before the others knew what happened.

'Why only six hundred?' Baz asked.

'Cause I'm not getting me full whack either.'

'It's fuck all if there's any trouble,' Squash said.

'Listen. I told ya. It's a piss-easy job. Probably don't even need you.'

'Talk to us first next time.'

Rickshaw stopped with his back to the bag and poked Squash in the chest. 'I'm talking to ya right now, cunt. When the club knocks on your door to do collecting, then you can ask all the questions ya want. I do the business round here, don't fuck'n forget it.' He lifted Squash's smokes from his top pocket and lit one using the end of Squash's burning cigarette. 'Plus, when we walk into the club and hand over the cash, the sarge's badge is all mine.'

'You reckon you'll get voted?' Baz asked.

'Why the fuck not?'

There was no reply.

'Got something to say Baz?'

'We'll vote for ya.' Baz pulled out a fat joint and fired it up.

'Ya think I don't know that?'

Rickshaw dragged on his smoke and said to Squash, 'How about me and Baz do this job alone. You go to work with ya broken hand.'

Squash didn't reply. He just dragged on his smoke, kicking up more dust. The men rounded the corner of the shed into the open paddock near the silent dogs. Carlo retrieved the bag.

——

The typical farmhouse layout led from the laundry, through to a passage and into the kitchen. Dishes were piled high, the rubbish bin overflowed with crushed bourbon cans, pizza boxes and cheese wrappers.

Boots thudded on the lino floor, the three men entered.

'Need you cunts on the weekend,' Rickshaw said. 'We'll do a tip run. Clear out that shit from the side of the house. Mum come out the other day, started bitching about seeing rats out there.' Piles of green rubbish bags were stacked along the blind side of the home. The stench was horrible.

'You been saying that for months,' Squash replied. 'Garbo comes Tuesday. Give 'im a bag of shard, we'll back the truck up, clear the fuck'n lot out.'

'You fork out for the meth, I'm good to go' Rickshaw said.

Squash didn't answer. The fridge snapped, followed by the crisp sound of cracked cans. Someone slid a drawer open, then shut it, the men walked into the dining room. Baz and Rickshaw took up seats at the table. Squash picked up a dirty glass and disappeared back into the kitchen. A tap ran followed by the hollow pelting of water in the sink. Squash returned and sat at the table beneath a solitary globe casting enough light for the men to operate in the small dining room.

Rickshaw tipped white powder onto a mirror. The only sound was the awkward hiss of Squash's breathing. With the concentration of a surgeon Rickshaw cut the powder into three thick lines with a credit card, snorting his first through a rolled up fifty-dollar note. He dropped his head back, closed his eyes. Baz slid the mirror over and blew his line before passing the remainder to Squash, who scraped his share into the glass.

Rickshaw pressed one nostril shut, sniffing hard through the other, drawing every last spec into his system. He then opened his eyes and focussed on the gun, blinking rapidly. Then he focussed again. 'WHAT THE FUCK—?'

'Remain in your seat,' Carlo said.

Chairs scraped loudly, but then thoughts seemed to freeze on the disbelieving faces of Baz and Squash. They remained half seated at the sight of Carlo who stood up from the recliner, pointing the Glock. The table stretched widthways across the dining room. Baz and Squash at either end, Rickshaw sat rigid in his seat over on the far side facing Carlo. A move could only come from left or right, Baz or Squash. Carlo recognised the blue star on Rickshaw's right ear, the spider web on his elbow, HATE, etched on the knuckles. The silver rings. Baz's lips curled, a cocky snarl. He stroked his goatee, then tilted his head back and confidently scratched at the faded scorpion tattoo on his pockmarked neck.

Carlo met the cocky gaze. 'Hands flat on the table, Baz. All of you.' All three men obeyed. Like a magnet, Carlo's attention was lured toward Squash. He'd never seen such a grotesque man. Shadowed eyes moved nervously in deep, primitive sockets beneath a fringe of oily hair. Cheeks ballooned out past the inverted, squashed nose.

How could this freak be alive?

Carlo was unable to tell if it was a defect or an injury, recalling the man's irregular breathing on that day in the bar. A distant memory flooded in of a comic strip from the Griffith Times. As a young boy he followed the cartoon adventures of a scrawny bush kid named Twig who lived in the fictional town of Narranjoop. The nose on his faithful dog, Charger was pushed in square from chasing cars up and down the main street.

Rickshaw's eyes narrowed. 'You … you've been following me.'

'Research, Greg.' Carlo moved further into the light, pressing each step into the floor, heel to toe, he raised his eyebrows at Rickshaw. 'People watching, I call it. It's nice to learn their habits, their daily rituals.'

'And why the fuck would you do that?'

'Seems to be a pastime of late.'

Rickshaw caressed his beard. 'That's not an answer.' He placed one hand on the back of his chair to stand.

Carlo raised the gun. 'I wouldn't.'

Rickshaw ignored him, only offering a laconic expression before standing fully. Eyes became fierce slits. He leaned forward, resting knuckles on the table. 'Whoever sent you, we can pay more.'

'I seriously doubt that.'

'My brother—'

'Is not here and has nothing to do with this.'

'He's the guy from the bar ya dumb cunt,' Baz said.

Rickshaw turned. 'What bar?'

'Maxine's, Christmas, or just before.'

Rickshaw gave a vacant look. His tongue began to move behind the bottom lip, left right, right to left, just like in the bar that day; processing. Then his eyes lit up with recognition, the mouth sagged to an arch.

'So you took a beatin', learn to take it like a man.'

'Oh I did, Greg. Thought I took it rather well. Perhaps I should've kept my head down at my beer, too late for all that now. I copped mine. We're going to find out a little about you.'

Rickshaw's nostrils flared like steam holes in Anita's pea soup. 'You arrogant cunt. I've had enough. You're way out of ya depth, son. You got one chance and one chance only to piss off. Nothing will come of this. You got—'

Carlo shot Baz in the stomach.

Eyes bulged in shock. Hands clasped the wound, he slumped forward. 'You fuck'n shot me,' he said in broken words.

Carlo pointed the Glock and motioned his head sideways towards Rickshaw's seat. The tongue halted midstream, the big man lowered himself back onto the chair.

'That's better, Greg.'

Squash's petrified eyeballs darted between Carlo, Baz and Rickshaw. Fingers gripped the edge of the table. Breathing became heavier. Carlo warned himself not to be complacent. Squash had long arms.

'Who are you?' Rickshaw asked, sniggering a foul leer, showing little concern for his wounded mate.

'My name is Carlo Caruso.'

'Caruso?' Rickshaw said, shrugging.

But Squash's shoulders slumped, eyes lifted. 'You plugged those two pigs in Sydney.'

'You can read, Squash. I'd prefer you to not bring that up again.'

Squash began to scratch at the tattoo of a snake winding up his forearm. Baz was making wincing noises. Lips shook.

Carlo reached into his pocket. 'Brought you a gift, Greg.'

'A gift? What in fucks name—?'

'My father taught me to always bring a gift. Took it from your former colleague, Ian 'Tinny' Pewter. He told me a lot about you, Pugsley.'

Rickshaw's face reddened, pronounced by thin blood vessels mapping beneath the skin.

Carlo guessed no one other than the hierarchy of the Sons of Cain dared to use his childhood nickname, including Squash or Baz.

'What the fuck has Tinny got to do with this?' His voice withered, the futility of the question appeared to dawn on him.

'Heard you're after this.' Carlo tossed the badge on the table, embroidered with,

No. 3 Original
Sergeant–at–Arms
1%er.

'You?' Rickshaw said.

'Made him cut it off with his own knife. Surely the cops told you he died on his knees.'

Rickshaw studied the badge, raking a hand through his hair. 'There's no way—'

'I bet Tinny told you that badge meant more to him than his life. I knew different.'

'How ... how did you get him to—?' Squash stammered through the words. 'He was like six foot eight.'

'The bigger they are the deeper the hole, Squash. That's all it means. Told him he'd live if he cut his precious badge off.'

Squash was now scratching the arm rigorously. Red blotches appeared on the few sections of naked skin.

'Bet he was the most dangerous man you ever met. How does that make you feel now, Squash?'

The scratching ceased.

'You say you killed a mate of mine,' Rickshaw said. 'Guy never even laid a fuck'n hand on you.'

'I only shot him once.' Carlo eyeballed Rickshaw. No reply came. 'And he was no mate of yours, Greg. Said he would've put a bullet in you years ago if not for your brother.'

Squash's long fingers were bent, pressing hard onto the table surface. Breathing accelerated.

'What would the Sons do if they found out he died because he was with you at that bar?' Rickshaw's tongue started up again, left right, left right. Thinking. 'What would they say if they knew this is all over ... what ... few hundred bucks of whatever the hell you were selling that day?

'But Greg, I'm not here to drive a wedge. I'm at a point in my life where I don't need this.'

Baz groaned, easing himself off the chair onto the floor.
'Patience, Baz. You'll bleed out soon enough.' Carlo eyed off Squash's hands. Fingers stretched out, then crunched into fists, leaving round moisture marks on the veneer surface. The rhythmic breathing increased further to a wheezing, asthmatic level, yet his face remained expressionless. Carlo turned, showed his back with the 9mm stuck in his belt.

The chair cartwheeled, Squash charged into his second last step. Carlo spun on his left heel, shifting his weight, chest and shoulders squared up, hips drove the thrust, the fist caught the nose flush. Bones cracked and Carlo immediately felt the man's face had caved in even further. Marco Sabina would have been proud of the perfect timing.

Legs buckled, the head hit the floor.

Carlo aimed the Glock at Rickshaw, daring him to move.

Squash's hands cupped his face muffling wild, spasmodic squeals. Blood flowed like a stream through the fingers. He gagged and kicked his right foot up and down, then started banging his head on the lino in some sort of desperate attempt to offset the pain. Carlo studied his fist.

It was only a punch.

He thrust his boot down on Squash's hands. Hysterical screams rose. Legs thrashed out searching blindly for his attacker.

'He was much braver than you,' Carlo said to Rickshaw. Lifting his boot he shot Squash in the forehead. The right leg fell with a final thud as the table toppled toward Carlo. He leapt back and fired at Rickshaw, who – for such a big man – moved fast to his left into the kitchen and down the passage toward his room where he kept the pistol. The bedroom door slammed. Seconds later came the sound of glass crashing. Rickshaw had tossed his mattress and found the Browning beside the empty magazine. Carlo shouldered the door open. Rickshaw had also leapt straight through the window.

Carlo walked calmly back to the living room, retrieved the backpack, switched on the stovetop gas burners and headed out through the laundry into the fledgling dawn.

———

The thirty-metre dash to the shed exhausted Rickshaw. Short breaths whistled through narrowed airways. Only life preserving urgency carried him the last few steps.

His mind raced. THINK.

All his firearms were buried on another farm since his last arrest. After Tinny's murder his brother had provided the Browning as a precaution. Norman also warned him to buy more ammo, but he hadn't bothered. Caruso had not only found the gun, he unloaded it and left the empty magazine under the mattress like this was some sort of a game. He stared at the extra jerry can. Caruso had planned this.

THINK.

The daunting reality struck. Rickshaw couldn't escape. He'd provide an easy target if he tried to ride out on his bike.

A toolbox covered in cobwebs sat beneath the steel shelving rack bolted to the far wall.

The old shotty, was it still under there?

He ran over, knelt down and shoved the toolbox out of the way, found the taping and tore the shotgun loose. Caruso hadn't covered all his bases. Rickshaw cocked the weapon. Both barrels were loaded.

It wouldn't be enough.

Spare cartridges were kept in the steel cabinet above the workbench, padlocked with a chain through the doors.

Keys were inside the house.

FUCK. THINK.

Spare keys were inside too.

Keeping one eye on the door, he turned his attention to the shadow board above the bench. For once the jimmy bar sat in its rightful place. He slipped it inside the chain and twisted with all his might, the chain refused to snap. More leverage was required.

For the past month he'd been busy making a side gate for the house, a job that should have taken only a day or two. He scrounged around, found an offcut of gal pipe, slid it over the jimmy bar and heaved downward. The handles gave way. Momentum slammed his elbow down onto the bench. Ignoring the shooting pain, he flung the cabinet open and shovelled handfuls of shells into his front pockets. He replaced the old shells in both barrels and slipped the chain into the back pocket of his jeans.

Possessed with newfound confidence, Rickshaw exited the rear of the shed and inched along the back wall to the corner where he obtained full view of the yard. The dogs remained silent. The shed door creaked. He spun.

No sign of Caruso.

A magpie curdled in the hiding dawn. A dog chain jangled. He swept the yard from tree line to verandah, from the shed to the driveway, far as he could see.

No one.

Rickshaw passed the kennels. Wings broke. A bird fluttered out from the eucalypts along the driveway. He levelled the shotgun.

Caruso was hiding there. Sunlight could only be minutes away.

He crept to the gum trees behind the kennels, knowing he had to reach the house to find cover. Caruso's only means of escape was through the neighbouring paddock or down the driveway.

Open ground.

Both barrels.

Blow the cocksucker's head off.

The Sons would clean up.

No pigs involved.

Stop daydreaming.

Concentrate, he warned himself.

Rickshaw moved in front of the tree line, wary of the exposed roots and strips of bark lying about.

More flapping overhead. He swung the gun upwards. Instincts ran wild. Dark wings of a crow left the branches and settled on the roof.

Speed had worn off, replaced by adrenaline. He ignored the rising tickle in his throat.

Grass rustled behind.

A twig snapped.

Air cracked.

The shotgun left his hands. White-hot pain scorched through to the bones. But there was no blood, only cut skin, ripped flesh, reddening, rising before his eyes. Air cracked twice more. His right leg collapsed like he'd been shot, yet there was no gunfire. Searing pain set in.

Caruso stepped in front, kicking the shotgun away, brandishing a whip. Another sickening crack split the tee shirt and his gut, exposed beneath his vest. The whip lashed again, this time to his cheek. Rickshaw raised a hand and was struck across his eyes, nose and forehead. His face was on fire.

'I went home for Christmas to see my mother. All I could think of was you. I was delighted to find this old whip. Took me about a week before I could nip the horseflies from the air.' The whip lashed again and again. Skin tore on his back beneath the tail of his vest. Rickshaw flung himself into the dirt, only to have his gut slashed again.

'One for your dogs.'

Rickshaw knew he somehow had to stand. When he first joined the club as a prospect, he'd been taught to always get to his feet no matter how bad the beating. He struggled onto all fours. Finally he managed to get upright, a hand wrenched his hair. A hand more powerful than any – even he – had ever known. Another hand clasped the back of his jeans, ramming him forward into the verandah post so hard he bounced off. Mercilessly he was slung forward again. This time the post split, so did his shoulder. Rickshaw felt the crack but ignored it when he saw a face. He threw a punch with his good arm. It struck nothing. A combination of fists hammered his body side to side. Each one so deep, so penetrating it felt like his spine was being tapped. The last punch knocked the wind out. Rickshaw bent over gasping, searching for air. Caruso turned and stepped away, perhaps to gather his own breath. Rickshaw could only see the man's boots through blurred vision, but it was enough.

Lungs filled with air. Mustering all his remaining strength he slipped the chain out and struck Caruso across the back of the head, forcing him to stumble forward. Rickshaw lunged, ready to strike again when he saw two pistols in the back of Caruso's jeans. He grabbed a handle as Caruso spun, pushing Rickshaw's hand down. Gunfire echoed. More heat, this time in his foot. A mighty blow landed between his eyes, followed by another. Most of Rickshaw's senses departed, the gun was eased from his fingers.

———

Carlo breathed a sigh of relief. He had no idea what had hit him, but knew how close he'd come to being shot. He dragged Rickshaw by the hair onto the verandah and heaved him through the laundry door. It burst off the hinges. Momentum carried the biker forward over the door. To Carlo's surprise, someone was beneath it, groaning.

A body?

Baz had crawled all the way from the kitchen.

Some men refused to die.

Carlo followed Rickshaw, treading over the door and the half dead Baz. He slammed Rickshaw into the doorjamb of the kitchen, twice. The floor quaked momentarily on old stumps.

Rickshaw's legs sagged but before he could fall, Carlo ran the biker by the scruff of the neck into the living room, shoving him forward so he tripped over Squash's body. He fell into a heap on the floor. Carlo eased the Glock out, lined up the head then sniffed the air.

Gas.

Instead he brought the butt of the gun into the biker's skull.

Sunrays were only minutes away. He raced outside. Baz had crawled from under the door onto the verandah. Carlo ignored him and retrieved the jerry can from the shed, then splashed the baseboards around the entire perimeter of the house. When he reached the back door again, Baz had toppled off the verandah onto the grass.

He managed to roll onto his back, palms to the sky. 'Don't burn me … please?'

Carlo shook the can.

Out of petrol.

Baz's blood drained face was locked in horror. Lips blue as the ink on his neck, yet somehow he still lived. There'd been one shot too many let off outside, so Carlo went back down the sidewall where he'd doused the garbage bags. A large gas bottle hissed away, filling the house. A shovel, a crowbar, a rusty wood splitter leaned against the wall. Carlo climbed over the bags, grabbed the splitter and returned to Baz, who was lying face down in the dirt.

The sound was a dull, moist *thwack*.

He hurled the bloodied splitter into the laundry, then spotted the chain in the grass and realised what he'd been struck with. Touching the back of his head, he felt a lump, no blood. He tossed the chain, the can, the bag and the whip through the door, washed up and torched the house.

As he fled past the front door, it opened. Rickshaw stumbled out. Carlo prepared to shoot when the fireball engulfed Blackbeard as the top of the sun shimmered over eastern fields.

Carlo drove west, not taking the turn off to the northern Victorian town of Kilmore, though the irony teased. On the half hour, media reports were already spruiking of imminent underworld and bikie wars. Mid-morning sunshine provided a pleasant drive. Soon he became hungry again. It seemed like forever since his last meal at the restaurant. At a service station he filled up, purchasing food for the drive south where life would be slowing down for the off-season.

Slow like a Murrumbidgee sunset.

15

Homicide, Melbourne

A red light flashed, the commander buzzed, a lifeless summoning monotone. Senior Constable Eva Hollander had to wrench her eyes from the face in the third monitor.

Bardsley's line, she answered. 'Sir?'

'Need you in here.'

'Can it wait? I'm half way—'

'Immediately.' The line went dead. She checked the time, quarter past seven. The day had been long, Friday night drinks, a distant memory. She went back to studying the face.

Male.

Caucasian.

Unidentifiable.

The eyes tracked her every move. 'Who are you?'

She entered Bardsley's office. The handset was pressed into one ear, he motioned to a chair, she sat.

'Certainly John,' he said into the phone. 'You will be briefed on arrival.' He listened some more, tapped the desk, intensity rose in his face, crevices defining the cheeks tightened with strain, leaving her to wonder who was on the other end of the line.

'Under no circumstances, Inspector.

—

'I cannot permit that.'

—

'I'll have a car waiting.'

He hung up, reclined back, all ten fingers steepled below his nose. 'That was Inspector John Ingliss, New South Wales.'

'Ingliss?' She'd been to a couple of Ingliss's seminars on organised crime.

'We've had a win, a print, rear wall of the shed next to the door. Four fingers upside down belonging to Carlo Caruso.'

The name registered along with a kaleidoscope of clashing thoughts.

Caruso?

Ingliss.

Operation Janis.

'Most wanted man in the country. What the hell's going on? How are the Mafia involved in this?' She'd only met with Bardsley three hours ago when he returned from the scene. His last hunch was they were dealing with the violent implosion of an outlaw motorcycle gang.

'We'll find out soon enough. Ingliss is on the next flight.'

'There's two million dollars on his head,' said Eva. 'No one's heard from Caruso, in what—?'

'Eight years. I've sped the ballistics up. Priority is to find the link to this other murder, Ian 'Tinny' Pewter. Can't be a coincidence his Sergeant-at-Arms badge was found in the grass next to Barry Cornes's body.' He swivelled the monitor so she could see the face. 'Caruso's our prime, obviously you're familiar with the murders of New South Wales officers Benson and Welham.'

'Mainly from training, studied the setup. The girlfriend decoded the mobile phone of one of the murdered detectives. Changed our procedures regarding the use of mobiles.'

'Yes it did. At the time we were beginning to lean towards the digital network as an alternate means of communication. Wouldn't have thought they'd let on which investigation it's from, though.'

'Every cop in the country knows how Operation Janus ended.'

'Never even got off the ground. You are not to mention it to Ingliss under any circumstances.'

'Yes sir.' She decided not to question why he made that comment because the face on her own computer screen tapped her mind.

The blue four-wheel drive.

'Can you email this photo over, I'm working on the Garland lead. Running footage, café, street.'

'The stockbroker right?' Bardsley said, emailing the photo.

'Correct. We've confirmed the sighting of Rickshaw parked at Garland's office building yesterday, just before the café.'

'Whoever did this may not have acted alone.' He slid over a photo. 'Timothy Clarke, AKA Squash. They found a spider web like fracture spanning cheeks, eye sockets, the jaw. According to his file it's an old birth fracture, been re-opened, possibly a blunt object. Caruso may well have had company. Could be connected to Garland.'

'Might be, but sheet's clean, certainly don't look the type, seventy kilos wringing wet. We're running finance, it'll be messy, Garland probably owes this club money. There's something else, sir.' She cleared her throat. 'I have a man I cannot identify who's come up on footage.'

Bardsley sat up. 'How can you not identify him, Detective?'

'Ran him through every database in the country.'

'Nothing? How can there be nothing?'

'Come into my office, sir.'

Bardsley followed. Once they were seated she led him through the café footage. 'This is our man here,' Eva said. 'Enters the café after Rickshaw, then sits in the corner, watches the exchange with Garland. Rickshaw gets up to leave and notices this guy. Take a look.'

'Rickshaw certainly appears to recognise him,' Bardsley said.

'No doubt about it, sir.' She fast-forwarded the footage. 'Leaves straight after Rickshaw. I want you to see this.'

She clicked on the street footage. 'Rickshaw's sitting on his bike, looking down, adjusting something. Doesn't appear to notice that our man walks right up, stares him down as he passes. He's not intimidated by Rickshaw at all. Then he goes through to this carpark.'

'Izett St, right?' Bardsley said.

'Correct. Gets into a dark four-wheel drive. Appears to be a Toyota. Could be our link. Hard to tell, footage isn't clear but a similar vehicle came up in surveillance from the Pewter funeral.' She clicked open another tab.

Bardsley rose from his seat and leant in close to the screen, studying the photo of the blue four-wheel drive circled in red texta. 'Rego?'

'No. Apparently they only took bikes.'

'Slack arses.'

She zoomed in. 'Looks like the same model. Both have identical bull-bars. It's marked because someone's sitting in the driver's side at the exact time of the funeral.'

Bardsley's phone buzzed. He read it. 'Ingliss is about to board.'

Eva opened the email, Caruso's photo appeared. They compared both screens.

'Definitely two different men,' Bardsley said.

'Not too dissimilar. Surgery, maybe?'

'Can't be ruled out. Could be undercover, ASIO, perhaps? Might explain why he's not coming up.'

'Want me to send it off?'

'No. Not yet. Wait for Ingliss.' He stretched his neck and rubbed his throat using a circular motion.

'You okay, sir?'

'Air-con in here, messes with me glands. A whisker under forty out at that farmhouse today, then we're stuck in a perfect twenty-four degree environment back here. Just hasta screw with ya. Bio-climatic Syndrome I call it. They'll recognise it one day. Should patent it, make my fortune.'

'Probably already been done.'

'Knowing my luck,' Bardsley said, casting a hapless grin.

'Have this stockbroker, Garland brought in tonight. When Ingliss arrives I want you in on the briefing. Keep working on this for now.'

'Yes sir.'

Bardsley turned to leave.

Unable to wrest her eyes from the photos, she whispered, 'Mason?'

Bardsley stopped, turned. 'What?'

'Mason. Audio Visual, out at Macleod. Was in here this afternoon working on this. He's the one who recalled seeing this vehicle amongst photos from Pewter's funeral. Maybe the same car, maybe not, but what if this guy's not a cop? Why would he be following Rickshaw? What if this is Caruso and he's had surgery?'

'Where are you going with this, Detective?'

'We may have a means of identifying him.'

Bardsley folded his arms. 'I'm listening.'

She bit down on her smile. 'It's a long shot, but there's a program I'd like to run these pictures through. Mason's been working with the F.B.I., only got back before Christmas.'

'You're not talking about sending this to the States?'

'No. Says he's got access.'

'If you can tell me this man is or is not Caruso, then—'

'Mason can do it, sir.'

'Where is he?'

'Gone home.'

'Get him back, now Detective.'

———

Eva enjoyed Mason's company, when he wasn't being too forward. They often did coffee whenever he came to St Kilda Road and since his return from the U. S., he'd asked her out, twice. However being four years her junior, she was more interested in his work. In particular, an identification program he worked on in the U.S., he'd bragged about having access. Now she was calling him on a Friday evening after spending the bulk of the afternoon together.

She found his number in her mobile. Mason answered on the first ring. 'Eva! I'm at the Y and J. You in for a drink?'

She imagined his face lighting up, an awkward moment. She pushed through. 'Ummm, no, not exactly, but glad to hear you're not far away. I really need your help.'

'Sure ... anything.'

'Can you return to the office?'

'What for?'

'We need to access Iceberg.'

She waited through the extended pause.

'I said anything ... didn't say that.'

'I can't tell you how important this is.'

'Can't be important enough.'

'Not asking you, Mason.'

'It's to do with those kebabs today, yeah?'

She shut her eyes. 'We have a suspect. Think national importance. If Iceberg can do what you say it can, we could break this wide open.'

'If I get caught I'll lose my job, my career, probably see the inside of Guantanamo freek'n Bay, they'll wire my head up.'

'I know you can help me.'

Another long pause. 'Have to be tomorrow, everything's out at forensics, Macleod. My department's locked—'

'That's all you can come up with, Mason? Anything from anywhere you once told me. Use my computer. I need you more than ever.' She envisioned his head drooping.

———

Mason arrived in under an hour.

Eva waited by the elevator, expressing a wide grin at the laptop tucked under his arm. She took him up to Homicide and briefed him on trying to match Caruso to the man in the café.

'Need a few minutes to set up.'

'I'll get coffees.' But as she stepped into the hallway, Bardsley approached and introduced Inspector John Ingliss, a greying, sleek man with sagging fifty plus jowls, a cropped moustache. Discerningly quiet.

She briefed them both on Mason and Iceberg, as much as she knew. Mason poked his head out the door. 'Okay, I'm in.'

'In where?' Bardsley asked as they entered the office.

Mason glanced up at Eva. 'Do I tell him?'

'No.'

'Might exonerate us both if we're busted.'

'Your call.'

'Okay. We're into an F.B.I. porthole. One way or another you will have your result tonight, sir.'

'I get the feeling this is illegal.' Bardsley said.

'Program's not illegal, what we're tapping into is.'

'What department you from, Mason?'

'Technically it's Audio Visual Forensics, but I'm ever expanding, sir.'

'I'll take full responsibility,' Bardsley said, 'just get my result.'

'Okay,' Mason began, 'the software measures all the components of any section of the human body, using a 3D grid format. Putting it simply, anything we can measure on the dead, this will calibrate on the living. All we need are photos, or in this case, footage. Cranium size, shoulder widths, rotator cuffs, legs, arms, basically any part of the body really. Once it's fully developed, Iceberg will open up a whole new field of forensic science based on information we put on file today. Similar to what we did pre-DNA. If this program gets over the line, criminals won't be able rely on surgery anymore.'

'Why haven't we used it before?' Bardsley asked.

'Most suspects pop up somewhere on a database, plus it's still under development,' Eva said. 'If Caruso's had surgery, then this program has been designed for this specific reason.'

'Glad you've been listening.' Mason typed as he spoke. 'Sometimes I think I'm talking to your coffee mug.'

Eva smiled, his index fingers were the fastest she'd ever seen over a keyboard.

Mason leaned back. 'Now that the footage is loaded, Iceberg will compile thousands of frames and compare body mass against people and objects we know the size of in the background.'

'Kind of like the B.M.I. used in the fitness industry?' Ingliss said.

'Nah, nothing like it, sir. This software uses a human template.' Mason paused in thought. 'In layman's terms it's like determining that this person takes up so much space, or volume. Iceberg creates a 3D image by building its own grids and layers, then compares the data against a template, which is another person in the frame who we already have data on. In this case, the template will be our deceased biker.'

Eva opened up the file. 'Rickshaw's weight—'

Mason's hand shot up. 'Don't tell me yet. Come on Google Earth.' He typed in the address and the street view of the café popped up. 'There's our café. Old converted single storey house with a pitched roof.'

'Why are you using Google when none of their captions have our suspect in it?' Bardsley asked.

'Look how clear it is,' Eva said.

Mason nodded. 'Very good, Detective. Iceberg relies on Google's clarity to calculate precisely. It can override the Google caption, allowing me to upload any footage on to it. Normally we can only see about ten per cent of Google Earth's capability and only through a stationary image, but as we all know, their satellites cover every square inch of every major city. This program allows us to view the other ninety per cent without Google knowing, not yet anyway, or at least that's what the F.B.I. tell us. Once it's online every law enforcement agency will have to purchase it. For now, Google and the F.B.I. are apparently bickering over rights. They tell us they're not working together, but yeah, right.' He zoomed in. 'Let's superimpose our man onto Google's footage. Iceberg is very creative, can size up anything, you watch. Now we need measurements for reference points.' Two fingers flew.

'Measurements?' Bardsley said. 'How are you going to obtain measurements without us actually going out there?'

'It's all online, sir. Twice.'

'Twice?'

'Yup. Thank 9/11 for it.'

Bardsley turned to Eva. 'What the hell's he on about?'

She shook her head, then shrugged. Ingliss remained quiet, arms folded.

'Well sir,' Mason continued. 'When 9/11 occurred, insurance companies had to foot the bill and they don't like paying. Business premiums have tripled since, underwriters have become a lot more cautious. So to activate policies they now look at major future concerns like global warming and in turn, flooding. Plans showing updated floor levels are required to be submitted with all business applications. Everything's online. Speeds up their processes, similar to what they do when you insure a second hand car. You buy the car, ring them, they already have all the details. Easy as picking cherries off a tree, you just have to know where the tree is.' He clicked on a webpage already opened in another tab. 'This is a website where surveyors, builders, architects, and the like log both street contours and most importantly to us, finished floor levels, which are—'

'R L's,' Bardsley said.

'Yeah, adjusted to the height datum, zero at sea-level, all that.'

'How's that stuff going to help us?' Bardsley asked. He winked at Eva; he seemed to enjoy prodding Mason's mind.

'Have some confidence in me, sir. Not here for my looks, ask the lovely lady beside you.'

Eva chuckled. 'Mason, if you get me a result tonight, I'm definitely taking you to dinner.'

'Cool, you'll be buying for three.'

'Mason! You didn't tell me.'

'You'll like her, straight out of the academy. Had to stand her up tonight so let's make sure you get your answer. A double date, wow! Now I got somethin' to work toward.' Mason was clearly on a high. 'Anyway, it's all recorded against the height datum on this website. Now we type in the address of the café.'

They waited.

After a few seconds, Mason said. 'We have our levels inside and outside the café. There's a 90mm difference, which is the step down from the inside to the outdoor area. We only need the outside so we now have our two recorded measurements.'

'That's only one,' Bardsley said. 'Our guys remain on the outside of the café.'

'Good observation, sir, watch this.' Mason clicked on a drop down and crosshairs appeared. 'Those crosshairs are on the Google cameras as they pass the café; they also give us a height measurement referenced to sea level, no matter what angle the car's on. When Joe Citizen sees a normal Google map, they don't see the crosshairs. Iceberg does and records a difference between our two measurements, allowing it to calibrate the size of any object in that café. All we have to do is wait for Iceberg to do its thing.'

Mason relaxed with his hands behind his head. 'Where we doing dinner, Detective?'

'Hardware Lane.' She gladly resigned herself to losing. 'Love the way they grab you off the street and literally push a chair under you, like Europe.'

'Hardware Lane it is. Tonight? I can call her back.'

'If you get a result, I won't even be sleeping tonight.'

'Well you won't have to wait too long,' he said. 'Results are up. In Elvis speak, Iceberg is in the building. Now let's check. See that table in front of the café.' He clicked on the table, a layer of measurements appeared. 'Standard chair height is forty-eight to fifty centimetres, a table is around seventy-five.' He clicked the icons on the bottom of the screen, chairs and tables that were against the wall earlier, reappeared. Mason then clicked the top of each item. Numbers and lines with arrows showing heights and widths and perpendicular distances appeared all over the screen. 'All stacks up. The more standard heights and widths we have, the quicker Iceberg establishes reference points.'

'How do you know what's a standard measurement?' Bardsley asked.

'We load 'em in. I worked on this program in the States for six months, that was part of our job, loading up the database. Tables, chairs, door and window heights, ashtrays, anything, you name it. Including people. If there are any abnormal measurements, Iceberg has the ability to convert. This is easy. It's a café. All the furniture's the same anyway. I'll give you an example. See the bricks on the wall of the adjoining shop.' He clicked on a brick and rolled back his chair. 'Any drafting software can do this nowadays and will provide an exact metric conversion of the amount of bricks required in a wall. Then your budget volume builder's bean counter, who never even steps foot on a building site, can relay that to an exact cost per thousand bricks and not pay the poor brickies one cent more. It's tough out there. Most bricks are around 75 millimetres in height. Iceberg's already clarified that the average brick in that wall is 76 mills. Probably a pressed red, Melbourne's built on 'em. Check it tomorrow, you'll find it's spot on.'

'Might just do that,' Bardsley said.

Ingliss chuckled at Bardsley. 'Is there anything he doesn't know?'

'I'm too scared to ask.'

Mason kept talking. 'See how accurate this system is. Let's go to people. Our bikie's now a template.' He dragged Rickshaw's image to the first screen and typed. 'Iceberg will build our template. A man can get shorter by stooping or sitting, but he can't get taller, the software calibrates a reference to scale.

He waited. 'Pity we can't work on the one with the busted face. Heard his mother was a junky slash pro. He couldn't make expressions, now this. They're saying his face got smashed in by a cricket bat or something. If he could, he'd probably say he's glad it's all over.'

'Concentrate Mason,' Eva said.

'Just saying. Here comes our man.' An upright shot of Rickshaw appeared with a chart on the middle screen. 'Homo erectus. In colour, too.'

Eva didn't want to ask how that happened, neither Bardsley nor Ingliss posed the question.

'Now you can open the file and tell me if I'm right about Mr. Rickshaw. The software says he's one ninety-five, weighs in at one fifty-three kaygees.'

'Spot on height wise,' Eva said. 'Prison records from twenty months ago have him at one hundred and forty-four kilos. Don't think his diet was too flash.'

'Probably dropped a couple of k's each time he took a dump, anyway, we know it's Rickshaw, Iceberg's data is correct, guaranteed.'

'One thing's concerning me,' Ingliss said. 'I can understand how it works with inanimate objects that you've been able to load in. But people? How can you have such a data base on people?'

'You're all over it, sir.' Mason tilted his head with a wry smile. 'That's the scary part. Iceberg has created its own human database. In the U.S. we had this massive amount of data to work off, but that's all they'd tell us, and when we tested the system we found it to be extraordinarily accurate.

'There were varying opinions floating around. Some of us reckon they used U.S. government employee or military records. Others said it had to be based on medical records, but I can't bring myself to believe even the F.B.I. would stoop so low. It's likely they used prison records. There's something like two and a half million prisoners incarcerated at any one time in the States. If they've been secretly collecting this data for as long as we suspect, who knows how many millions have gone through the system.'

'Imagine if the civil rights nutters get wind of this,' Bardsley said.

'Yeah. It'll never get past the goalkeeper,' Mason replied, 'despite the fact we're trying to identify the country's most wanted man. All I know is we have this wealth of human statistical information at our fingertips. We dubbed it Iceberg cause there's so much data below the surface we'll never get to see. Anyway, that's beyond control. We have enough information. Let's see if it's Caruso, the man they call the Fox who's been following our template.'

'Mason, he's just a lousy cop killer,' Ingliss said.

'Sorry sir.' Mason found an image of the man, typed in a command and sat back. In a matter of seconds the data appeared in the clear box at the bottom of the screen.

'This man is one ninety-three centimetres, six four in the old, an inch below Rickshaw in height and weighs one hundred and fifteen kilos. Puts him up there with, wow, a rugby prop or a juiced up wrestler. This is one strong mother.'

'There's only one problem,' Ingliss said. 'Caruso didn't have a criminal record. We used old gym records.'

'Iceberg is accurate, sir. It not only measures components that can't be enhanced by surgery, it will also compile a list of features altered by surgery.'

As he spoke a chart appeared. 'You see, the software has logged his measurements against both his New South Wales and Interpol files.'

Eva read the bottom line. 'Ninety-six per cent.'

'Woh ... shit!' Mason blurted out, gently shaking his head. 'That's ... that's incredibly high. Margin for error's fifteen per cent. Oh man! Check this out.' He clicked on a drop down in the left corner of the screen, and clicked again. Three photos of Caruso appeared. One of the old, one of the new, another with all the surgical alterations listed. 'This is the most sophisticated identification software in the world.' He pointed to the screen. 'That's your man. There's no doubt about it.'

Ingliss drew a long breath. 'This is the first positive sighting of Caruso since the murders of my two officers.'

'I can do some more work on this tomorrow,' Mason said. 'I have a colleague who—'

'No,' Bardsley replied, 'I've seen enough, we have a print.' He rubbed his chin, eyes dancing between Ingliss and Eva. She pressed her lips, fighting off a grin. Bardsley lowered one hand and placed it on Mason's shoulder. 'Not one word of this leaves the room, Mason.'

'Ditto, sir.'

———

'Motive, any thoughts, Inspector?' Bardsley asked. Mason had packed up and left. 'Could he be supplying chemicals, drugs? Someone contracted him?'

Ingliss paced to the door and turned. 'No. He could have sent any number of men down here. His father is a powerful man with global interests.'

'Is it true he's the head of the Honoured Society?' Eva asked.

Ingliss nodded, several times. 'Yes, Detective.'

Her breath jolted.

'But Caruso's Sicilian, isn't he?' Bardsley said. 'Thought they were Calabrian, 'Ndrangheta out in Griffith.'

'It's both,' Ingliss replied.

Eva's phone buzzed. A message. 'They've just brought Garland in.'

'Good. Room seven,' Bardsley replied, turning to Ingliss. 'Why does he come down here and kill four members of the same club. Need something before I grill this stockbroker.'

'Nothing makes sense, Lance. I think all you're going to find is the guy's in debt to this club, probably shittin' bricks.'

'Are you saying Caruso acted alone?' Bardsley said. 'These men were hardened crims.'

'Oh he's capable all right,' Ingliss said. 'You haven't shown me any evidence of another party being involved. Caruso is a brutal criminal, but also intelligent and resourceful. He wouldn't stick his neck out like this without good reason.'

'If it's not business, then what else?' Eva said.

'If you ask me, something's happened here, an altercation of some sort, something he couldn't let go of. If they've crossed an associate, I can't believe he'd be prepared to commit multiple murders for someone else's problem. Leads me to believe it's personal.'

'Like what?' Eva asked.

'Who knows, but I have an idea Caruso is also down here for a different reason.'

'What could that be?' Bardsley replied.

'His former partner, Isabelle Kelly is living in a Victorian coastal town, St Claire, in the south west.'

'The model?' said Bardsley, neck craning forward.

'That's right.'

'When were you going to tell us this, Inspector?'

'I mentioned to you on the phone earlier, if this is a positive sighting there is someone who must be notified.'

'This is a homicide investigation, John.'

'I haven't made the call yet Lance, but she must be informed. I have an obligation.' His voice seemed void of his previously authoritative tone, his face, uneasy.

'Could that be where Caruso's staying?' Eva asked Ingliss.

'Definitely not, Detective. His family will be protecting him.'

'How could you possibly assume that?' Bardsley said. 'She might be in touch with him or—' Bardsley snapped his fingers. 'Shit, John! Perth! Wasn't there an investigation into Caruso living over there? Couple of years ago.'

Eva detected the outcome of this.

'That's correct, Lance. I was involved. Turned out to be just media speculation. If he's approached her in any way I'd be the first to know.'

'You cannot say that for sure.'

'I guarantee you I can, Detective,' Ingliss replied, firmly.

Bardsley glared at him, hands on hips. 'If this gets out the media will be all over us like a rash. Caruso will disappear again.'

'She's an innocent party. You have to consider the danger she's in.'

'I don't buy it,' Bardsley shot back. 'What if she's the one hiding him?'

Ingliss shook his head. 'Impossible. It's likely he's only recently returned to the country, what we've seen tonight is evidence of that. Otherwise he would have been down here much sooner than this.'

'For a former partner you're saying he hasn't contacted in almost eight years,' Bardsley said, shaking his head. 'I'm sorry John. Think about it. If you're right and she has nothing to do with this, why would I risk my investigation? If you're wrong and we make contact with her—'

'I'm not wrong, Detective.'

'Either way you know I can't risk it. I plan on taking Special Ops out to tear the Sons' clubhouse apart with sledgehammers piece by piece until I find the connection to Caruso. We will investigate her in due course.'

'This is a mistake. I've hunted Caruso around the world. I knew he'd come back for her.'

'That's an assumption.'

Ingliss glared at him. 'I have a duty to inform her.'

'No. No, you don't. Nobody does, Inspector. We invited you in. This is my investigation.' He matched Ingliss's stare. 'Under no circumstances are you to make that call.'

16

'**D**on't be so down on him,' Eva said. 'He's one of our finest.'

'I know,' Ingliss replied, 'bothered the shit out of me all night. In his position I'd have done the same.'

It was midday the following day. Eva had just picked up Ingliss from his hotel. Garland, the stockbroker was a dead-end. After the interview all three officers remained at Homicide until after three in the morning. Bardsley offered the spare room at his house, Ingliss politely refused.

Traffic eased once Eva reached the City Link freeway, they settled into the drive north to Buchannon.

'Lance contacted the sergeant in St Claire this morning,' she said, 'turns out he knows the boyfriend, Lucas Maddigan. They drink coffee at the same place. He checked in on Isabelle Kelly too. She's fine. Nothing's out of the ordinary.'

Ingliss only nodded.

'They'll keep an eye on her.'

'That does not alleviate my concerns, Detective.'

'Lance mulls on things, you know, not too proud to change his mind if he thinks he's made a wrong decision.'

'All I know is she must be informed.'

'I'm sorry, sir.'

He clamped his lips, gave a defeated look then said. 'How far's Buchannon?'

'An hour.'

'St Claire's what, three hours south? What'd he say, don't let me out of your sight?'

She sighed. 'You said you wanted to visit the crime scene, all I can do is my job.'

Ingliss cut a grin. 'I apologise. My shout for lunch.'

'You're on. Tell me about Caruso.'

'Had it all, penthouse, sixty foot ocean cruiser, 'A' list cocktail parties. You name it. Money's no object.'

'And a woman like Isabelle Kelly.'

'High profile couple, Caruso was obsessed with her.'

'I read up on her. Lots of info out there.'

'Most if it's press-related bullshit.'

'There's some positive stuff too. One article described her as the next Elle.'

'You can believe that. Her old bosses all agreed she would also have been a successful businesswoman. Surprised you didn't know of her, wouldn't be much younger than you.'

'Oh I knew of her, just don't get into those trashy mags.'

Through the corner of her eye she saw his smile lift.

'I have to introduce you to my wife. She's always telling me those mags are full of rubbish, then on the other hand always knows what's in 'em.'

'Catch 22. I'm sure she's lovely.'

His phone rang.

'John—'

Ingliss was clearly part deaf. The volume, perhaps turned up all the way.

'—it's Assistant Commissioner Mersche.' Eva heard.

'Hang on.' He pulled out an earpiece, fumbled about until it was attached to the phone, then said, 'It's a positive sighting.'

—

'We've discussed it, thoroughly.'

—

'I understand, Tony.' Ingliss ended the call. 'Bardsley has finished mulling it over.'

Eva winced. 'Your boss?'

He nodded. 'Where was I?'

'Isabelle Kelly.'

'Always looked professional. The rich model they said either didn't understand or care about the trouble she found herself in. Media's like a dog with a bone once they get hold of a story like that.'

'And you believed her?'

'Absolutely, Detective. Could've travelled anywhere in the world to re-ignite her career, yet she stayed in Australia. Never refused us an interview. Not one word to the media, either.'

'Disappeared right off the radar, as I remember. I also recall her arrogance at the time, or how it was portrayed, anyway. Pardon me for calling it as I see it, but you're rather defensive of her.'

Ingliss shrugged. 'She was just being the person she'd trained herself to be. Isabelle knew no other way, held her head high. That pissed a lot of people off, including my superiors. There was a lot of internal pressure to pin something on her.'

'So you're telling me she had no idea who Caruso was?'

'That's correct. I don't think it's a coincidence Caruso is also in Victoria. Scares the hell outa me. She's finally found happiness, a good life down there.'

Operation Janus. Eva knew she had to ask, but how? Bardsley's warning was clear.

'The day your officers were killed,' she began, choosing words carefully, 'the cocaine in that truck had a street value, some say between four and five hundred million.'

'Never recovered it. We also didn't let that type of information out.'

'Common knowledge round the traps, sir.'

Janus. She swallowed hard.

'You're a natural antagonist aren't you?'

Eva laughed aloud, more out of nervousness. 'My father used to say that. Guess it led me straight to the job. Can't deny myself.'

'Don't hold back on my account.'

'Take that to the bank.' She licked her lips. 'There's an elephant in the room here sir. Yesterday we began an investigation into murdered bikers, today I'm driving you to the murder scene, this country's foremost expert on the Mafia, the man appointed to command Operation Janus.'

His head snapped toward her.

She absorbed his glare. 'Do I get an answer?'

'What do you know about Janus?'

'Supposed to have been the largest organised crime investigation this country has ever seen. One of the murdered detectives, Craig Welham was your leading investigator. His girlfriend, a Mafia plant, swapped the sim card in his phone resulting in your officers being killed in a location they were never supposed to be at.'

Ingliss sighed. 'That's correct, Detective.'

'Which part?'

'All of it.'

———

'Sure mate,' Lucas said, pressing the end button on the phone. He'd been sweeping the downstairs living room of his construction site in Gloucester Street when he took the call from his carpenter, Patto. Nat appeared from the kitchen, leaning on another broom.

'You right to help Patto with the skirts and arcs over the next few days?'

'No drama,' Nat said. 'Surf's ordinary, need the cash.'

'Might get you to start cleaning upstairs.'

'What about lunch?'

'Isabelle's bringing something out soon.'

226

'Shit hot. Freek'n starving.'

Lucas smiled. 'Be right up to give you a hand when I'm finished here.'

Nat disappeared up the stairs. Lucas turned, watching in dismay as a man slipped broad shoulders through the narrow opening in the gate of the temporary fence, despite the signs. The stranger moseyed around the front of the house, wearing a long sleeved tee and denims.

He stepped over a puddle by the front door, strolled through the garage opening and entered the hallway where Lucas now stood. A rush of sea breeze followed, bringing up dust. Lucas shut the door.

The man ignored him.

'Can I help you?'

'Just looking around, pal.'

Pal? Lucas didn't offer his hand; neither did the stranger. He only cast a dismissive look, raked his gaze across the ceiling and down the walls before wandering away up the passage. 'Excuse me, this is a building site, you walked right past the sign.'

'I won't get in anyone's way.'

'Not the point, you're not allowed on site.'

The man scuffed his boot on the floor. Dust cleared, exposing the concrete. 'Terrazzo?'

Lucas gave up. 'We don't call it that anymore, it's just polished concrete.'

'I prefer Terrazzo.' The man glanced at the broom. His hands hadn't moved from his pockets. 'You the owner?'

'I'm the architect.'

'An architect, sweeping?'

'How can I help you?'

'Looking at buying, this is nice, overlooks the bay.'

'Not for sale yet.'

The man turned, dark, penetrating eyes. 'Everything's for sale, Lucas.'

'How do you know my name?'

'A lady told me who you were.'

'A lady? What lady?'

'Does it matter?'

'It does.'

'A lady from the pub.' Eyes bore down on him. 'A very attractive lady, Lucas. Told her I'm interested in something with an ocean view. She said this would be coming on the market, I should take a look.'

Isabelle?

He hadn't exactly told her to not mention the house to anyone, and couldn't really blame her, but he was tiring of this man. 'Listen, should be on the market within three months. Once the landscaping's done the agent can show you through.'

The man drifted away again, pacing slowly until he stood in the kitchen at the rear of the home. 'Why involve an agent, I like what I see, why can't we deal direct?' The man spun on his heel. 'You and I, Lucas. I get to choose colours, the fit out. You save on agent's fees. Seems logical.'

The face? There was something about the man's face, fake, like it was carved out of wood.

Lucas cringed. Fingers gripped the broom handle.

'Margins are tight nowadays, Lucas. Market's not too buoyant, I'm cashed up.'

'Haven't done my figures yet.' He was wondering how to get this man off site when a car door slammed. 'Excuse me.' He walked away to the front window. Isabelle carried a plate of sandwiches and stepped over the same puddle. He opened the front door.

'Hi babe,' she said. They kissed. 'Sandwiches from leftovers in the kitchen. Had to fight the cook's dog.'

'Great, the Bos is upstairs.'

'Yeah.' She gave her delightful smile. 'I knew Nat was here. Grabbed as much food as I could.'

'Hey, ah, you spoke to some guy, you mentioned the house, he's here looking around at the moment.'

Lucas turned his head but couldn't see the man.

'What guy?'

'Some guy, fit looking, dark hair, says he spoke to a woman in the bar, was told to take a look at this house.'

She shook her head. 'Haven't mentioned it to anyone.'

'You sure?'

'I'd remember. Might've been one of the waitresses.'

A gush of wind rushed by, he walked back into the kitchen area to see the sliding door open. The man was nowhere. 'Wait here,' he said to Isabelle who placed the plate down on Patto's makeshift workbench, set up in the corner. Lucas walked outside, checked down both sides of the house before returning.

Nat was downstairs already with a sandwich in one hand and another jammed in his mouth. Lucas grabbed a sandwich and took a bite. Through the living room a blue four-wheel drive accelerated down the road.

———

'Do you expect me to believe it's a coincidence Welham was one of the officers killed?' Eva asked.

Ingliss faced the window, glaring out at the passing countryside. Without turning he said. 'Never believe in coincidences.'

'How did they end up where they were if—?'

'How long to Buchannon?'

'Fifty something minutes.'

He offered a mild, uncomfortable chuckle. 'They were redirected.'

'Redirected? How? Internally? Are you talking corruption?'

'Never found out.'

'The second detective, Benson, could he have been turned?'

'No. Just horribly unlucky.'

'How do you know they didn't turn him, then killed him after he served his purpose.'

'You know about Welham's girlfriend, right. We caught up with her hiding out in a caravan park in Darwin. She was more scared of them than us and came clean.'

'Why were they re-directed? And if it's corruption, who would send two officers to the location where a haul of cocaine was kept, without backup, knowing they could be killed?'

'Powerful men who could not let Janus get off the ground. Criminals who had a lot to gain when Carlo Caruso was supposed to be found dead at the scene of two murdered detectives, one being Craig Welham. It was a tough time for the force. We'd just been through a Royal Commission into corruption, then these murders tore us open again.'

'But Caruso lived and Welham didn't, why was he so important?'

'This has little to do with your investigation, Detective.'

'Any information to do with a murder suspect is relevant, sir.'

A pause, he seemed to be studying a new plague of suburban rooftops creeping over the retired farmland.

'Who is your super with, Detective?'

'What? My superannuation? What's that got to do—?'

'Just tell me.'

'Emergency Services. Why?'

'Stick with them.'

'What the hell are you talking about?'

'Janus was not the first investigation of its type. In the mid nineties I led an initial organised crime investigation primarily focussed on the L'ombrello Superannuation Trust, originally set up by businesses in the Riverina District of New South Wales. Super had become compulsory, all of a sudden this fund gathered money like wildfire. Industries right across the nation began investing with L'ombrello.'

Her mind tweaked. 'L'ombrello, there's an office tower in Sydney isn't there?'

'Built from super funds controlled by the Mafia.'

Eva gasped. 'Can't the government stop them, I mean, can't they bring in laws?'

'No. It's legitimate. Super is a financial windfall for the government, helping to drive the Australian economy while the rest of the world is falling into an economic black hole. Sometimes I think we're fighting more than organised crime.'

'Why would anyone invest with them?'

'Returns are excellent. It's tough out in the country. Major banks are sending farmers to the wall. Suicide rates are sky high. L'ombrello have set up a finance arm to keep farmers on the land. They get the sympathy vote.'

'And the super funds flow back through.'

'That's correct. Craig Welham was an integral part of my team. A brilliant analyst who was to be promoted within Janus.'

'My guess is you found out the Mafia were laundering money through their super funds.'

'No we didn't. That's the catch. Rules are too tight. Welham believed they set it up as a legitimate revenue stream to invest back into their own businesses, and he was right. Think about it. There's over a trillion dollars invested in super right across the nation, L'ombrello is one of the best performers.

'When the Government introduced compulsory super, one of the major criticisms was the lack of regulations controlling where funds could be invested. It's all so simple, entirely legal and untouchable. I remember Welham came to my office one day saying the horse has bolted. We're too late.'

'So, what were you hoping to uncover through Janus?'

'Janus was designed to track the funds utilising advanced forensic accounting resources with new, wide ranging powers incorporating all government departments for the first time. We set up investigative units in each state. Welham's murder sent shockwaves through them all, Janus died with him.'

'So you're telling me Italians in outback Griffith came up with this scheme.'

'Don't underestimate the Griffith Mafia, most powerful criminal network in this country. Franco Caruso's interests are worth billions. Ever been out there?'

'No.'

'Dry as all hell, but for the rivers and the irrigation system. Water flows from the Snowy River Scheme. Money too. Marijuana was grown on a massive scale until satellites began detecting their crops in the late eighties, costing hundreds of millions of dollars along with bad publicity over certain murders. On top of that, new laws meant they were going to have to begin paying superannuation. Why not exploit it. L'ombrello's birth was at a meeting popularly known in the Riverina as the Murrumbidgee Meeting.'

'Never heard of it.'

'The meeting was held at Franco Caruso's property on the Murrumbidgee River, south of Griffith on the fifth and sixth of February, Nineteen ninety-one. Twenty-nine of the most powerful Mafia families from all over Australia attended.'

'I've heard of the Apalachin meeting in the U.S. where the Mafia families carved up their rackets across North America. Didn't know it happened here.'

'Certainly did, only difference was cops in the U.S. got wind and raided them. Half were chased into the woods, unlike our own meeting where the local cops stood by and watched, then let us know after all parties had left.'

'Carlo's father set up such a meeting?'

'Yes, however it was chaired by a young man named James Riggs.'

'Doesn't sound Italian to me.'

'He's not. Just a local boy from Griffith. His old man did time for a commercial marijuana crop back in the early eighties. At thirteen he was forced to leave school to help his mother keep the farm. Shortly after the father was released, young James went on to be privately educated in Sydney then studied economics and law at Oxford.'

'Some turnaround.'

'Sure was. At a very young age Riggs became CEO of Caruso Industries. He's the man behind setting up their super funds, which have since blossomed into what L'ombrello is today.'

'How the hell does that happen?'

Ingliss shrugged. 'Riggs is closely associated with the Caruso family. We don't know how.'

'What has this got to do with the murders?'

'As you know Franco Caruso is Sicilian, Cosa Nostra. Our previous investigations concentrated on the Calabrian 'Ndrangheta. Franco told them they couldn't continue business the old way. So they thrashed out their differences at the meeting and voted on moving in on super funds, legislation was about to be passed.'

'The 'Ndrangheta, tell me, is it true they were taxing the major supermarkets around the country something like thirty to forty cents a crate on fruit and vegetables?'

'Wetting the beak, they call it. That racket went on for decades until Riggs capped it. We looked into it but he was always one step ahead. In one of his biggest deals, he brought in a company to take over the distribution network, and then to appease the 'Ndrangheta he increased the flow of funds back through their associated businesses.'

'Didn't think Sicilians and Calabrians worked together.'

'They'd rather have us believe they don't. However, the two organisations are also closely associated in Italy, too. Franco Caruso snuck under our radar. Previous investigations looked into where they could hide dope crops. Caruso's business is livestock and abattoirs.'

'Abattoirs?'

'Abattoirs.'

'That's handy,' Eva said.

'Carlo's older brother Nicky runs that side of the business now. Welham believed Franco Caruso is the financial brains behind the entire organisation. You may be a little bit young to know they were investigated for passing horse meat off as beef, sold it to the Japs back in the eighties.'

'No, I don't remember.'

'Sent our bi-laterals back a few pegs. Welham's theory was the trustees controlling L'ombrello represent factions within the Mafia, same as Liberal and Labor within our government. The two major factions are Sicilian and Calabrian.'

'Where does Carlo Caruso fit into this?'

'Franco's rogue son moved to Sydney four years before he murdered Benson and Welham. A young man with all the money in the world and no need to get involved in importing drugs.'

'Other than ambition.'

'Total ambition. Carlo wanted to carve out his own empire. He had contacts with a Mexican cartel, organised a large shipment but couldn't finance it through his usual channels in Sydney. So he approached the Santoli brothers, property developers from Queensland.'

'The Santoli brothers.' Her mind registered. 'Killed in a boating accident off the Gold Coast, right?'

'Blown sky high ten kilometres out to sea, part of the clean up after the murders. The Santoli brothers were also present at the Murrumbidgee meeting years earlier. At first Caruso trusted them despite their 'Ndrangheta connections. They distributed cocaine through South East Queensland. Caruso was their major supplier. Then he brings them in on the shipment. They agreed to help finance him and went to senior members of the 'Ndrangheta for the cash. The 'Ndrangheta saw their chance and devised an elaborate plan that very nearly came off. They had inside knowledge of Janus, knew it had to be stopped, so they put the girl in place to keep eyes on Welham and financed the Santoli Brothers. But on the day of the murders there was a third man killed.'

'The hit man, the driver, forgotten his name.'

'Gregory Reynolds, hired by the 'Ndrangheta to kill Caruso.'

'So they could get their hands on the shipment?'

Ingliss thinned his smile. 'For a truck load of coke?'

'What's that look for?'

'That wasn't the prize, Detective. They even intended to leave most of it behind.'

'I have no idea why someone would do that.'

'Think about what would happen if Franco's boy was found dead in possession of Mexican cocaine worth hundreds of millions, and at the scene of two murdered detectives, one being Welham, my lead investigator under Janus. Imagine the media circus. Franco was not supposed to survive the internal rift. Your colleague, Mason used a soccer analogy last night. Think of it like this, the Sicilians have the ball, the 'Ndrangheta want possession. Control of L'ombrello means they can pump an even larger percentage of investment dollars back through their own businesses, criminal and legitimate. The prize was billions of dollars held in super funds.'

Eva gasped. 'Of course—'

'Carlo Caruso was becoming a very rich and powerful man in his own right, but he was also feared. You need to know the man you're up against. They knew if they sent my officers to that industrial estate, they wouldn't make it out. If you come up against him, he will kill you. You saw what he did to those bikers. It's my bet he acted alone. His father and older brother, Nicky are only interested in the money, but Carlo Caruso is a sadistic, ruthless criminal. Even the 'Ndrangheta feared him.

They know they'll never gain control of L'ombrello while he's alive. It was supposed to be a three-way win, but Caruso outsmarted them all. We believed the cocaine was to move off the docks on the Sunday evening and organised our surveillance. Turns out the shipment was delivered three days earlier, sitting safely in a container on the back of a truck.'

'How did your investigation uncover all this?'

'They still went ahead and tipped us off.'

'So that's how you found out Caruso killed your detectives.'

'We already knew that. Sam Benson had a camera. Last photo he took was of Caruso coming at them with a machine gun. We also made several arrests including one of Caruso's associates named Joey Avola. He opened up, we had a statement ready, but he refused to sign. Family owned car dealerships throughout the Riverina. A boy riding to school found the oldest brother on the side of a road on the outskirts of Griffith with a bullet in his head. Avola has two more brothers, never spoke another word. Gets out of Long Bay next year. Said he'd rather face God than Carlo Caruso.'

'That's some elephant.'

'Tramples through my head every day, Detective. The whole structure of the Honoured Society changed at the Murrumbidgee meeting. Welham believed Franco tried to lead them out of their old ways, but the 'Ndrangheta are powerful. Welham's analogy was it's like owning a vicious dog you can never let off the chain. He predicted there had to be a takeover one day. Never got to live to see how accurate he was.'

———

Eva took the first turnoff into Buchannon, still processing everything. 'Bardsley's asked me to visit petrol stations first.'

'It's unlikely,' Ingliss replied. 'Do that through the week. According to the notes, the victims spent their last afternoon in the pub.'

'That's correct. It's up ahead, next set of lights. You don't think we'd get a sighting there do you?'

'Maybe the bistro,' Ingliss said. 'Could've been stalking these guys for weeks.'

'Worth a try, don't forget, your shout for lunch.'

Eva pulled up in the only space she could find opposite the pub. Cars lined both sides of the road. Hagan's Hotel was a horrible box on a box double storey building. She couldn't quite work out the colour, pastel or peach, maybe?

'Don't think we'll be eating here.' Heads filled the windows. 'Place is jam-packed. Guess a triple murder will do that to a small town.'

'Want to know anything, go to the pub.' Ingliss said, pointing. 'Take a look, furthest table along.'

Men and women were drinking outside, chatting, laughing beneath a wrought iron laced balcony. Clothes were too casual, too country for country wear, camera bags at their feet. 'Bardsley warned me, we can't let the media see you.' She drove off and parked down the road. They swapped seats. Ingliss drove back and pulled into a gravel carpark at the rear, also full of cars.

'Be careful,' he said, as she opened the door. 'Waitresses only, don't show that photo to any barmen. They're different creatures, amazing memory skills, sell their mothers for a dollar. If the press get a sniff—'

'Don't worry, I'll be careful.' She stepped out, her brain still racing. The hot wind hit her like a furnace, so too did another thought. She stopped with the door half open.

'What's the problem?'

'Something's been bothering me. If they want control, why don't they go after Riggs?'

'Riggs is untouchable, along with the entire board, all respectable businessmen under Mafia protection. L'ombrello is their goose that lays the golden egg. Superannuation is easily transferrable, they can't risk a run on funds. Seen it happen to many smaller lending institutions over the years, cripples 'em.'

She nodded and shut the door, tucking her satchel under her arm. Unfortunately, it made sense.

Ingliss took off. Eva entered through a back door leading past the toilets. She opened another door at the end of a dark passage, straight into the main bar. Not exactly to plan, she thought. All eyes descended on her so she walked in. Voices hushed. Curious locals stood side by side, hairy faces, hairy ears, dusty wide brimmed hats, blue truckie singlets holding pregnant looking stomachs all parted as she brushed her way through, feeling every bit a female detective in her suit. Incessant whispers rose behind her. Thoughts turned to Rickshaw, how he would've stood out in a café in upmarket Prahran. Murder, the most intriguing of all crimes had visited here. They would claim it as their own, even though the killings happened several kilometres out of town. Lips poised over rims of pots. Rumours of bikie wars would strengthen with each downed beer. Eva approached the bar and asked the barman if she could speak to the manager in private.

He pointed to the bistro door. 'Through there, I'll come around.'

She couldn't see the media crew for the thick crowd, then heard, 'Detective!' Eve turned. Linda Scholes from the Herald Sun was pushing through the crowd, so she hurried through, shutting the door and stomping the locking bolt down. From behind the glass door, the reporter shot a look of betrayal. Eva didn't have long before they found another entrance. The barman appeared, motioning with his head toward a flight of stairs. 'He's coming down.'

'Thank you. Keep that woman out, please?'

White tablecloths stood out against the old world, wood panelled walls. An empty dining room.

No way would Caruso have eaten here.

A short, portly man dressed in black came down the stairs preceded by a mingling of nose hairs and the stench of tobacco. 'Pete Cavanaugh. Publican 'ere, miss.' He thrust out both his chest and a hand.

'Detective Senior Constable Hollander.' She shook the hand, it felt moist, it held on a little too long. She passed over her card.

He read it. 'Fella from yesterday, must 'a been ya boss.'

'Yes, Detective Senior Sergeant Bardsley.'

'Sumptin' like that.' He looked her up and down. 'He coming out today or what?'

'No.' She changed her tack. 'I will need to organise a time to talk to your staff, maybe not today.'

'Good. Pumpin' out bar meals like hot cakes. Never been busier. Can schedule it for tomorrow, or later in the week.' He waved the card. 'I'll call ya on this.'

'Thank you.' Instincts told her the interviews might not be necessary at all.

'Can you excuse me?' She sent a text to Ingliss —HURRY UP—.

When she finished, she smiled back at Cavanaugh, who was busily tucking his shirt in using his thumbs. The chest came out further.

'Ya got sumptin' already?'

'Just a routine enquiry.'

How do I approach this? She wondered.

'No one round 'ere's gonna miss those arseholes. Anything else I can help ya with?'

'Uhmm, yes, tell me, if I wanted to experience the finest dining in town, where would I go?'

His hands lifted, then slapped down on the sides of his thighs. 'We can look afta' ya here. Be our pleasure.'

'I appreciate that Mr. Cavanaugh, was thinking more of a restaurant.'

He rubbed his chin. 'S'pose there's either of the two Chinese joints. Indian on Cobble Street's all right, but me and the wife like the Takari Winery bout fifteen minutes south on the Templeton Road. Best in town, try the duck risotto.' He checked his watch. 'It's two now. Pretty sure they stop serving lunch at two.'

'Uhmm, that's—' she pointed over her shoulder '—back through the lights?'

'Yeah, straight through to the next roundabout, instead of turning left 'n back onto the highway, head right, winery's up on the hill. Can't miss it.'

'Thank you Mr. Cavanaugh, you've been a great help. Please don't repeat a word of this to the media.'

'Course not.'

'Can we get out the back from here?'

'Follow me.'

He led her to another rear door, opening onto the carpark.

Ingliss had the car running. She hurried over.

'Detective!'

'Oh shit!'

Scholes walked out from behind the pub wall.

'Linda, not at the moment.'

'Eva, come on, need a break here.'

'Please? I'll call, soon as I have something.'

Fortunately the reporter was blindsided by the bulk of the car and didn't appear to take any notice of the driver. Without waiting for a reply, Eva jumped in. 'Move, and shield your face.'

Ingliss spun the visor ninety degrees and sped off.

Eva pointed south. 'Back through the lights.'

'I thought the farmhouse was out on the Northern highway.'

'We're going to a winery.'

'A winery?'

'Nothing but the best.'

Ingliss slowed for the red light.

'Go straight through.'

He ran the light.

'Right at the roundabout.' She glanced over her shoulder, making sure they weren't followed.

Ingliss gave a curious look. 'You going to make me buy you lunch at a winery?'

'Wouldn't normally do that to a guest of the State. Just drive as fast as you can.'

They found the Takari Winery and pulled into the long driveway running up through the vines on a sundrenched hillside. The sign read,

CELLAR DOOR OPEN / RESTAURANT CLOSED

They found the restaurant. A pretty, red-headed waitress greeted them.

'Good afternoon,' she said, a pleasant country smile. 'We're closed until six. You're welcome to taste some of our wines through the cellar door.'

'Thank you.' Eva showed her badge. 'May we speak with the manager, please?'

'You're Police?'

'Homicide, Miss.'

'I'll get her.' Sally started to walk out of the room, then spun. Can I get you a drink?'

'No, thank you, official business.'

'I know,' the young woman replied. Her voice suddenly lowered. 'Everyone in town knows.' Then she innocently munched her lips together making a hollow, pucking like sound, almost like she was trying to cover up either her goofiness or uncertainty at her own comment. 'Back in a sec.' She left through the door, reappearing moments later with another woman and a man who introduced themselves as the owners.

'We apologise for coming unannounced,' Eva said. 'We'd like to talk to your staff, please.'

'We're all here,' Heather, the female owner replied. Within minutes, she assembled her small staff in the dining room. One chef and a young cook's hand were accompanied by another, older waitress. Eva showed the photo to Kate, the elder waitress. She studied it. During a lengthy, silent pause, her gaze flicked to her younger colleague; then back to the photo, hands held at her waist. The left hand was holding her right wrist, tight. The right hand crunched up in a nervous ball.

'Kate. Do you recognise the man in the photo?' Eva asked.

'Kate?'

'He was here,' she said, her voice, low. 'Thursday night, I think. He ... he sat over in the corner.'

A gasp came from Sally, the redhead standing further away with the rest of the staff, and yet to see the photo. The young woman's head dropped, a hand lifted over her mouth. Gentle sobbing filled the room.

'Thank you Kate, please take a seat,' Ingliss said. Kate went to speak, he raised a hand and silenced her.

Eva turned the photo face down on the table. 'Could you all please leave the room,' she said to the remaining members of the staff. 'Sally, please remain, take a seat.' It all made bizarre sense, Caruso had left a presence here, perhaps more.

The cooks left, the husband started to follow, Heather put her hand on his forearm, saying to the officers, 'They're our staff.'

'Please?' Eva said.

'Come on,' the husband urged. His wife gave her two waitresses a forlorn look and left.

Sally stood alone, an isolated figure.

'Please take a seat,' Eva repeated.

Sally shuffled forward, head down. 'What's happened?' she whispered, amidst weeping.

Eva took pity on her. Despite their age differences these two colleagues were close, apparent by the look the older Kate cast toward Sally. Caruso's interest would only be in the younger, curvaceous figure.

'I served him,' Kate said. There was a long silence. Eva watched Sally.

'No ... no.' Sally's voice was soft, distant. Hands gripped the back of the chair. 'You don't have to do this, Kate.'

Realising she might only have only one chance at full disclosure, Eva looked to Ingliss and nodded toward the door. He left the room.

———

'We had nothing to work with Lance and your detective walks away with a confirmed sighting,' Ingliss said, elbows resting on the bar.

Eva drained her beer, hiding her modest appreciation. They had returned from Buchannon and met up with Bardsley at Opey's Bar on Little Flinders Street in the heart of Melbourne.

'Don't you think of poaching her,' Bardsley warned.

'You've got our old boss.'

'Welcome to have that woman back any day.'

'All yours, mate.'

'Cut it out you two,' Eva said, 'woman present.'

Bardsley grinned. 'So what do we have? Caruso sleeps with a waitress the night he kills three people.'

'The restaurant and the murder scene are forty minutes apart,' Eva said. 'Caruso used the name Wayne. Said he was travelling to Melbourne. She has a one-night stand with a clean-cut, good-looking guy who just didn't look the type to go out and murder bikers. She's terrified. Don't think she'll ever go back to her house again.'

'How sure are you about the car?' Bardsley asked.

'Matches the four-wheel drive from the footage. Even though Caruso arrived after dark, she's confident it was a blue Landcruiser. Got lucky with the wine bottle, too. Meant to put her recycle bins out yesterday, slept in.'

'Good work, Ballistics also match,' Bardsley said. 'The bullet in Rickshaw's foot came from the same gun that killed Pewter. They're finding marks on Rickshaw's body they've best described as welts, don't know what to make of it all just yet. Visited the brother, Norman Rickshaw today at his Harley dealership in Preston, said they're making their own enquiries. The remaining club members were all out there. If he really has no idea who did this, then he'll have his own list of suspects. This could get out of hand.' He signalled to the barman for another round of beers. Bardsley eyeballed Ingliss. 'You sticking around? We're going in, possibly as early as Thursday morning.'

'I'll be here, if my presence is warranted,' Ingliss said.

Bardsley nodded, taking a long sip. 'Listen John, sorry things got a little heated last night.'

'It's understandable,' Ingliss said. 'We're close, I can feel it, still there's no motive.'

'Yeah, I want you to know the local sergeant in St Claire phoned a short time ago. Isabelle Kelly worked in the hotel most of the day. She's fine mate, and listen, I've also had a good re-think.'

'I have grave concerns, Lance.'

'I know, Inspector. I'm gonna up the man power, we'll hit em hard, but if things don't turn out this week like I plan, then—' he paused and cast a look toward Eva. 'I have another idea you may be interested in.'

Part 3
All Mine

"St Claire looks after her own,"
so the locals say.

PETER EDWARDS

17

Waves exploded, a rich booming, cracking sound above the constant echoing rumble of the groundswell, this ocean's deep bass. It surrounded, encompassed, almost threatened the landscape causing the earth to hum from within. Despite its isolation this house was not a peaceful setting. Yet the wall of sound was so welcome, so familiar now, buffeting her mind from realities of the past. Lucas had explained how the bedroom window was angled slightly so he could see the surf, in particular the offshore wave they spoke of with such excitement, such enthusiasm. The big wave they curiously called All Mine.

The blind never closed. Isabelle woke, bathing in the joy of radiating sunlight.

Beneath her was a towel, evidence of last night's dream. Lucas would wake her, often placing a towel on her side of the bed so she wouldn't be lying in cold sweat. She struggled to recall the dream, or even being woken up.

Was I screaming again? She asked herself, rolling over, washing a hand over the wrinkles in the sheet where Lucas had slept. Drawing in his scent, laughing mildly as she found herself doing each morning at the sight of tee shirts and shorts draped without care over the bed rail.

Naked, she wandered over to the window appreciating a morning without clouds. Dew droplets sliced through the salt crust she cleaned off only a week ago. It took several minutes to find the men. Dark, tiny figures somehow paddled through mountainous seas over to the reef, into the bowels of the mighty wave.

All Mine.

A name for a wave. Somehow it didn't seem so ridiculous any more.

Trampling was heard up the stairs down the far end of the deck. She slipped on a top, a woollen jumper, trackies, Ugg boots and went outside. Horry was leaning on the rail patting Clyde.

'Morning Horry.'

'Hey.'

'Thought you'd already be out there.'

'Some poor suckers have to work. Bakery door's been open all morning, swell's breaking over the sea wall in the bay. Man, check this set out.' A surfer took off inside a falling wave and disappeared behind a veil of water then shot out. 'The Bos is ripping out there.'

'How'd you know it's Nat?'

'Only one goofy footer gets barrelled that deep, on his backhand too. She's all time out there.'

Isabelle wanted to ask what a goofy footer was, or even what backhand meant, but thought, one step first. 'All time?' she asked.

Horry grinned. 'Means sick, going off, cranking, good as it gets.'

'Oh. Why not just say *real good* then?'

He gave a sideways glance. 'We'll make a surfing wife out of you yet.'

'Yeah. Can't wait. Want coffee?'

'Nah. I'm out there. Biggest day we've had since last winter.' With two hands on the rail he hoisted himself over and jumped off the deck, both feet plugged into the soft sand below with an acrobatic-like landing.

'You're a show off.'

'A natural performer, Connie says.'

She heard the distinct grumble of the downstairs sliding door. Horry soon appeared in his wetsuit, running down the beach with a board tucked under his arm. He launched himself into the water, duck diving through the shorebreak to begin the long paddle out over to the reef. A short time later more surfers arrived, two groups of two she didn't recognise, already suited up. They waved while strapping on their leg ropes down at the water's edge.

Just after nine the front door sprung open, Connie barged through without knocking. Isabelle reminded herself once again she'd have to get used to that. Dimi leapt out of her lap, yapping fiercely.

'Hi,' Connie called, dumping more food on the table next to the meatrays Lucas left out to defrost.

'You've come prepared.'

'Course darl, you know what they're like. Despite all that macho bullshit, they don't get fed, they whinge like little bitches.'

'Can we not cook today so we can listen to that?'

'There's a plan. Horry reckons this'll be an *ipic day*. She thrust her teeth out, trying to mimic his grin, making fun of her husband's accent. 'I bit he said the sirf 'll be crinking ill day.'

Isabelle laughed aloud. 'Every time he says cranking I imagine God with a long white beard and all, out past the horizon cranking a machine with wheels and cogs and pegs, like the one in Mousetrap, churning out big waves, singing mystical tunes.'

'I hear ya.'

'Been watching them surf all morning. It's thrilling.'

'No need to watch, Horry'll give us detailed running commentary of each wave when he gets in.'

They laughed again before Connie's look turned somewhat serious. 'Hey, there'll be lots of crew out here today. Used to have days like this all the time with ... with Sue. Just wanted you to know, darl. You gonna be okay with this?'

'I'll be fine.' Isabelle knew Connie and Sue had been best friends. Despite Connie being several years older, they too had formed their own close relationship since she began dating Lucas. For a bit of fun in between breaks through her shifts at the pub, Isabelle often went into the bakery and helped Connie serve. Everyone in town was called either darl or kiddo.

'Where are your two boys?'

'Sleepovers. One of the girls from the shop will bring 'em out later on. Let's cook. I'm starving.' Connie tapped her belly. 'Gotta get off bakery food again.'

Before long the men paddled in, stripped off their suits and the wind was soon alive with barbequed food and the chatter of families who arrived throughout the morning.

Isabelle was cuddled up next to Lucas on the deck lounge when a text came through on her phone.

'Hey. That's a friend. She called before for coffee, told her we were all out here and she should come over. Hope you don't mind?'

'Course not,' Lucas replied, 'you don't have to ask that.'

'I know, it's just that she's new in town. Met her at Tom's, comes into the pub too. I'm meeting her at the road, otherwise she'll never find the place.'

'Want me to come?'

'I'll be fine.'

———

Eva acted surprised when Isabelle showed her around, despite having been to the house on two other occasions on her own. She'd driven down the track once before and walked along the cliff tops from town.

Wives and girlfriends lazed about sipping coffee and wine, kids and dogs ran ragged through the bush. She took her jumper off to soak up late morning rays, the deck on the ocean side was sheltered from the autumn winds.

'Hey Connie. Got what's probably a really dumb question,' Eva said.

'Expect a dumb answer kiddo, but fire away.'

She knew Connie from the bakery, a chatty woman, dry humour. 'No seriously, why name a wave?'

'So they can brag.' Connie let out a delicious cackle.

Another woman further along the deck lifted her sunglasses. 'They're men, honey. They name their God-damned cocks.' Laughter rose over the deck.

'So true,' Connie replied. 'Horry calls his Kong. Likes the movie so much, named his old fella after it. Would you believe it— "here comes Kong," he says in this deep voice, stamping around the bedroom like a sumo wrestler with it in his hand. It's so wrong. Kids busted him once.'

Isabelle giggled. 'Come on, Connie, I invited Eva cause someone's got to ask the dumb questions.'

Eva twisted her face. 'Bitch.'

'Booyah,' Isabelle squealed aloud.

'That's what I was thinking,' Connie replied, 'but hey seriously, it's an ownership type thing. First person to surf the wave, names it. Dad surfed this coast for years, there's a name for every break.'

Isabelle broke out laughing again.

'What's so funny about that?' Connie said.

'I imagined someone else coming along and naming their dicks for them.'

'Nah, nah, that's different, darl. They're always the first ones to use that.'

They all laughed so hard Eva had to wipe the tears rolling down her face. The banter was rife amidst the heart in mouth screams as they watched their men dropping into huge waves. Eva could no longer be judgmental of Isabelle's perfection. It tracked through her smile, her personality, so easy to befriend, the delightful person Ingliss spoke so fondly of and she often spoke of Lucas. Today was the first day Eva had met him.

Under the guise of a redundant bank teller opting for a sea change, she'd rented a house in town. But despite her constant surveillance over three weeks there was no sign of Caruso.

Perhaps Bardsley was right after all.

Each time she saw a dark Landcruiser the trace led to a legitimate owner.

Eva finally gathered herself. 'So, Lucas named it? The wave, I mean.'

'Nat reckons he did,' Connie said.

'Nat?' Eva's chest tightened. She'd met him at the pub, only her professionalism had held her back.

'So why would Nat call it All Mine?' Isabelle asked.

'Don't try and understand, darl. He just likes to stir the shit out of Lucas at times.'

'Seems pointless to me,' Eva said, 'so does paddling so far out, risking themselves to do the same thing over and over again on such dangerous waves.'

'If my husband's not out there, he'd be off doing stupid shit like base jumping or snowboarding,' another woman said. 'All his dickhead mates have got one leg shorter than the other from accidents, so I won't let him go, bastard's gotta work.'

'Don't blame ya,' Connie said.

'Tell me how they knew the swell was coming, Connie?' Isabelle asked.

'They just know. Horry's tried to show me on the weather maps, all I see is a bunch of warped circles.'

Isabelle turned toward Eva. 'Should've seen them through the week, worked twelve to fourteen hour days to finish cause they knew the swell was arriving on Wednesday. And sure enough, Wednesday arvo, Nat, Lucas, Horry and Patto drank beer and carried on like school kids each time a wave broke. All they've done is surf every day since.'

Eva decided to get adventurous. 'Lucas called Nat "the Bos" before. Why?'

Isabelle shrugged. 'Cause he's the best surfer, I guess?'

'Partly right,' Connie said. 'Means balls of steel.'

Eva became confused. 'What the—?'

'An acronym, darl.'

'Oh.'

'Guy's got no fear. Short too, perfect build for a surfer. Horry didn't take up surfing till he arrived in Australia at eighteen. Reckons his parents never even took him to the beach. Now he'll surf waves any size, like the others, but Nat's different. He lives and breathes that vagabond life every surfer – and Horry – dreams of.'

'But Horry's got everything in life,' Isabelle said. 'Good home, family, a business. Nat's only got a beaten up old car.'

'I know my Horry wouldn't change a thing, but Nat looks at life differently to anyone else I've ever known. No road most travelled bullshit for him. When he reaches the crossroads, he hides in the water. Said to me one day, when he's on a wave he imagines all the people who've told him what to do in life are behind him, school teachers, bosses, bank tellers, whatever, all getting pumped and smashed on the reef while he rides a clean face.'

Eva's curiosity drove her on. 'Some philosophy, where's he live?'

'Sometimes here with Lucas,' Connie said. 'At the moment he's staying at our house. It's like having an extra pair of hands around. Picks up the kids from school, does house work, all that stuff. Gets enough work just to go to Hawaii for the season, then comes back broke and brown as shit ready for the big swells that hit down here.'

'So he's a bum?'

'No way, kiddo. We all love him to bits. Packs a lot into his life, but when they get out there together on a day like today, nothing else matters to any of them.'

'What about women?'

'You're asking a lot of questions about Nat.'

Eva swallowed. 'Got thighs like tree trunks.'

'I'll let him know,' Connie said. 'If you wanna have a conversation with him, just talk surfing. You'll be fine.'

'Don't know if I'll go that far.'

Isabelle lowered her sunglasses. 'Hey, didn't I see you having a beer with him last week?'

'Just a beer, stop prying.'

'Work behind a bar in a small town. Get paid to pry.'

Eva cast her mind back to Ingliss. 'Been warned before about bartenders.'

'Tread carefully, darl,' Connie warned. 'Women come second to Nat, literally.' She cackled at her own comment. 'He's never got it together like the others. Lucas is set up so he can surf when he wants, and then there's Horry, my precious. He's still gotta work twelve hours most days. Domesticated, like a dog. Never wanting for the life it doesn't know. But he does know where he eats and craps, where he gets loved. That's why I let him off the leash when the surf's up.' She held up her glass of white in triumph as the women around burst out in raptures of laughter again.

They were interrupted by a squeal from Leigh, the only one of the women holding binoculars.

'What's the matter?' Connie said, though she seemed to know there was a problem because she stood, peering out over at the reef.

'Nat always does this,' Leigh said.

'What's going on?' Isabelle asked.

'He always pushes up too far on the inside,' Leigh said. 'It becomes a duel to see who can take off deepest and then … Christ … take a look at the third wave in line to hit the reef.'

A surfer rode down a monstrous face. 'Who's that?' Isabelle asked.

Connie craned her neck. 'Patto, and that's an even bigger wave out the back. It's feathering already.'

Eva turned. 'Feathering?'

'Means it's about to break on their heads. They'll get cleaned up.'

Concern swept over the faces on the deck, yet Eva also felt a sense of excitement in the air. She grabbed some binoculars off the barbeque side tray. They all seemed to know what was happening except her and perhaps Isabelle, who held a hand over her mouth.

Humour deserted Connie, replaced by worry as she said, 'That wave 'll break wide and sweep the whole reef. Most of 'em have seen it, they're paddling out to sea. They'll make it over the shoulder, but take a look.' She pointed, Eva's binoculars followed, two lone figures were stuck on the far right of the reef.

'They're caught on the inside. It's Nat and someone else.'

'Mike, my husband,' Leigh replied.

'They're in trouble, aren't they?' Isabelle said.

Leigh gave a look of concern. 'It's a dangerous spot to be caught in. They'll cop it on the head big time if they don't catch this wave in front, and they're both paddling for it.'

Both surfers took off down the face. They collided, the wave shut down. A body and a board got sucked up and over the top then got pummelled back under. The women gave a collective sigh, worried faces waited, silent. The ocean churned and rolled, leaving a wake of froth and foam. One board shot up, spiralling on a feverish gust before landing back in the water. Eva judged a full minute might have passed before a head broke the surface, arms scrambled for the board.

'It's Nat,' Connie said. Eva felt relief, mixed with a sense of hopelessness. Another board appeared above the surface with no one attached. The big wave peaked wide over the reef, it seemed to grow double in size drawing the shifting black waters in front, its journey across vast ocean ended on Nat. He paddled, suicidal, straight inside the pitching, almost waiting ribbed wall of water. He tried to push the nose of his board under as it lurched and hollowed, collapsing over him, over the reef, spitting spray and thunder. Body and board disappeared then reappeared as it was thrown up over the waterfall like face and dragged back under mercilessly beneath the force of what she imagined was tons of white foaming ocean.

Leigh bit her lip. 'I can't see Mike, he's still under. Got worked pretty bad, lost his board.'

'That was twenty foot, twenty five maybe,' someone said.

Connie rubbed her shoulder. 'He'll be fine.' Nat surfaced and scrambled onto his board again, then began paddling across the reef.

'Mike hasn't come up yet,' Leigh said.

Seconds later Connie pointed to the right. 'I got him. Over there.'

'Look at Nat,' someone else yelled. Eva focussed the binoculars, found a hand and a head above the water. Nat was paddling over from a long distance away when the next wave, smaller than the last hit the reef. Both men dived under, then re-appeared. A lull came. Nat finally reached Mike, hauling him onto the surfboard. It took several minutes before another set of pulsating lines hit the reef, the first wave swallowed them both. Then cheers rose from the deck as they were spat out and launched forward, racing in front of the white water over the reef until it petered out into deeper water.

Leigh wiped her eyes.

Connie placed an arm around her. 'Nat wouldn't let anything happen to him.'

'I know. After seeing so many wipe outs, I still get scared. He was under a while.'

'They're all coming in,' Connie said, the women raced down to the beach. It took several minutes before Nat and Mike negotiated the shore break where waves were still well above head high.

Mike seemed okay despite his face being drained of colour. Nat dragged himself out of the water and slumped onto the sand. Connie checked him over, brushing thick clumps of wiry hair from his face. Nat remained quiet. The type to keep it all inside, Eva thought as a large group of bare chested kids ran down the beach, calling Lucas's name. They resembled street urchins from a Dickens novel. Heaving ribcages threatened to punch through skin.

'Lucas ... Lucas ... we saw someone! We saw a man—'

'Wo, wo ... guys. One at a time.' He pointed at Freddy, Connie's eldest. 'Freddy, what's going on?'

'We saw a man over the creek heading up the side of the cliff,' Freddie said.

Horry moved in, slipped an arm around his boy. 'How long ago?'

'Bout ten minutes. Jamie and Zach saw him, Dad.'

'What about you Freddie, did you see him?' Lucas asked.

'Only when he was a fair way up.'

'How close to the creek were you guys?'

'None of us crossed it, I made sure.'

'Good boy. You guys know not to cross the creek,' Horry said.

'Yeah, yeah, we know,' came the replies.

Lucas bent down to the eye level of the younger boy. 'Okay then Zach, what'd he look like?'

Zach drew in a lungful, stretched his arm high, 'TALL. REAL TALL. Like Patto. He crossed the creek.'

Eva listened in.

'Did he see you?' Lucas asked.

'Yeah. He looked right back at us.'

'Did he carry a bag?'

'Yehhh. A back pack.'

'Just a bushwalker, boys. Go get some lunch, stay away from the creek for the rest of the day.'

The kids ran up to the house. 'How do you know it's a bushwalker?' Eva asked.

'Get 'em all the time round here. The creek forms my eastern boundary, there's signs up, most people don't care. Normally I don't mind because Clyde's around, but there's kids.'

Looking up toward the cliff, he shielded the midday sun with his hand.

'Can you see anyone?' Horry asked.

'Nah. But someone's still up there.'

'How can you tell?' Eva said.

Lucas moved closer. 'Look straight up over the edge of the face.'

She focussed, seeing only blue sky. 'What am I looking at?'

'See that bird up there. Circling?'

She picked up a black spec. 'Oh … yes.'

'It's a falcon.'

'Yeah. Isabelle mentioned falcons live around here.'

'See how high she is? Someone's up there for sure. Noticed her over the same spot when we paddled out a couple of hours ago. Whoever's up there could've been up there earlier, and if the boys are right, then he's come down while we were in the water and gone back up.'

Caruso plunged into her thoughts. She tried to hide her alarm. 'Why would someone do that?'

Lucas didn't appear overly concerned. 'No idea. Might've parked up near the road. Could've been watching the surf, who knows? He'll probably head off down the other side.' Lucas and Horry carried their boards up the beach leaving Eva to focus on the cliff.

————

Eternity happens right here.

The ocean forges, it carves, it etches, it pounds, still the cliff withstands the onslaught forever, waves retreat then surge washing rock to granules, pumping ocean spray high up the

jagged face, it falls, spreading like tossed linen into the
swirling back-wash, all through the days of time.
Eternity happens right here.
'Have some food.'
A voice.
'Eva?'
Isabelle held out a plate.
'Oh ... hey, must've been miles away. Thanks'
'You okay?' Isabelle asked.
'Yeah, should've told me to bring some food.'
'Don't be silly.'
Everyone on the deck seemed busy, eating or chatting. Nat
was in charge of the barbeque. Eva watched on, unable to
wrest her mind from the tall cliff. Or Caruso.

Despite her love for the job she could see herself living
along this unforgiving coastline. Air was often thick with a
silent chill, suspended mist, not smog or road rage, pounding
horns, no sobering arseholes, cowards pleading for a cheap ten
to fifteen, no idea how wives, partners, kids, parents,
mistresses were stabbed, beaten to pulp, disappeared, tossed
off balconies, off bridges, found their way into creeks, one
stuffed in a barrel, weighted, never to surface, until it surfaced.
There were fewer arseholes, anyway, they were everywhere,
murderers. Dams were preferred in the country, not creeks or
drains. Eighty five percent were labelled in-house, they knew
their killer, most domestic, figures don't lie, eighty-eight
percent clearance rate, bar the odd druggie, the odd dealer, not
the odd neighbourly murder over a parking space in a West
Meadows street, she cleared that one off her desk two days
before Rickshaw and his crew were dispatched so
methodically by the most wanted man in the country. Lessons
of almost a year in Homicide, still, she felt green.

Raids on the Sons of Cain's clubhouse and other properties
found no leads to Caruso, only guns, speed, e's, a press, mull,
hot bikes, hot parts, a meth lab, most were stashed on an

abandoned farm in the name of Norman Rickshaw's wife. Ingliss was right, there was no apparent motive for the murders, Ingliss seemed right about everything. She ate in effort, salad went down easily, meat lumped in her throat. Clyde got lucky.

Lucas's bushwalker explanation appeared sensible.

Part of her brief was to keep an eye on Isabelle. Bardsley was yet to be fully swayed she was not in touch with Caruso, despite Eva's strongly worded reports to the contrary. Bardsley had also agreed to show Isabelle the photo if there was no sighting within two weeks. That was one week ago.

Her orders were not to engage, only report. S.O.G. backup was a helicopter ride away. Crime Units stationed in Warrnambool, Colac, Geelong, were all nearby. *Do not engage*. Still, she found a quiet moment and stole off to her car, slipped her gun in a jacket and hurried over the creek.

Avoiding the track, she made her way through the sand up the spine of the cliff. Gnarly twisted saltbushes hid her from both the deck and eyes of anyone who might be on the cliff top. The ground soon became hard sandstone. She paused, surveying the area around the crown. From below it appeared like a god had dumped a huge rock on top. Up close it was just a part of the cliff, honed and weathered by time.

Instincts warned she was not alone.

Eyes darted about.

Drawing her gun she stepped forward toward the crown.

Footprints not yet wind-blown were visible in the dirt, the trek pattern of hiking boots leading nowhere specific. The crown was about two metres high, with enough clearance to easily walk around the edge. Wind gusted in short, fast whistles, it almost spoke, such was the strength up here. Eva studied the prints. A track twisted down eastward toward a lonely stretch of beach ringed by an inland maroon-coloured precipice covered in a fringe of matted heath. Sun gleamed off a distant guardrail beneath the road cutting, which disappeared around a remote point further east high above the ocean.

Was someone behind the crown?

With the gun poised, she stepped half way around, crouching. Breeze whipped hair in her face, lashed her eyes, she brushed it away.

No one.

One hand gripped the rock, the other slipped her gun inside the jacket, she crept toward the edge.

Down below, waves thrashed the black rock. The sound, a gentle deep, energy filled thaaahhhhwwooomp, dominating this battlefield of elements. Clawed fingers dug into the crown. She stepped out to an arm's length, daring herself to look down. A hiss of spray, slow and effortless, powered to its zenith, leapt back and tumbled. Fear raised a notch. The drop tapered slightly, then squared off. She envisioned her own body broken backwards on the rocks below, ready to be claimed and tossed like air trapped in the mass of foam shifting about. Her grip tightened.

A noise. A flap?

Menacing black eyes ringed by yellow, locked on. She gasped.

The bird hovered low and close adjacent to the cliff top out over the sea, long, tapered wings, almost motionless.

Peregrines were rumoured to nest on the ledges of skyscrapers in Melbourne. Was there a nest up here instead of over in the Bluff, as Isabelle had told her? Would it attack?'

With an effortless press of wings the bird banked, arrowing straight for her. She flung her arms back into the crown, but the bird manoeuvred, disappearing down the cliff side so close it cut the air. Everything moved. Ocean. Wind. The clouds. All but the ground she stood upon and then it too appeared to sway. Below, black shiny rocks waited. Thaaahhhhwwooomp. Hiss. Her legs, concrete.

The bird circled once more, swooping again down the other side before retreating with grace out over the ocean.

Carefully she moved back to the safety of flat ground. She checked the other side of the cliff, peering down to the water. Her foot slipped, kicking stones and dirt over the edge, they bounced and disappeared. She reached for the crown, her hand latched on.

She caught a breath.

Just a hiker.

———

Fingers were white to the knuckles, arms taught as he clung to the rock face above the ledge. He pressed his body against the wall. Small stones toppled over, some missed, some fell through his hair. He froze.

A cop?

He'd seen her climbing up through the scrub and barely had time to scramble down onto the ledge. Heights never worried him. The bird did. It swooped so close he felt the pressure, the swooshing of wings, half expecting the thing to land on his back.

But it missed.

Twice.

He'd been unable to get his gun out to wave it off and feared another attack.

She couldn't be a cop. They had no idea he was even in the country.

The kids had seen him. Perhaps she was just a foolish mother with balls for brains.

Nothing made sense.

A cop? The thought refused to escape.

Had she turned a quarter way he would have been seen on the ledge. Luckily the bird had transfixed her, saving him, in some strange way.

He crept along the ledge, fingers first, feet last, even though it was barely wide enough to stand on. He found a good foothold and hoisted himself up, just enough to see the ground above. Whoever she was, had left.

A cop?

Carlo brushed dirt from his hair and thought of his mother. The right decision was to hide. He looked out over the ocean. No sign of that evil bird.

———

'Didn't know you're so popular,' Isabelle said.

Lucas stretched his legs on the deck lounge beside her, the day had faded around them. 'Never see most of these guys until the surf's going off like this, being the weekend they can bring their families out as well. It's been a cool day. Reckon they came to suss you out too.'

'Me?'

He gave her a playful squeeze. 'Why not? Tales of your beauty stretch to Adelaide.'

She slapped his thigh. 'Don't be an arsehole.'

'And I thought that's what a girl like you would like to hear.'

'It is, kind of.' Her eyes lit up. 'Hey, teach me to surf one day.'

'Really! You?'

'What's wrong with that?'

'Just kidding. It'll be fun. Something we can do together.'

'That's what I thought.' She leant forward and kissed him.

He groaned as she pressed on his thigh. 'Legs are killing me.' They'd surfed for the third time on the late afternoon low tide. Out on the reef, All Mine threw more unridden barrels beneath a sky burnt by rich pink and orange belts until they paled into the backdrop of smoky layers of fading blues. Only a core group remained on the deck along with Big Steve and Thumbtack, who'd arrived with a box of beer each.

'You remember waking up early this morning?'

Her eyes lowered. 'Sort of. Was I screaming?'

'No. Just yelling out. Thought I'd wake you before the screaming started.'

'I'm sorry, Luke—'

'It's okay. I'm here for you.'

She nodded. 'I remember now, the dreams are becoming weirder, like they're building up.'

'Building up? You sure you're all right?'

'Yeah, I'm fine.'

'Tell me about it.'

'It's the same dream. It's like … getting bigger and bigger in my head. I see him, but it's different … his eyes look up at me. There's a clown with tears, but then I see the clown with no make-up … and him … he's always in the forefront. There's a boat. Blackness beyond. Total darkness. And white. Glistening white. That's all I can remember. Whiteness moving all about like rolling clouds.'

He brushed the hair from her face. 'It's best we talk about it.'

'I know.'

'It's just a dream. We both have things to get over.' He felt guilty about going surfing so early and leaving her to wake on her own. Another part of himself he didn't like. 'Were you okay when you woke this morning?'

'Yeah but—'

'But what?'

'I'm uncomfortable right now. Can I say something you may not like?'

'Whatever it is, I can handle it,' he said.

'Little Thumbtack creeps me out. He reminds me of a face in my dream. It's silly, I know. Who has a tattoo under his eye? When I'm working in the bar he stares at me. I pretend not to look back, but I can't help it. He's doing it now.'

Lucas glanced down the deck, Thumbtack's eyes diverted away. 'He's harmless. Once you get to know him he's the kind of guy who'll do anything for you. Want me to just mention something?'

'No, no. I know he's your friend and ... I'll try ... really.'

He rubbed her back, she rested her head on his chest. They listened to the waves, and Horry. He grew louder. Nat and Eva thought they'd found a quiet end of the deck, until Horry moved in and started telling Eva how he'd seen a shark out on the reef some years ago.

'Serious!' Horry told her. 'White Pointer, twelve, maybe fourteen footer and you know what? Knew the thing was there before I even saw it.'

'That's ridiculous, how could you?' Eva said.

'Don't ask,' Connie warned. 'He tells this stupid shark story every time he gets pissed.'

Horry ignored his wife and tapped his head, facing Eva. 'Instinct my dear, that's how I knew.'

'Eva's the only one who hasn't heard this story,' Lucas said.

'I haven't yet.' Isabelle's smile had returned.

Lucas appreciated the distraction.

'You're next.'

'Do you believe him?'

'Hey, I love the guy. If he says he saw it, then he saw it, no matter what anyone thinks.'

'It's true,' Horry said to Eva. 'I knew the shark was there first, so I just paddled over to the reef where it's shallower.'

'Yeah right, so you're what ... telepathic or something?' Eva asked, dripping sarcasm.

'Don't take the piss. Told you. It's instinct. In South Africa we got grass taller than you and sometimes you can't use your eyes to know what's nearby. You ... you Aussies have kangaroos and snakes that run and hide with the bunnies.

When there's big cats, you develop a hunter's instinct. Only Africans have it, don't we Clyde. We know, eh boy.' At the sound of his name Clyde walked over and stood up on his hind legs. Horry supported him with a forearm, stroking his head. 'We know, ja boy.'

'What a croc of shit, Affffreeeekaaaans,' Steve said. 'Old Noah would still be using your scrawny bones for a tooth pick out there, with half a chance.'

'Ja. My father bought me a 303 for my fourteenth birthday, what'd your daddy buy you … a fishing rod … wasn't an ape suit. You were born in one of those you—'

'Fuck'n little Boer,' Steve yelled and those in the way moved aside as he lunged for Horry, who ditched Clyde and leapt over the balcony. He tumbled on the sand, spilling his beer. Big Steve couldn't follow. Horry taunted him from below.

Everyone laughed, none harder than Isabelle. 'Today's been so much fun.' Her eyes lit up. 'Hey, you noticed Nat and Eva?'

'I think it's cool,' Lucas replied. 'Know Nat pretty well, though.'

'Give 'em a chance. You have wonderful friends.'

'I've spent my life with these people. You're the person I want to spend the rest of my life with.'

Her gaze softened. 'Babe … one day at a time, remember.'

'Yeah, I understand. Sometimes I just want to tell you every chance I get.'

'I'm sorry, Luke. I'm … I'm not good at this. Everything in my life used to be wrong and since I came here, everything is so right. It's a feeling I'm struggling to deal with. I'm working hard because I love you. Someone once told me real love is hard work.'

'Who told you that?'

'John Ingliss.'

'Sounds like a smart guy.'

'I really want him to meet you one day.'

A drunken voice interrupted, 'We're off to the trough.' Horry had snuck up on them. A fresh beer in one hand, a cold sausage in the other, sauce dripped on the deck. 'If you two wanna stop swappin' spit, come join us.'

She twisted her nose. 'The trough?'

'The pub.' Laughter burst through Horry's slack, moist lips. 'During all my years of bar work, never heard it called that. In an Asperger's moment I see a line of surfers, arse up, drinking beer from a dirty big trough. Better go, Luke. Don't wanna miss out on that. I'll stay and tidy up.'

'Oh come on,' Lucas said, grinning. 'We'll have something to eat at Reno's.'

'How can you guys still eat?'

'Patto's organised some musos to play in the bar,' Horry said, pointing to Lucas. 'He'll help ya tidy up later ... or in the morning. Who gives a shit?' Then he held up his beer like a trophy and swigged.

'You guys go. Connie will help me, we'll come down later?'

'Sure,' Lucas said and soon after, he loaded the drunken mob into the old four-wheel drive.

18

Wafer thin clouds drifted beneath the black canvas ablaze with stars. Eyes quickly became accustomed to the darkness, despite the absence of the constant glow of man's presence in this valley. There was no need for the torchlight once he crossed the creek.

The dog habitually slept on the front, north deck.

He walked the deck on the ocean side stepping carefully on the rows of nails, aware the smallest creak would sound his presence. Offshore winds and pounding seas protected him from being heard, but the dog knew his scent.

A ridgeback, possibly a greyhound cross, probably some mastiff in there too. The powerful physique reminded him of pig hunting dogs of great speed and agility from almost a lifetime ago. Jaws so powerful they could hold a wild adult boar, or strip a man's calf from the bone. This animal's most dangerous trait was the freedom to roam, allowing it to process and make forthright decisions to protect its home. He had not attempted to bribe it, choosing instead to elude its senses.

A light shone over the wall unit, enough for him to view the dog sleeping peacefully through the floor-to-ceiling windows.

He'd deliberately kept away from the main part of town since his return. Izy rarely spent time at her home anymore. Each night he'd been forced to leave here, knowing she was in the arms of another man, knowing his own time would come. Lately he found his mind torn. Could it still be possible to speak with her, offer her a chance to come with him? Maddigan did not have real wealth. The more he resolved, the more he realised there was still a chance to tell her of this madness.

She would listen.

Her car was parked beside the old Porsche, the only two cars left from the day. Maddigan was out, a rare event. Barbeque odours lurked, bringing on hunger. He paused for a wave to blanket the air before gently placing the key in the lock.

Perhaps she was in bed.

The heavy glass door rolled effortlessly on well-oiled tracks. He slipped through, easing the door back, leaving only a small gap.

Inside, the familiar scents of Izy flourished his nostrils. Aromatic candles and fresh wildflowers – vased on the wooden table – laced the room. She'd added her touch since he was last here. Empty bottles were stacked neatly for recycle, the environment, still all the rage with her.

He heard a noise and checked the dog through the window. It remained still.

He heard it again. Breathing. Light reflected off a dark veil of hair draped over the headrest of the white modular. His stomach knotted, he moved closer, watching the rise and fall of her breasts through an orange, floral patterned dress ending over her sun glazed thighs. He slipped off his gloves.

Was the journey over?

In the penthouse he would sit on the edge of the bed and marvel at her sleeping. He closed his eyes, smelt her hair, yet warned himself that once he touched her there was no turning back. He eased the pistol out.

A corner of her lips lifted into a sleepy smile. A tingle livened the skin on the back of his neck. Now he truly desired to touch her – Izy – more beautiful with age, mature. He'd had the girl, now he must have the woman. Her presence had drawn him as a moth was drawn to light, or a man's life to the void of another world, denied the beauty that obsessed his mind.

The fate of lesser men.

End this now.

She was ruined. Soiled. Kill her. Kill the desire. Leave this country.

Find a new lover.

He longed for the peace of mind he'd known in Europe and the States. He thought of his mother, his father.

Izy was different too.

Resolve.

Papà would resolve.

He shut his eyes again. Am I a coward? He questioned.

Don't touch her.

Maddigan must die tonight.

She stirred, he realised the barrel of the gun *had* touched her hair.

'Stop,' she whispered, rolling halfway onto her side.

Another whisper. 'No'. Movement, inside her eyelids.

Nostrils fluttered. 'No.'

Her hand moved down, fingers caressing her inner thigh. 'Stop.'

———

Isabelle sat bolt upright.

Her dress, cold, wet against the modular.

Barking. Furious barking.

Clyde slapped his paw at the pane, foggy from hot, angry breath. Lips retracted, teeth snapping.

A presence? She turned, not knowing what to expect.

'Lucas?' she called. 'Lucas?'

No answer.

No one about.

Her mind questioned. Was I screaming again?

The barking. What was he barking at? Had her screaming woken him?

The dream. Sydney Harbour, mystic lights over black waters. The view was from the penthouse.

The clown.

Him.

He came home.

The boat.

At the forefront of her mind she tried to grasp the scene of white, it was moving forward, rolling, shadowed by immense darkness, stretching forever.

She smelt the air, not knowing why. A fragrance arrested her senses, distant yet familiar.

Was someone outside?

Or worse still, inside?

Fear struck like a thunderclap.

Clyde galloped around the deck, barking wildly.

She noticed the door open, only a touch, but still open.

Open?

She recalled locking it.

Get out of the house, her mind ordered.

She fled onto the deck. Terrified.

Behind her, a door slammed.

She gasped, spun, bleating a short squeal. The front door was closed. Solid.

The wind?

She struggled to remember locking the front door, though she couldn't imagine falling asleep out here without doing so.

Was someone inside?

The black ocean boomed and crashed in the night behind her

Clyde raced past. She clutched at his collar. He pulled and pulled, trying to get inside, almost dragging her along the deck. She held tight. He struggled harder, rearing on his back legs then he turned and snapped, eyes fierce and elsewhere.

She reefed her head back and he let out a desperate, sorrowful whine when he recognised her. Wild eyes danced side to side. He made one last effort, she released her hold and he bolted through the door.

She watched, questioning if it was her that had left the door open.

No, she assured herself again.

Clyde would have nuzzled through a small gap earlier if it had been open.

Someone was inside the house.

The thought grew potent.

Dimi appeared from the bedroom, seemingly barking at nothing. Clyde pounced over the couch in one leap, hackles up, ears pricked, lips curled sniffing the cushions, the air.

He followed his nose to the front door, body taut, strutting like a prize-fighter along the window, staring out, whining, growling. Warning anyone out there.

She stood half in the door, half out, not knowing which was safer. Her right cheek stung. She touched it then pulled her hand away, studied the trickle of warm blood on the print of her middle finger and realised she'd scratched herself.

Switching the floodlights on, she saw the deck was clear.

She stepped inside, grabbed a knife off the magnetic rack, with her back pressed into the stove she clutched the knife, watching the door, watching the kitchen end wall beside the fridge.

No one came.

Clyde sniffed the passage, the bedrooms, the stairwell. Dimi followed close behind. Clyde snapped at him, then prowled around the glass door, rumbling still came from deep within, his chest vibrating in anger. Isabelle shut and locked the glass door, safe in the knowledge no one was upstairs.

She pulled the lead off the wall and clipped his collar, patting him with long, pacifying strokes.

'What did you see boy?'

Satisfied, he licked her face. Normally it would repulse her enough to push him away. She knew his excited bark when he chased possums and rabbits.

Tonight, something had frightened him.

Lucas had told her the dog wouldn't jump on the bed when she was at the house. She would change that now.

She hugged him, recalling Lucas's strange words of months ago. *"He's come here for a reason."*

'Good boy, Clyde.'

Was it just her screaming? But her throat wasn't dry or sore, like it usually was afterwards.

She probed the hazy depths of a troubled sub consciousness, recalling only fragments.

A scent?

Him?

Was it possible to somehow dream a scent?

'Am I crazy?'

She tried to recollect, assuring herself she'd shut both doors before lying on the couch. The glass door had definitely been locked. The front door … maybe.

Dimi wandered about the kitchen looking for food. With the knife in one hand and Clyde still on the lead, she checked every room, every closet, bolting every door, closing every blind. Back in the kitchen, she picked up the phone and dialled Lucas's mobile.

Ringing came from the study.

———

Lucas heard his named called over the music. The barman held the phone up.

Isabelle? He glanced at the clock on the wall.

Nine o'clock.

The night reminded him of many nights through younger years, long days when All Mine cranked and they'd hit the pub at night. Patto was in a band back then. Sue had adored his music. He held the phone tight to his ear and stuck a finger in the other.

'Isabelle.'

'Lucas!'

'Hey, thought you were coming down. Patto's roped in a few mates, it's been a good night.'

'Sounds like fun …' Her voice was distant, reserved. Sharp?

'You okay?'

'Just another dream, I'm fine, babe. Clyde started barking. Must have scared him … screaming probably.'

'Where's Connie?'

'She left not long after you, I fell asleep.' She sounded despondent. Guilt flushed through him even though he hadn't left her alone.

'I'm coming home, now.'

'Thanks Luke, listen, I'm sorry.'

She didn't offer to pick him up, he wanted to ask why, then also thought it would be the first thing on her mind. He'd only been drinking mid-strength beer, but he didn't want to get in the car. It was only a dream.

'Be there as soon as I can.'

———

St Claire had eased down from the weekend, no traffic in sight. The Patrol was parked beneath a streetlight. Lucas walked past and hurried over to the beach. His mind drifted. These dreams were so regular. What if this was so deep her mind could not unravel? Many times he vowed not to let it destroy everything they had started together.

Once on the sand, he looked back at the Patrol, wondering if there was a torch under the front seat. He'd have to use the track along the top of the Bluff. Fifteen minutes, if he ran part of the way, although the last section led through heavy scrub.

The ocean roared, spray tingled on the rocks and in a moment of clarity he stood by the crystal waters of Modey's Creek and his urge to be with her heightened. It alarmed him. He headed back toward the car.

Beneath the backdrop of pier lights his straining eyes caught movement further down the beach. The silhouette of a broad-shouldered man walking in the other direction along the waterline, toward the surf club building, elbows stuck out as though hands were tucked in the rib pockets of a hoodie.

Lucas wondered how he didn't pass the man. And if they hadn't passed each other, then whoever it was must have walked only so far up the beach and turned around, almost at the same instance Lucas had.

Across the road lights were on in Reno's. Heads mingled through the windows of the pub. He reached the Patrol and followed the ocean road home as it trailed off, twisting through silent bends.

Headlights appeared from nowhere, almost as if the car behind had left town, *and then* put its lights on. Lucas kept one eye on the mirror, expecting blue lights. Sergeant Kowalski, the local officer also drove a four-wheel drive. Perhaps he could explain if he blew over the limit. The gap closed to nothing.

Cops don't road rage.

The driver seemed eager to pass, but there was no room on the narrow lanes. The road slithered up the steep slope of Scenic Hill, away from the ocean. Barely a metre from the passenger door, the rock cutting stretched upward. Trees protected by a steel guardrail lined the opposite side of the road.

Nowhere to pull over.

The Patrol chugged across the side of Scenic Hill. Cars passed by in the opposite lane from around a blind bend. Behind him, high beams flashed and stayed on, almost blinding him down through a series of "s" bends. No more cars approached, Lucas slowed and pulled over to the left, the impatient driver had a slight chance to go through.

The car rammed him.

'What the—?' He gripped the wheel and accelerated.

Lucas and many of the townspeople had all experienced road rage along this infamous stretch, but not rammed. He longed for his Porsche.

Left with only one choice, he pulled into the centre of the road, knowing he'd have to enter his track from the wrong lane – if the road was clear.

Lights followed. The rear window exploded.

'What the hell is that?'

A hole appeared in the windscreen, then another.

Gunfire? This was crazy. Someone was *actually* shooting.

Something punctured the windscreen again, this time near his head. He swerved.

Caruso?

The name cannoned into his mind as he was shunted hard again.

The man was dead.

Rumoured to be dead.

He swerved left to right and slid down the seat knowing the spare wheel fixed to the rear door on the driver's side would offer protection. High beams filled his mirrors, penetrating his mind.

If this guy can shoot cops— 'Isabelle!'

The phone call … she's alive. He'd heard her voice.

His rear bumper was rammed again. If he swung into his driveway at this speed, he'd surely roll. Whistling air rushed by, so too did his property entrance.

The man on the beach?

He accelerated out of the high bend heading further east, away from home, away from Isabelle. He had to stay in front and keep his head down, powering through bend after bend.

The road hugged high over the dark ocean again. Another gunshot, the windscreen shattered.

The Old Loggers Road.

The entrance was up ahead, two bends away. His only hope was the gravel road leading deep into the forest. He could lose the guy on one of the four-wheel drive tracks. Eventually he'd make it out to the Blue Stone School Road and back into town.

Headlights came at him. He swung the wheel left, dodging another approaching car rounding a bend. A horn blared then trailed off.

Behind, the headlights followed, it had to be Caruso.

There was simply no-one else.

Was Caruso at the house when she called?

Was this a trap?

There was not enough time to get from the house to the beach.

Has he killed her?

She's alive, he recalled her voice, scared. Desperate thoughts pushed him on.

He took the next bend wide, dropping back to second and labouring up the hill. The Old Loggers Road – he had to make it. This could go on for miles across the front of the Otways until he was either shot or had crashed. He kept swerving, aware that his two and a half ton vehicle could easily penetrate the guardrail down to the ocean below. The Patrol had been his father's car. He'd contemplated upgrading; the sentimental value was too great.

Gunshots pinged beneath the car.

He was trying to shoot the tyres. Lucas kept on swerving.

The old dirt road met the ocean road at an obtuse angle, allowing log trucks to merge easily if there was no traffic. He'd have to be facing the wrong way to make the entrance without fully stopping. A daunting task, Caruso had to be taken by surprise.

With one hand gripping the handbrake he sped up and rounded the top of the last bend, veering across the white lines hoping no cars were coming. Thoughts turned to his own family, killed by a drunk driver. Thankfully no headlights came from head on. Overhead the cutting wall became a smaller embankment as he exited the bend. The car behind nudged him again, but Lucas was ready, the road opened up, he saw the dark gap in the embankment, wrenched the wheel hard left, ripping the handbrake up. The Patrol swung violently. Tyres screeched.

Panic struck, he braced, realising he'd mistimed the turn.

The car behind clipped his back corner spinning him a hundred and eighty degrees into the embankment. Impact shuddered every nut, bolt and bone. Remaining windows shattered. The Patrol teetered for an eternity on two wheels, he feared the vehicle would stay against the wall where he'd be helpless, waiting to be finished off. Then it toppled back onto four wheels, bouncing and settling. The bank had stopped him from rolling. Relieved, he threw the stick into first, dropped the clutch and the gutsy Patrol responded, lurching up the dirt road.

———

Carlo braked hard. The Landcruiser slid to a stop against the guardrail. Taillights disappeared up into the bush behind him. He pulled a three-point turn and shifted into four-wheel drive. The Toyota's wheel hubs locked automatically, Maddigan would have to stop and get out to lock his manually. Carlo had superior traction and power, and he'd pulled the fuse on his airbags before he left town.

He thought of giving Maddigan a little credit for the manoeuvre before killing him.

He roared up the graded road churning stones into the under-carriage. On the beach he'd rehearsed a little chat while planning to drown Maddigan in the surf, but the chase along one of the greatest scenic drives in the world allowed him to enjoy picturing the man's fear. A memory from his youth sprung to mind. Carlo and a schoolmate, Don Merinio, raced paddock bombs around the farm. Don was a good driver. Carlo couldn't beat him until the day he shot his tyres out. Don rolled and broke his arm, didn't come around after that.

Carlo grinned. Wonder what Don's up to now?

Beams from his own headlights bounced off Maddigan's dust, yet to settle. Carlo followed deep into the forest, knowing he was close. Corners were also tight, more perilous on the gravel, and there were no guardrails.

Maddigan's death would be a lonely experience.

———

Lucas knew the Otway Ranges well having spent his childhood years camping out with Nat. Old growth logging was outlawed years ago. Dense vegetation now thrived on Southern Ocean storms, reclaiming most of the tracks. Only gated fire trails remained, opened seasonally for four-wheel drives and barely wide enough for a single vehicle.

Cold forest air rushed through vacant windows. Manna gums lined the road, each one a solid pillar of death. Traction was good, but as he got deeper into the forest the shale binding the surface would become damper. The West Fyans Track, the first of the fire trails lay up ahead.

He powered through steep valleys and sharp bends, thundering over corrugations, hoping against hope the gate to the track was open. Strappings of slippery bark and foliage filled the roadside culverts. If he dug a wheel in he'd lose control, but if Caruso was following, he wouldn't dare drive like he had on the ocean road.

Lucas slowed at the signpost to the trail, lights shone on the padlocked gate, the bush, too thick to drive around. If he busted it open with the bullbar, Caruso would notice.

He glanced into the rear vision. No headlights.

Had Caruso crashed back on the road?

Isabelle was alive. Lucas had to reach her. His only chance was to push on to the Bluestone School Road, straight to the Police Station.

Would Sergeant Kowalski believe someone had actually shot at him?

Was Caruso dead?

Again.

More inquests. Except this time there might be a trial for an architect suspected of being drunk, scenarios, yet to happen.

Insanity.

Some fifteen minutes ago he'd been at the pub.

He prided himself as a rational person, but this man behind had to be Caruso. Why was he back?

Lucas couldn't rationalise. Isabelle had feared this killer might come back one day. She'd even told him of an incident near the pier where she'd mistaken somebody else for Caruso. Lucas had held her so tight while she cried, revisiting the trauma. But to him, the man only existed in her past. Her dreams.

Now, as he pushed on through the dark forest, he knew he had been so wrong. Horribly wrong.

The man on the beach.

The man on the cliff.

Headlights lit up the forest behind.

———

Carlo followed down through a steep ravine past an overgrown run off ramp. He slowed to cross an old bridge. Rickety planks that once held logging trucks, tottered and shuddered beneath, threatening to send him down onto the creek bed below. Maddigan took off up the other side. Carlo tailed close. They climbed and reached the crest where the road plateaued across a hill. Carlo sped up, nudging Maddigan through another bend, then backed off and accelerated again. The bull-bar slammed into the Patrol. Maddigan hugged the high side.

Carlo shot out the driver-side rear tyre. The Patrol slewed violently, wheels found the culvert. Maddigan overcorrected, Carlo clipped the backend, the Patrol squared up, lunging through the air off the shoulder into a gum tree. The crunch shattered the night.

Carlo skidded to a halt, letting the dust clear before reversing up. From the roadside he expected to find the car at the base of a tree with Maddigan dead inside. The Patrol was nowhere in sight, then came faint, settling noises from deep in the valley.

Maddigan could not have survived, still he had to go down and make sure, in case there was a need to tweak the man's neck. He retrieved his torch and hiking boots, lacing them up on the tailgate, then followed the carnage down the slope. Some twenty steps down, he paused at a distant sound. A crack.

He propped in silence, the report died off in the bush a long way off.

A gunshot? Impossible.

But Carlo knew it was definitely a gunshot.

Had Maddigan called the cops? But why would they be shooting?

Another shot rang out, echoing through the forest.

There was only one possible scenario. Hunters.

They could not be allowed to see his car.

He moved quickly back up the valley. At the car he gathered his breath, listening. The unmistakable faint rumble of another vehicle could be heard. He travelled a short way until he found a section of bank where he could get off the road and hide in the bush. Long minutes passed before beacons of light flicked through the trees. Spotlights. A HiLux ute passed slowly by. Men stood in the back – roo shooters – loud excited voices, unaware a pistol was aimed at them.

Carlo let them slip by. Once they were gone he left the Landcruiser in the bush in case they returned and walked back to where Maddigan had left the road.

———

Darkness. A seal. A blanket of fine wool. Icy winds of death are circling.

Lucas slipped further.

No one can hurt me in here.

Darkness, a fortified crib, isolating from fear, all harm beyond.

MOVE!

The voice startled him. Lips motioned.

MOVE!

His mind drowned in her familiarity.

MOVE!

The voice, so desperate, so passionate.

Where am I?

Beneath the blanket. Safe. Die here.

MOVE my darling.

Is she real?

He saw blue – sky blue. *The dress?*

High-pitched sounds of crushing metal filled his mind, drifting, screeching, scarring the air, echoing down roads between buildings, riding the wind like a cool change on a hot Melbourne afternoon.

The crash?

LUCAS, MOVE!

She is with me ... in a different time ... time, the thief that stole her.

A different kind of time. He would easily die for long moments with her in a place, non-existent.

He listened, desperate for her subtle tones so much a part of his daily life he'd become unaccustomed to her quaint peculiarities others spoke of so fondly.

MOVE, LUCAS!

Her voice fierce, then velvety soft, present yet harsh. He found her eyes and longed to stay in here with her.

MOVE NOW!

The blue dress she died in, torn, shredded, bloodied.

Sensuous lips sent ripples out onto a pond, somewhere, through the deepest caverns of his mind like the cold awakening waters of winter's first swell.

I can stay here forever safe, surrounded by the warmth of her rich, hoarse tones, sexy beyond the boundaries of innocence, full of her understanding. The silky lips of a thinker.

MOVE, MY DARLING.

A metallic taste, rustic, warm. Blood? His breath, rapid, light and short. He had punched through the wall like he was pushing his board up through the back of a wave on the reef. Eyelids refused to open, overwhelming sadness returned. He longed to go back to the hollow emptiness where death and Sue were closest.

'ISABELLE!'

Breathing was now a fast, pulse like rhythm.

Movement. On his leg. Fingertips? He pushed. A bolt of pain shot up through his leg, he let out an agonising howl.

Still, he had to move.

He lifted his hand, prised open his eyes. Blood was fresh and warm. Throbbing pounded inside his skull. He moved his neck. *Click, click.* He cried out in pain, yet content for a voice. He moved his neck again, purposely. Slowly left, slowly right.

One more click. This time it seemed to move with him, less painfully too. Vision cleared, enough to realise he was in the cabin of the Patrol. He fumbled for his seatbelt, managed to unclip it, then raised his arm, crying out again. Every action brought a reaction, currents of startling pain spread out. He stuck his hand through the window, felt a tree, perhaps a giant messmate. Its girth covered the whole door. The passenger door was gone, sheared off.

A way out.

Every muscle ached, still he slid past the gearstick, tumbling headfirst out the passenger side. He tried to get upright, legs buckled, a steadying hand shot out and caught the foot rail. He willed himself on, eventually stood, eyes focussed on the ground, which spun, rising fast. Something hit him. Pain seared deep inside his cheek. Fresh blood traced down into the corner of his lips, teeth crunched on sandy loam. He rolled forward, dizziness swamped him, but a hand found the foot rail once more.

He knew he had no balance, but still mustered enough strength to haul himself up, then took in several long breaths. Many times he had been beaten down by life; thoughts turned to his wife, his parents, his grandfather, a man who would forge his way out of this.

Isabelle. 'I will get out of the forest alive,' he murmured, twice.

The vehicle would be easier for rescuers to locate, but Caruso would also be near.

A torch. He struggled to remember. Was there a torch in the car?

He felt around under the passenger seat. Instead he only found a rag, perhaps an old tee shirt, he didn't really know because it lost all importance. Something heavy was inside. Desperate fingers wrapped around the weighty sheath.

His Mako.

ALL MINE

Lucas slipped it down his back and moved fast, scrambling on hands and knees and feet over damp leaves and twigs, ignoring the bracken fern stinging his facial wounds. Instincts drove him down deeper into the valley.

The canopy overhead was a mass of tangled wood and vines cutting Picasso-like oblongs of black sky. There was no moonlight.

Water trickled. A stream?

Listening, he also picked up distant rolling surf, so big, the rumble carried over offshore winds.

Realising he must be on the ocean side of the Loggers Track, his confidence rose. Wind only swirled in these valleys without direction, but the stream would lead to the ocean road.

Moisture dripped from branches, bracken fern, palm fronds, clothes became cold and damp after only minutes.

Sleep was a brief thought. Hyperthermia would bring death. Move or perish.

The eerie, grinding creak of a car door filled the forest. His chest tightened. Digging fingertips into a moss-covered trunk he dragged himself to his feet. From back up the valley, his worst fears were met when a torch beam appeared and passed over. He dropped, moved on, willing himself forward.

Circular light hit again, the bush in front lit up, he kept down.

The valley flattened, the creek was closer, trickling over a rocky bed.

No time to cross. He had to move, had to hide.

With his head raised as much as he dared, he found an enclave, darker than the surrounding bush. He crawled in, crouching beneath the widest fern. Birds woke, chattering above. Air was moist, heavy in his lungs, a wave hit the distant shore, this time the rolling boom was the unmistakable sound he'd heard over a lifetime. The fern would provide a safe haven until Caruso passed, enabling him to backtrack over the creek to the ocean.

285

To home. To Isabelle.

He pressed his spine against the trunk. Pain was welcome now to each vertebra, keeping nerves on edge, his mind alert, analysing each sound. Fronds stretched out above. Amidst the silence came the faint rushing of air in his right ear.

A wet stick cracked below the weight of a large boot, followed by the unmistakable sound of periodic, heavy footsteps. A tremble rattled his spine, he bit into the side of his hand to stop panting, to slow his breathing. Light appeared on a trunk in front. His mouth, vacuum dry. Lucas knew real terror, unlike the car chase where the iron cage protected him.

'Lucas. By now, you know who I am.'

It was strange to put a voice to the man. A clear voice, each word bore its own chilling purpose.

Evil.

Familiar?

Every nerve ending tightened. Caruso was behind, somewhere.

'We need to talk. To work this out.' A pause. 'Just a chat, Lucas, she's not for you.'

The voice? He knew the voice. From where?

He reached behind his back, unsheathed the Mako tucked in his jeans, his favourite diving knife.

'You'll die in the forest without my help, Lucas.'

The voice came from his left.

'I promise you'll live. Isabelle is alive. I did not harm her. I won't harm you, Lucas.'

Caruso had not seen him yet.

Lucas rose onto his haunches, lips clamped, breathing only through his nose, careful not to disturb a leaf. With the blade high in front of his face, he poised.

Light flooded the ground in front of the fern. A leg brushed fronds aside. A boot came down, followed by the dark shape of the gun pointed toward the ground. If Caruso moved forward and shone the light back, Lucas would be exposed. He drove the knife hard down to the hilt and twisted. The sound was like Clyde chewing gristle and bone.

Caruso cursed, a violent yell, a gunshot blast rang in Lucas's ear, he sprung up ordering his feet one after the other to run, head down, bent ape-like, arms searched for trees, hands bounced off trunks. Balance did not desert him this time as he ran blind. Palm slashed his cheeks. The gun went off again amidst many more angry, wretched cries of reprisals. Another bullet thudded into a tree to his right. With outstretched hands he fumbled his way through bush and reeds, lunging into the creek. Pain spiked his right knee, but he crawled and clawed and clutched at the rocks below the water, dragging himself out to the other side.

Another long, agonising cry came from somewhere behind.

He envisioned Caruso guiding, ripping eighteen centimetres of blade back up through bone and flesh. The back of the knife had a serrated edge with a lethal hook beneath the point.

Thumbtack often came around and sat on the deck, drinking free beer, sharpening Lucas's knives. Little Thumbtack had performed his task well. Lucas hadn't seen that Mako for a while. Things went into the Patrol, sometimes they didn't come out. He recalled how easily it sliced through the foot into the ground and laughed, a laughter, perhaps of disbelief. Perhaps even of insanity as he scampered up the other side of the valley.

19

An old car horn blared repeatedly, a dull sound, blanketed …
somewhere. Eva woke up, confused. After the noise wouldn't
go away, she rolled off the couch and poked her head into the
bedroom. Nat lay motionless on the bed. At some stage
through the night she found the couch, unable to sleep through
his snoring. The horn kept up its incessant honking. She
retrieved the phone from his jeans on the floor. The screen
said Lukey Luke, ten past three.

Why would Luke be calling so early?

She sat on the bed stroking Nat's forehead. 'It's your
phone.'

His eyes cracked awake, the phone stopped then started
blasting and flashing again so she nudged him.

'Hey, it's Lucas.'

Nat stirred, gave an unconvincing smile. 'Morning already?'

'Not really, just after three.' She passed the handset.

'Serious? In the morning?' He answered, 'Hello.'

'Nope, haven't seen him.' He listened some more.

'Checked Patto's, or Steve's?'

Nat's brow fell, eyes scrunched.

'What's going on?' she asked.

He motioned her to stop with his hand. 'Okay. Be there
soon.' He hung up and swung out of bed.

'What's up?'

'Lucas didn't make it home last night.'

———

Dave Hudson and his buddy Jarrod started the day just as poorly. Both were severely hung over after a great night in the Triple Finn Hotel and a hundred and fifty bucks lighter, busted for sleeping in their van. Dave watched the Bi-Law's Officer drive off into the rising sun, wishing it would drop on him.

'Nuthin' but a pocket Rambo with a badge.'

'Can't do fuck all about it mate,' Jarrod said. 'Let's find some grub and get outa here, swell's pumping.' He climbed into the front next to Dave. They drove out onto the ocean road, found a café. Minutes later Dave had just finished telling the owner about his run-in with the town's parking inspector when Duberly's car pulled up.

'Morning again, boys. Tom.'

'Good old Doob Doob Doobelly,' Jarrod said, throwing a smirk.

'Don't be a smartarse again, son.'

'Morning Nev,' Tom said. 'Hear you've been waking these lads up.'

'All got jobs to do. Take away, thanks.'

'Reckon ya might've learnt from the last beating ya copped,' said an old lady seated at the table next to the counter.

'Thought of it, meself,' Jarrod said, under his breath.

Duberly frowned. 'I don't have to put up with that from the likes of you, Betty.'

Betty ignored him, instead the cheeky grin set on the lads. 'Ended up in hospital 'e did. Second time it's happened so his fat-arsed council bosses decided he needed a hand, couldn't get no-one stupid enough to help him, so they bought a dog.' Her demonic cackle followed, it seemed to bounce off the walls.

Laughter rose from the three men who'd been reading quiz questions out to each other from a newspaper.

Duberly pointed a finger. 'Shut ya mouth, Betty.'

'What'll you do bout it, tell ya dad, ya uncle?' She turned back to Dave and Jarrod. 'Both drink out of the same pot in the pub.' The cackling rose to a new level, this time the young men laughed along.

'Knew there was something about that turd,' said Dave, 'even looks inbred.'

Tom pointed to the door. 'That's enough, Betty. Warned you about saying stuff like that. Take ya coffee and piss off if ya like.'

The old lady settled back down to her paper.

'Thanks, mate,' Duberly said. 'Bakery's closed.'

'There's a search on. Lucas Maddigan might've crashed on his way home from the pub last night. Cops are out too.'

'Lucas? Why didn't someone call me?'

'As if—' Betty said.

'Betty!' Tom warned, passing Duberly his coffee.

'Better go see if I can help,' the officer said, casting a dirty look at Betty as he left.

'Some guy from the pub's missing, don't remember meeting anyone named Lucas,' Dave said.

'If he's sleeping in his car, that wanka 'll find him,' Jarrod replied.

The café settled back down, Tom collected their plates. 'Where you guys heading?'

'Wanna surf Bells tomorrow, hang there for a few days before getting back to the smoke.'

'Safe trip, stay outa trouble.'

They headed east, leaving the town behind. 'S'posed to be awesome waves along this section,' Jarrod said.

Through the gaps in the passing trees Dave viewed the plateau of scrub to the cliff line. 'Not worth the effort, we'd have to find a track, climb down cliffs, or jump off. Fuck that. Swell's massive.'

'Guess so. Autumn Reef's meant to be around here somewhere. Some guys reckon it's the biggest wave in Victoria when it's on.'

'Don't have the boards,' Dave replied. 'Supposed to be on private property anyway. No doubt there'd be a few set ups round here that'll hold that size. Those fellas at the pub last night were pretty charged up, braggin' they'd been getting epic waves.'

'That South African dude was maggoted, in me face all night.'

'Still, we lucked it, shit hot music, what I can remember.'

Jarrod chuckled. 'Sure was, hey bad news buddy, turtle's awake, next chance you get pull over.'

'Couldn't you have gone at the café?'

'Sorry, mate.'

Dave drove through a few more bends before stopping at a small clearing near a bridge. 'Paper's under your seat.'

'Cheers.' Jarrod took himself behind a tree.

'Hey, go down to the creek mate, just in case that tosser comes along and books us again.'

'All right, back soon, pump out a Doo-oobelly, huh.' Jarrod's laughter echoed through the bush.

After waiting and listening to music for about ten minutes, Dave began to wonder what was taking so long. He stepped out of the van, calling Jarrod's name. No answer. He called twice more, walked further into the bush, got a low reply.

'Hurry up, over here.'

Dave found him at the edge of the creek. 'Hey, think I heard a voice, scared the fuck outa me.'

'Bullshit.'

'Listen,' Jarrod said, and then he called out aloud. 'HEY … YOU THERE?' Bird life stirred, Dave heard a weak voice.

'Help.'

'Shit! You're for real.' He took off, splashing down the centre of the creek. 'Hello?'

'Help.'

The voice came from his right. 'In here.' Dave trampled through reeds and a crop of thorn bushes to find a man lying in the grass, saturated. He knelt down. 'We got ya, buddy.' He looked up at Jarrod. 'That guy, they said someone's missing. We gotcha mate, what's your name?

'Luke ... Lucas.'

'It's him, Lucas!' Dave said. 'Lucas, can you hear me?'

'Yeah.'

'We're here to get you out.' Dave lifted the matted hair to see a large gash and dried blood over his eye, a plum red hole in the man's cheek. He turned to Jarrod in disbelief. 'He's been shot.'

———

Isabelle watched the ambulance leave. An arm slipped over her shoulders.

'Get some things together,' Horry said, 'I'll take you in.'

She burst into tears. 'Oh Horry! This is all my fault.'

'Luke's okay, it's all that matters.' He pulled her in closer.

She nestled her face into his chest, gripping his shirt so tight she heard it rip a little. Her first opportunity to cry since the two surfers brought Lucas back.

'I know but ... this would never have happened if I wasn't here.'

'Listen, I don't quite know what's going on,' Horry said, 'but Lucas has told me some things. Those boys found him at Pale Creek, that's a few kilometres past here. They thought he'd been shot. The ambos say it looks like a palm frond had gone through his cheek, must've fallen on one up in the rainforest. Where the hell's he been? Has this got anything to do with that guy ... your ex?'

'What has he told you?'

'We have these chats, there's no secrets.'

Isabelle felt an overwhelming sense of relief, she nodded. 'Carlo did this. Lucas told me he somehow stabbed him in the foot to get away. He's supposed to be dead, now he's back, look what he's done Horry … look what I've done. It's all my fault … I … I have to leave.'

Horry didn't reply straight away, he only hugged her tighter for long seconds, then held her at arm's length. 'That's not the way we handle things down here.'

'You have to understand Horry, yesterday was … just … the best day I ever spent with Lucas and so many of his friends … now look … how can I tell him?'

'You don't. You're not leaving. That's not how it's going to be. Darkness can't get rid of darkness, only sunshine can do that, Lucas was in a very dark place before you came along. He's also told me how strong you are.' With a coiled finger Horry lifted her chin. 'Look at me.' She did. 'Those guys told me Lucas reckoned he walked all night to reach you. They wanted to take him straight to the hospital but he became hysterical, started screaming your name, trying to open the car door. He's more concerned for you than he is for himself.' With his thumbs he wiped back her tears. 'When I first met him I was just a kook on a surfboard drowning off the rocks in Fishhook Bay. Some guys in the line-up were ready to belt the crap outa me. Apparently I was getting in the way, so he helped me get in. Then we went over to the pub, had a few beers, you know the story, ja.'

She found a meek smile. Horry always made her smile, even now.

'He taught me to surf, taught me the water. Also introduced me to Connie and when I came back to this country to marry her, he got his grandfather to be guarantor for a loan so Connie and I could start the bakery. Bet he didn't tell you that, did he?'

'No.'

'Now when Lucas needed help, these boys were there for him. That's how this coast works. We stick together down here. Lucas loves you. He's lost everything before, now he has you, he'll only want to see you when he wakes up, the lady who's survived all of this. I remember the first day he met you. We look back and laugh now, but you really got your back up. *That's* the lady Lucas fell in love with.' He eyeballed her. Strong hands firmed on her shoulders. 'I need to know where that lady is right now.'

She bowed her head. Sheila's voice flooded her mind. *"Love the ones who love you, most important thing in life."*

She steeled herself. 'I'm here Horry … I'm sorry—'

'Where is she?'

'Right here.'

'Good. No more talk of this, ja.'

She nodded. 'I love him, Horry, so much.'

'I know. You're one of us now. We'll figure this out, together. We'll deal with this, I promise you, but for now all I need you to do is get some things organised for him.'

She wiped her face, went to the bedroom and packed some clothes and a toothbrush for Lucas. When she walked back out Nat was in the main room, the last of the searchers to arrive back.

'How is he?'

'Yeah, he's okay,' Isabelle replied. 'They've taken him to hospital. Horry and the others are on the deck.' Out the window she saw the roof of a police car.

'Followed us in,' Nat said. 'They're coming up in a minute.'

Isabelle stepped closer to the window. Her hands started shaking, she placed her palms flat on the glass. 'Oh my God,' she yelled.

Eva showed the uniformed officers her badge.

———

After a long day, Isabelle's mood was as sombre as the overcast sky. The late afternoon chill had already begun to creep in. Eva sat opposite.

Yesterday, a friend. Today, a detective.

Tom brought their coffees out. Isabelle tasted hers immediately. 'That's so good after the hospital coffee.'

'Reminded me of the rubbish they serve at headquarters,' Eva said. She had suggested earlier it was best to have the meeting at the local station, but Isabelle refused.

'How long will they be?'

'Should be here any minute. Isabelle, I'd still like to help you through this.'

'I don't know if that's possible, I'm not angry, actually I've learnt not to make enemies of the police. I'm glad you're here today, but—'

'I'm not your enemy.'

'I know, just don't understand why you're here in the first place.'

Eva nodded. 'As I said before, I'm not authorised to provide any details.'

A silver Commodore pulled up, John Ingliss stepped out of the passenger side wearing a grey jumper and denims.

'Hello, Isabelle.'

'John.' Lips quavered, she stood and embraced him, crying into his shoulder, not wanting to let go. Strong hands calmed her, pressing her biceps. 'I'm so glad you're here. Thank you … thank you for coming.'

'You okay?'

'No … ' She wiped her tears.

He introduced her to the taller detective, Bardsley. Tom took their orders and disappeared inside. Isabelle spent several minutes explaining as much as she knew, then caught Ingliss focussing on something behind her. Instinctively she turned. Lucas limped barefoot down the path wearing a neck brace. Surgical gauze covered half his partly bruised face. He was recognisable only by the clothes she'd taken to hospital. An officer followed.

Isabelle rushed to him. 'Lucas, you can't leave the hospital. Aren't you cold?' Fresh blood seeped through the bandage on his forehead.

'Checked out.'

'I tried to stop him,' the officer said.

'Thank you, Constable,' Bardsley replied, 'we'll handle this from here.'

Isabelle held Lucas's arm.

Bloodshot, marble hard eyes fixed on Eva.

'Yesterday you disappeared after lunch, told us you went for a bushwalk.'

Eva shifted in her seat. 'Lucas I—'

'I'm not an overly complicated man, Detective. However, I do take exception to being lied to. You were a guest in my home.'

After the events of the day, Isabelle had forgotten Eva had gone for a walk on her own.

'He was up there, wasn't he? Watching us.'

'Lucas, I did not see anyone.'

'But you went up there to look for the man who attempted to murder me last night.'

Eva held his stare. Finally, her lips parted. 'Yes … that's true.'

Isabelle gasped, no words escaped.

'Mr. Maddigan,' Bardsley said. 'I think it's best we continue this at—'

'I'm going home. If you want to talk, follow me out there.' His tone was as cold and uninviting as the brooding clouds marshalling in from the west. 'Better hurry too, storm's coming.'

'Mr. Maddigan—'

He showed his back and walked inside the café.

Despite Isabelle's protests, Lucas drove. They turned onto the track.

'Lucas—' Time hung between her words. '—he was in the house last night.'

He braked, hard. The Hyundai squeaked and jittered, sliding to a halt in a wheel rut beside the small clay belt, a section of track his grandfather dug by hand between the wars. Bardsley's car skidded behind. Lucas thought they might hit him.

Her lips shook. 'I'm sure of it now. I … I thought it was just a dream but when I woke up, I was certain Clyde had seen someone. That's when I rang you.'

Drowsiness and guilt entwined. He reached over and hugged her.

'I'll never leave you alone again.'

'No, no, no,' she whispered, her warm breath pounding his perforated eardrum. 'None of this is your fault.'

'I need to know we're in this together.'

She nodded. 'Of course … but I'm scared. They knew he was back. How do we deal with this?'

'I got some ideas. Steve will organise another car. Let's get through this first. When did you contact Ingliss?' He checked the side mirror. Bardsley opened his door, began to approach.

'This morning, once I found out Carlo—' She froze when she spoke his name, cast a blank, helpless look then closed her eyes, gathered herself. 'I had to know why there was an undercover officer down here, too.'

'What did he say?'

'He would explain everything when he got here.'

'Do you know who this other detective is?'

'No. Why?'

'He's homicide.'

'How do you know? He introduced himself as—'

'Tom recognised him, called me at the hospital, watches telly all day, seen his press conferences. There's a lot they're not telling us. We need answers, trust me, we'll get them.'

Bardsley tapped on the window. 'Is something wrong?'

'Everything's fine,' Lucas said and continued driving toward the house.

———

He parked in between Horry's ute and Dave and Jarrod's white van. Upstairs, he made sure Horry had put their fines under a fridge magnet.

Smiling became an effort. From his hospital bed, Lucas had to plead with Horry to take the boys out. When they'd brought him home that morning, despite his situation, he appreciated their hidden joy at witnessing perfect, un-ridden barrels peeling across a lonely reef.

He grabbed the binoculars, Clyde followed onto the deck. The ocean boiled and swirled over the rock pools, the fresh smell of approaching rain, dormant in the air. Out on the reef he recognised Jarrod's long blond hair, paddling the Jim Banks eight-foot pintail. Banks, a former pro had presented the board to Lucas after an amazing tube riding session last winter. Nat and Banks had jostled and sparred all afternoon, trying to take off deeper than each other inside the barrel. The Bos held his own with the pros.

Lucas cast the binoculars wide. Dave was sitting in the safety of the deep channel on another of Lucas's boards, a Sloth gun shaped by a mate in Queensland.

Ingliss rested his elbows on the handrail, clasping his hands. 'Very impressive.'

'Not a day goes by when I don't think that, sir.'

'Grew up in Narrabeen.'

'Know it well. Some pretty good surfers have come out of there.'

'Used to watch Tom Carroll, he's something else.'

'He's surfed here. A good mate of mine, another pro named Ross Clarke Jones brings him down when it's pumping like this.'

'Really?'

'Both missed their heats at Bells one year because this was going off its nut. We get lots of visitors here. If they respect my privacy, they're welcome back.'

'Seems fair. What do you call it?'

Lucas studied the inspector. Isabelle placed her trust in this man. 'Western Reef, Razorback, Autumn Reef. Depends on who we're talking to.'

Ingliss cut a wary smile.

'Made up so many names over the years. Lots of crew come looking, but mostly the swell rolls over the top of the reef. Needs to be big before it starts breaking.'

'My son raves about this wave in California,' Ingliss said. 'Can't think of the name, but apparently one guy surfed it for fifteen years on his own because no one believed it was there.'

'Mavericks,' Lucas said. 'Now it's a circus, we keep our secrets down here.

Lucas handed him the binoculars. 'Take a look.'

Ingliss steadied his elbows on the rail and fixed the glasses.

'See the two surfers to the far left. One is my mate, Horry. The other is one of the young fellas who found me this morning.'

The wave approached the reef, both men paddled toward it.

'That's one hell of a wave. Who's going to take it?'

'Neither of them.'

Horry paddled over the back. Jarrod made an attempt to paddle into the face, the wave passed beneath him.

Ingliss lowered the binoculars. 'How'd you know that?'

'We all went through it. Fear's got him. Horry's helping him so he knows the right waves to consider. May have to come back a few times before he pulls into one, but that's okay.'

'There's another man out to the left,' Ingliss said, 'never going to get a wave out there.'

'That's the other fella that found me. Neither of 'em have surfed this size. Now, see the guy paddling over to the far right, inside the others.'

Ingliss swung the binoculars, took a few seconds. 'Yeah.'

'Watch.'

The next wave approached the reef. Nat paddled over the peak, letting it pass. 'Keep focussed on this wave coming, biggest of the set.' As he spoke Nat turned and stroked effortlessly into the face. Spray whisked high off the top. Nat pulled in with barely a bottom turn and charged into the hollow pit, disappearing behind the thick, juicy lip.

'He's had it.'

'Not the Bos.'

Five or six seconds later Nat flew out of the barrel, as always finding his precious timing to plant the front foot. He cut back with typical cat like balance into a swooping bottom turn, raced down the line through the long walled section across the centre of the reef, tucked into another short tube. Lucas heard the noise, not that he really heard it because they were a long way offshore, but the sweet sound of The Bos's power as he smacked the lip was embedded in his memory; often heard if Lucas was paddling close enough when Nat raced past.

'Incredible,' Ingliss said. 'The wave seems to break below the waterline.'

"Optical illusion. There's so much water moving around out there. That's a gnarly section where Nat took off. Real shallow. Swell's swung slightly west in front of this storm and wedges at the top of the reef. On low tide it can almost suck the reef dry.'

'How did you know he'd take it and not one of the other two?'

Lucas smiled. 'Nat's a selfish bastard. There's no way he'd waste a wave like that on anyone. Not so flash on land, but faces his issues out there head on, the way issues should be met, sir.'

Ingliss lowered the binoculars.

'I can't tell you how pissed off I am.'

The Inspector nodded. 'Come inside, storm looks like it's about to hit.'

'Storm's not the issue. Watch 'em in the night just to see the light show across the horizon. No matter how big they are, storms always pass, sir.'

Ingliss nodded. 'Guess they do.'

'Isabelle spoke about you, just yesterday. She trusts you, but something's going on we don't understand. Isabelle and I are going to have to leave this place.'

'We'll explain everything inside, Lucas.'

'One thing first.' He didn't wait for Ingliss to reply. 'That detective's not here to investigate someone who crashed his car on the way home from the pub last night. I stabbed Caruso through the foot. Unless you've found a body, that's not murder, sir. Are you going to explain why Victorian Homicide are in my house?'

Ingliss pursed his lips. 'It's not my investigation.'

'All right, but do not let her down again. When I go in there, it's all on the table.'

Ingliss nodded, then walked inside. Lucas watched through the window as he went directly to Bardsley and pulled him aside.

———

Isabelle fought back tears, Lucas finally entered, his expression, galvanised, a morbid state hung in the room. He sat next to her and took her hand. Clyde banked at his feet, head resting on paws. The three officers sat opposite, backs to the ocean.

Bardsley started. 'Lucas, we need to know what happened from the time you left the hotel last night, please.'

Eva placed a small recording device on the table. 'Do you mind?'

'Course not.'

Isabelle tried hard to keep her emotions in check, listening to Lucas's full account of the previous night.

'Were you drinking at the hotel?' Bardsley asked. He turned the recorder off. 'It's a formality.' He pushed record.

'Only mid-strength.'

'You're sure this man followed you onto the beach?'

'The more I think about it, the more I realise he would've attempted to kill me down there if I didn't turn back.' He paused, shaking his head slightly. 'What about hospitals?'

'They've been alerted. Nothing so far.' Bardsley locked his fingers together.

'Lucas, Isabelle, I must inform you earlier this year three men were murdered just outside the town of Buchannon. A fourth man was killed two weeks prior in Melbourne. We believe Carlo Caruso committed these murders.'

'What?' Isabelle gasped. 'Why would he? And … and you knew he was back.' Lightheadedness swamped her. She opened her mouth to demand why she wasn't told, when Lucas tightened his grip on her hand.

'Buchannon,' Lucas said. 'Bikers, weren't they? Their house burnt to the ground.'

Confusion surrounded Isabelle. She recalled the pub chatter at the time regarding the murders, and for one of the few times in her life, wished she had watched the television.

'That's correct,' Bardsley said. 'We believe Caruso has had extensive plastic surgery.'

Bardsley handed her a photo. 'This was taken a day before the murders.' He passed another photo. 'This is an enhanced image of what he looks like now.'

She forced herself to look. Burning hatred rose within for the man who tried to kill Lucas. Then the shock of recognition struck, the pier, the man, the crowd. It *was* him.

Unable to control herself, she screamed. 'How long have you known?'

Lucas placed an arm around her. 'Isabelle—'

'No, no … Lucas! I saw him. You remember. I told you what happened on the foreshore near the pier when you came back from Hawaii. It *was* him!' She could feel her chest fluttering wildly. She breathed in deep, fists clamped tight in an effort to find calmness.

She told the officers of the events on the beach.

'He's been in this town, John. You knew about these murders.'

Ingliss gave a tentative nod. 'Yes, Isabelle.'

Immediately she recognised his frustration. 'After all we've been through.'

'Isabelle, you must understand—'

'When were you going to tell me?'

Ingliss gave Bardsley a fleeting glance.

Bardsley cleared his throat. 'This is my investigation and—'

'And you set us up as bait,' Lucas said.

'No I did not. I put an officer down here to protect you.' Bardsley's voice was dry, stolid. 'This man's profile is eight years old. My investigation was into the murders of other criminals. I had evidence to follow. We believed it was entirely remote—"

'REMOTE!' The word leapt from Isabelle's tongue. 'He nearly killed Lucas. You knew Carlo murdered four people only a few hours from here. I have never felt more betrayed.' Her head sagged, eyes looked back at Ingliss. 'You're the one person I trusted.'

'We judged he did not have the capabilities to find where you were living,' Bardsley said.

But Isabelle turned on Ingliss. 'John, that is not true, you … you know that's not true.'

'Isabelle, as an investigative unit we can only work with the information at hand,' Ingliss said.

'But John, this … none of this explains why you didn't inform me he was back. You have always promised. That's why I called you this morning first thing. Because you promised me, if he ever returned—' She struggled to hold off an impending torrent of tears, but also she felt Lucas's grip tighten on her hand even more.

'Did you believe he wouldn't come down here?' Lucas asked Ingliss.

'There were extenuating circumstances that led—'

'Answer my question!' he yelled, slamming his fist down on the table. The stubby candleholders jumped, the vase of bush flowers would have tipped had Eva not reached out and grabbed hold.

'Mr. Maddigan, please.' Bardsley said.

'No, sir! He told you. Didn't he?' Every muscle in Lucas's face tensed, veins on his neck were like roads. He thrust his finger at Bardsley, yet he faced Ingliss as though Bardsley was a painting on the wall. 'You warned him, didn't you. You knew he'd come. You knew, and you told him because your profile told you he is some sick demented murdering obsessive psycho who is alive and back in this country and he *would* come after her. You were gagged, weren't you?' He turned on Bardsley. 'You risked our lives. This could have been avoided if you had've fucking listened—'

'Mr. Maddigan, I made a decision based on evidence,' Bardsley said.

Lucas now squeezed Isabelle's hand. He too was trying to keep his anger in check.

'Can you identify him as the man who tried to kill you last night, Lucas?' Bardsley asked.

Outside the squall hit, the house shook, fat drops of rain pelted the windows, drumming the tin roof, deadening his voice. He spoke a little louder. 'I didn't see his face, he told me who he was.' He paused, closed his eyes. Isabelle felt an energy pass, like the anger was leaving him.

Lucas had his answer.

'I've seen him before, too,' he said in a quiet voice.

Isabelle was horrified. 'What? Lucas, where?'

'Last night I recognised his voice, just couldn't recall where from. Several weeks ago, remember, I asked you about some guy who said he spoke to you about my house at Gloucester Street, that's the same guy.' Lucas bowed his head again, straining to think. 'I remember now. He left when you arrived, didn't think anything of it at the time.' He turned to the officers. 'He came to my building site, in town.'

'My God, Lucas! He could have killed you then. How could you do this to us, John? After all we have been through.' Crusty tears prickled the corners of her eyes, she saw the compressed lips on the man opposite.

Lucas was right. He'd been gagged. She held her head in her hands, absorbing everything.

'How could he find me, John? After all these years? Everything's still the same.'

'You must have put your real name to something.'

She gritted her teeth, looking back up at Ingliss. 'It's my name. When do I have the right to use my name? He's supposed to be dead, or … or gone, not here, not in St Claire.'

'He may well have found you regardless,' Ingliss said.

'I know.' She lowered her head again, studying a knot in the wooden table. 'Lucas and I have to find a way to move forward from this. I have to know I can still rely on you, John.'

'Of course, you have my … our full support.'

'Could he be living close by?'

'I don't believe so,' Ingliss said.

'But up until now,' said Isabelle, 'anything you have guessed or assumed, has been wrong. Except for one thing.'

'What's that?' Lucas asked.

'That one day he would come back for me.'

Ingliss only nodded.

'Caruso cannot know we have a positive facial,' Bardsley said. 'I need you both in witness protection.'

'Witness protection—?' Lucas said. 'What … exist in some dumpy caravan park? I've heard the stories. Remember reading of a woman, years ago in Victoria who testified in a murder case against bikers. Despite the protection program and her new name, they caught up with her years later, shot her in her own bed. This family is a lot more powerful.'

'Caruso cannot know we have connected him to the murders in Melbourne,' Eva said. 'He doesn't know we can I.D. him. But he may suspect you can, Lucas. You met him at your other house. In his eyes, that makes you the only person in the country who can identify him. Now he has another reason to come after you. For your own sake and for Isabelle's, you must come in.'

———

Lucas's head throbbed. He stood, walked over to the old rocking chair, ran his hands along the crafted wood, so smooth, so old. He closed his eyes, wrapped a balled fist in a tight hand, saw the face, the cheek lines, so deep, so close, an eternity away. 'Old man,' he whispered, pushing hard on his knuckles. He walked to the far wall, picked up his wife's photo.

Police protection.

He recalled Isabelle's words. *"His family has contacts throughout every business sector, even government."*

His grandfather stared back from the wall unit. 'What would you do, old man?' With his back to the officers he glared out at the bush. The big old gums were bent to almost breaking point by the wind. He took solace in the fact that like his grandfather, they had survived far worse squalls. Branches and leaves ripped and fell, bark shed and anger simmered, tomorrow those trees would be rooted where they stood.

"Storms always pass son," came his grandfather's crisp, clear voice.

He moved toward the glass door, each step, each knee, each rib, each torn muscle owned its own pang, he ignored the jarring stabs.

'Lucas, this is your only option,' Bardsley said.

With all his might Lucas flung the door on its rollers so hard it crashed loudly into the support and bounced back toward him. 'Are you going to tell me I won't survive without your help?' he yelled. 'I heard that last night, sir. The decisions you have made nearly cost my life, sorry, that just doesn't cut it. You had a responsibility toward us.'

Ocean and sky had turned the colour of bruising. Lucas felt grim pleasure. Gone were the uniformed lines of swell. Stone-sized drops of biting rain pocked the swirling waters, soaking his bandages. He tasted blood. Howling south-westerlies ironed out the white caps, driving them in all directions, they breathed an aggressive chill into the room.

Horry, Nat and the lads negotiated the shore break. Dave, weary from the long paddle was picked up and dumped headfirst onto the sand. He scrambled onto the beach with Nat's help. Clyde placed two paws on the rail, pushing his head beneath his master's elbow, whining. Lucas tightened his arm around the dog's neck. Dark clouds circled their brooding centres, thunder cracked, lightning nailed the sky out to sea but he stayed out on the deck welcoming the temperature drop as the squall lashed the coast, driving rain through the open door.

Horry dropped his board in the sand and sprinted up to the deck. 'Luke ... hey ... how are ya, mate?' Cold water dripped from blue nostrils, red cheeks puffed, shivering fingers gripped the handrail.

Lucas remained quiet.

Horry looked past into the house. 'What's going on?'

'We're done here mate,' he finally said, loud enough for his voice to carry on the wind.

———

'You must try and talk him out of this,' Ingliss said.

Isabelle shook her head. 'We've decided this together. Lucas will make sure we're not found.'

They stood at the foot of the stairs in front of a second-hand, green Land Rover Steve had purchased for their trip. Two days had passed with Police swarming over the land. Sheila promised to look after Dimi. Clyde sat in the back, ready to travel.

'You'll always be looking over your shoulder.'

She saw the defeated look in his eyes. 'You'll catch him soon. You're the closest you've ever been. I believe in you, John.'

'After what's happened, I can only say I'll do my best.'

The last of the forensic trucks slammed their doors and drove out. 'Did they find much?'

'Don't think so,' Ingliss said.' Rain's been too heavy. Yesterday I walked from the crash site to the creek where Lucas was found. Took over two hours through some of the thickest bush I've ever seen.'

'He's very fit ... his will's just as strong. I can't change his mind and to be honest, I don't want to. You know how to reach us. Please ... please let me know if anything happens.'

Ingliss nodded, then touched her elbow because voices were heard from upstairs. She allowed herself to be led toward the back of the car.

'Guess all that's left is to wish you good luck.'

'Thanks. Means a lot.' After a pause she said, 'Hey, what went on the other day, Lucas has accepted everything, he just wants to leave.'

'We've spoken.' He frowned, like a thought attacked him. She recognised the old, uncomfortable look.

'What is it?'

He tilted his head. 'For him to come back after all this time? You ... you have this hold on him like I've never seen before.'

'John, we're about to leave. Why are you saying this now?'

He rubbed his chin. 'Caruso is the most ruthless criminal I've ever encountered, yet he was alone with you in the house and couldn't confront you. He came so far, and when the moment presented, he couldn't bring himself to wake you. He sees you as being unfaithful. That would normally mean he could harm you, but he seems willing to be able to forgive you.'

'Do you really think that's true?'

Ingliss wiped his hands over his face, and when they finally lifted, the strain showed. 'I know it sounds crazy. I've played it over many times in my mind, it all makes sense, you don't see it do you?'

She watched his searching eyes. 'See what?'

'You were the most successful model of your generation. To a man like Caruso, it's all about what you did for him. People admired him because of you. You gave him a profile he couldn't get any other way. He could have lived a life with more money than most people could ever dream of, but it wasn't enough. You tie it all in for him.'

'Are you saying I've driven him mad?'

'No. He's a product of the world he lives in. What I'm saying is he thinks he can start to rebuild his old life and the first step is getting you back. Even if he has to live in hiding for the rest of his life, as long as he's got you. Somewhere inside that demented mind you two never really separated. He won't stop until we catch him.'

Her shoulders slumped. Thoughts turned to the open road ahead. 'John … I'm so tired, we've been over this. Why now?'

'I'm scared for you, it's all I've got.' A door opened. He glanced up the stairs. Bardsley stepped onto the deck, Horry and Lucas followed. 'Listen. There's a memorandum of understanding being drafted. I'll be in charge of a joint investigation. If you and Lucas come in, I'll be the one protecting you. We've done it successfully before.'

'Our minds are made up.'

Ingliss nodded. 'Okay, just remember, you know the rules.'

'Yeah.'

'Take care. Like I said, you deserve him.'

She gave him a hug.

The three men came down the stairs. Lucas wore fresh bandages. Gone were the bloodstains that had been seeping through over the last two days.

'You ready?' Bardsley said. Ingliss gave her a longing look before the two officers sat in their car and waited while Lucas locked the house. Both vehicles followed Horry's dusty old ute down the track.

20

The Inner Melbourne Suburb of Kensington, Six Weeks Later

For Gary Kernot, life was over for another cold bastard of a day. Despite the light rain, he needed the rush of air so he kept the window down in the truck all the way back to the yard. Didn't really matter. The sweats always came just before knock off, regardless. He parked his truck in the same bay as he did yesterday, and every other day.

Hands jackhammered away, they shook the lid and it closed on his knuckles as he reached into his lunchbox for his flask.

Finally, hot whisky tinged his lips. Lovely, burning streaks of fire passed through his chest into his belly. The day had been long. Carting sand, dirt and tan bark all day on seven hundred bucks a week *was* long. Interstate runs, the big dollars, a distant memory.

Better than being inside.

The only abuse he copped nowadays was from angry concreters, like the mad Yugo who'd rung his boss this morning and lagged him in for dumping ten metres of sand in the wrong spot. The last delivery had also taken way too long, the boss would be pissed off again. There'd be an argument about the overtime, Kernot wasn't up for it so he decided he wouldn't even bother to clock off.

He lit a smoke, inhaled long and lapped up another swill, half the flask was already gone. Though he suffered no physical illnesses, each day was a day closer to death's welcome mat.

He shuffled through six blocks, counting the steps through each one before reaching home. Once inside, he cracked open another bottle from the top cupboard where he always put it from the night before. If he saw it on the bench in the mornings he'd never make it to work. No work. No Pay. No whisky. No smokes. He even had to prepare his flask the night before. The news was on the telly, he watched for no particular reason. Nothing on the news could affect him. He finished the whisky, butted the smoke and rested his head back.

When he woke he didn't know why.

A noise?

His mouth was dehydrated, the bottle empty, he had to get up, regardless.

———

A narrow footpath separated the house from the high red brick walls of the neighbouring printing factory. Carlo had to turn his shoulders to slip past the hot water unit and the meter box. Paint was peeling. Palings were either missing or split. Weeds thrived in the overhead gutter.

An old mustardy diesel tank rusted away on its angle iron stand in the back yard, amidst grass seeds, over four feet tall. Lights from the factory picked out the dark form of a black cat sitting up on a pile of old tires, watching through wary eyes. Across the road a stagnant creek lay beside a rail line; both shadowed beneath the dominant overpass of the City Link freeway. He figured if Kernot fed the cat, then the cat would keep rats from the creek away. A scratch-each-other's-back existence, eked out of necessity, rather than any form of want.

Carlo didn't bother to twist the knob on the back door. He just shouldered it open, then grimaced in pain. The effort involved weight through his right foot. Stitches had been removed; bones and ligaments and muscles were yet to fully heal.

Inside, the home was rather neat despite the dank circle formations of mould on the ceilings. Smells of age violated his nostrils.

As the groggy form of Kernot entered his kitchen, Carlo smashed his forearm across the man's face. Kernot crumpled to the floor. Carlo rag-dolled him back onto the couch. Kernot's mind seemed slow to regain his senses, or perhaps he was so beaten by life he couldn't quite absorb what had happened.

Eyes drooped, his look passive. He wiped the blood from his bent nose onto his sleeve.

'Who are you?'

'We have a mutual friend in St Claire,' Carlo said as he walked behind the couch.

'Who? Fuck!'

Kernot jumped up to run, Carlo collared him and snapped his neck.

21

Sicily
Two Months Later

John Ingliss touched down at Catania-Fontanarossa Airport on the east coast of the island of Sicily. Compared to Rome, the airport was a clean, modern glass fronted building and not nearly as busy. After only a few minutes waiting in the shade of the domestic terminal, a dark blue BMW sedan pulled up at a reckless angle in the front of the taxi stand. An attendant stepped forward, launching a verbal tirade at the driver. Ingliss watched the exchange. The officer, dressed in a dark suit, produced his badge. The attendant kept yelling, aided by contorted facial muscles and virtually speaking fingers and hands, sweat stains ringed the pits of his flailing arms. With an arrogant wave of his own hand, the officer brushed the attendant off.

'Inspector Ingliss?' he said on approach. 'Superintendent Arturo Meyanne, Interpol. Welcome to Sicily.'

Ingliss extended his hand. 'Thank you for coming out, Superintendent.'

They loaded his bags to more abuse. Ingliss struggled to place the man's accent as they sped out of the airport, onto the motorway and eventually past the turn off to the city of Catania.

'You're not Italian?'

'I was raised in France,' Meyanne said. 'My mother is Italian, my father is part Spanish and French, my wife is Sicilian. Me, I am a modern day European.'

Ingliss smiled, nodding at the dominant mountain to his right. 'Mt Etna?'

'The volcano, she's beautiful, yes. Like a mother, we live in her shadow, as Catanians say.' He passed an envelope. 'These top photos were taken in a restaurant in Catania four days ago.'

'Yes, I've seen them. Your report stated he's still in Catania, why aren't we heading there? I was told we had a meeting scheduled.'

'We did, at the Questura in Catania, but take a look at those photos underneath.' He reached over and flicked through until he found a shot of Caruso with two men on a rooftop of an apartment building. 'This was taken on a condominio in the city of Gela. Your fugitive has been moved there. It's a port city on the Mediterranean coastline in the Province of Caltanissetta. We will meet with the Questore himself in the main city, also called Caltanissetta, before we travel down to Gela.'

Ingliss studied the photos. Caruso was somewhere on the Island. 'Why meet with the Questore, we have our warrant, don't we?'

'Yes we do and he will tell you nothing more than I can, but he will want you to hear it from him.'

'When will you make the arrest?'

'It's complicated. I am an observer at the request of your government. This is a combined operation between the Polizia di Stato and the Carabinieri, could take several days.'

Ingliss decided not to raise his concerns regarding the State Police because the involvement of the Carabinieri provided great confidence. They were a world class Police unit with an excellent, highly efficient anti-Mafia squad.

'Why haven't they arrested him already?'

'The mandato – the warrant – wasn't issued until yesterday. The Carabinieri have him under surveillance. At first we did not know who he was. You have only recently updated his file, yet this is normally due to more current crimes being committed. The file contained no such notes.'

Ingliss knew the man had done his homework. 'He is suspected of more crimes, yes, however we have our reasons for leaving them off the file.'

'Perhaps he knows he is a suspect in this new investigation. This would explain why he is now a guest of Don Vito Spinali.'

The name triggered Ingliss's memory, though he couldn't quite recall from where. 'Spinali?'

'You have heard of this man?'

'Yes.'

'He's from Palermo. Came from nothing until he married into a wealthy family from the province of Caltanissetta.'

'Why is he under surveillance?' Ingliss asked.

'Spinali's business interests are mainly transport and shipping throughout the Mediterranean. He is also an arms dealer to North Africa. Your fugitive has changed his appearance. Is he aware you can identify him?'

'We believe not.'

Meyanne grinned. 'Then you are lucky. We only picked him up because of the company he is keeping.'

'When do they plan to go in?'

'It's not that simple. There will be armed men protecting him. Rome has ordered the arrest must be made when they move him out of Gela.'

'Why, if they know where he is?'

'You haven't been to Sicily before?'

'No.'

Gela is a densely populated city full of condos crammed into tight streets. The government says they will promote tourism in Gela if they can wrest control from the Mafia. Truth is, Italy is struggling under the Euro, funds are spent on the mainland cities. Nothing to spare for poor old Sicily but they can't risk bad publicity either. Italy has a solid extradition treaty with your country. They will have the best lawyers so we cannot give them grounds to win a refusal.' He paused in thought, then said. 'You do know the difficulty will be in convincing an Italian judge he is the man you are after.'

'We can prove his identification,' Ingliss said, glancing at the speedo. Meyanne averaged a hundred and fifty kilometres an hour, drifting with careless ease between the lanes. The scenery changed from vineyards to dry, sun scorched hills and rocky outcrops of the Sicilian heartland.

And gum trees.

'You have gum trees?'

'What's a gum tree?'

'These trees on the side of the road, they're native to Australia.'

Meyanne pulled to the right, a white Audi shot past doing two hundred plus. 'Eucalypts.' He shrugged. 'I think we call them eucalypts, just trees, who cares.'

Who cares, Ingliss thought, staring at the rubbish littering both sides of the highway.

After a little over an hour's drive, they reached the bustling city of Caltanissetta. Buildings were stacked side by side, no evidence of any real town planning.

Typical Juliet balconies hung from apartments. Their main purpose seemed to be for drying clothes and sheets, growing potted herbs and smoking.

After the meeting with the Questore, which Meyanne translated, they drove an hour south into more wine country along the shores of the Mediterranean. They turned east toward Gela. Ingliss took an interest in the unfinished, double storey shells of dwellings lying to waste beneath the Mediterranean sun. Some had roofs; most had no windows or walls, only concrete columns.

'What's with all these unfinished houses?'

'Half built by the Mafia. Lots of arrests were made in the last couple of decades. The Government repossessed the properties, yet they don't use funds to tear them down.'

They reached the city, another metropolis of apartments and chaotic traffic. Meyanne negotiated pedestrians, cars and mopeds coming at him from all directions.

'I've driven in other parts of Europe,' Ingliss said, 'but this seems a lot worse down here. Are there any road rules at all?'

'Of course! We stop at red lights, but if there's nothing coming we go through, and there is also the rule of space. If there is space and you don't take it, someone else will. Just keep moving, take up space, they will stop for you.' Meyanne raised a finger. 'And be careful. White lines on the road are just that … white lines on the road. It's chaos, yet once you get used to it you will see how it works so effectively.' Meyanne grinned while navigating his way down toward the waterfront. He stopped on a corner and sifted through the file until he found another photo of Caruso on a distant roof top balcony. 'Hold this.' He took off again, turning down a narrow street with shaded modern condos on either side. A stark contrast to the grimy, water-stained buildings he'd seen so far. 'I'm not stopping here,' Meyanne said, 'but take a look as we pass the grey building up ahead with the blue shutters.'

Ingliss recognised the building from the photo.

'Now you understand why the Carabinieri will not storm the building. There are many families living below in close vicinity. Their tactics will also be to move him around. He could be staying in any one of these buildings. We will flush him out instead.'

'You seem sure of that.'

'Patience my friend, Spinali is a cautious man. In Gela, the whispers we create will travel faster than the wind. They will be forced to move him out, probably at nightfall.

They continued down toward the sea. Ingliss took notes of the streets. The Via Francia, left onto the Viale Indipendenza, right on Via Europa, left on Via Ettore Romagnoli, right into Via Borsellino and along the Lungomare Federico Il di Svevia; the waterfront road. With the Mediterranean to his left, his bearings were established and he would easily find his way back up the hill to the condo. After passing more rundown seaside apartments and restaurants along the beachfront, they finally reached a bend where Meyanne pulled up at the Hotel Sole.

'You will require this.' He passed Ingliss an English passport. We have you booked in under the name of John Stanford, a London businessman on holidays. You will have to show this to the desk. They need it for their records but they cannot validate it, of course. There is a credit card in there, legitimate, Bank of England. We have already provided details with the booking so you won't have to produce any other documents. I'll come by at seven o'clock tonight for dinner.

Ingliss checked into his room overlooking a large refinery. He fired up his MacBook. The name Spinali appeared in Craig Welham's files. Spinali was the maiden name of the wife of Eddy Mollica, a man whose olive oil business on the Murray River had grown to become the largest in Australia. Their eldest son Lou served on the board of L'ombrello.

———

A high-pressure system had lodged over the Tasman Sea, driving easterlies along the coast. When they arrived home that morning, the beach had changed. More of the shoreline reef was exposed. Lucas tried to explain to Isabelle that when these weather patterns clashed with the westerly currents, the ocean seemed to be turned upside down, resulting in steep, unsurfable south-easterly whitecaps. The air was unpleasant, tangy from piles of rotting kelp and weed torn off the reefs and dumped onto the beach. Steve and his crew would be holed up in the bar of the Triple Finn Hotel pondering over their pots, *"when the wind's from the east the fishing's least"*. Then, maybe tomorrow or the next day, the easterlies would disappear just as quickly and westerly patterns would return life back to normal along the coast.

Lucas assured her the kelp would wash away within days, but that didn't matter. They'd already decided to leave again tomorrow.

For three months they had travelled west, visiting friends in Robe, South Australia, then camped along endless beaches through The Great Australian Bight. They reached another friend, Bon Terrents in Margaret River, south of Perth before heading north to Exmouth for a month. Lucas borrowed an old mal off Bon. Isabelle could now stand up on small waves. They visited again on their way back south, then drove east across to Port Lincoln. Big Steve organised accommodation with a tuna fisherman, and that was when Isabelle received the call. Caruso had fled the country.

———

Lucas rocked gently in his grandfather's chair. Isabelle played with Clyde down on the beach, she'd taught him to return a stick.

Clyde rarely left her side now and would often choose to nestle into her by the campfire at night.

He rocked slowly. Headaches were a constant. He'd slept a lot through their travels. Physically he felt good, ribs and the eardrum had healed, though the scars on his face were a permanent reminder. He tolerated the floating piece of bone in his right kneecap. But he *had* noticed on their long drive back, the more he thought of St Claire, the worse the headaches became.

The motor of Horry's old ute strained and churned in low range through the sand, dragging logs chained to the back.

Lucas rocked slowly as his good mate piled the wood up on the beach.

Soon after, tapping on the window made him realise he must have drifted off to sleep. Isabelle wore her red woollen beanie with the loose knitted balls dangling down the sides. Within seconds she was kneeling on the timber floor beside him. 'I've never seen you in this chair before.'

'It's three or four times older than me,' Lucas replied. He bought it from a second-hand shop just before World War 2. Each time it broke, he fixed it better than new.'

'What are you thinking about?'

He rubbed his thumb over his grandfather's photo. 'What he'd do about this.'

'What do you think he'd do?'

'Know what … this old chair rocked a fighter. I only really knew him for thirty years. He'd lived almost two of my lifetimes before that. His father was a World War 1 digger. Together they worked on the road, cutting through some of the most rugged coastline in the world. Then they built the old house with their bare hands. My grandfather, at his age didn't have to go World War 2, especially after hearing the horrors from working with diggers. Still, he went over and fought the same army for the same fields.

'Did he ask what should he do, or ask what he thought someone else should do? Back then they made decisions I can't fathom. He always said a man's destiny is shaped by how hard he is prepared to push through adversity.'

She ran her fingers through his. 'Tell me more about him.'

'He loved this ocean, gave him energy. There's no way he'd ever let that scum on his property. Most stubborn man I ever knew.'

Aware his eyes were glassing over, he took a moment. 'You know, I never knew my grandma, but according to Grandpa she often complained about the cold and the noise from the surf. She put up with it though because they loved each other and made a life here. So, thank you for coming back with me.'

'I wouldn't have let you come back on your own.'

'I know. He would have liked you.'

'After all that's happened, how can you know that?'

Lucas gazed out at the deep blue surround. 'He didn't like Sue at first. She stayed in my room before we married. He couldn't accept it. I quickly learnt there are no guarantees you have to like the people who are thrust into your life. But Sue chipped away, didn't give up. She broke him down with her kind spirit and a curiosity to explore the depths of a mind so deep in the experiences of life, none of the generations after could ever provide her with the same answers, the same knowledge, the same stories. Then she'd come to bed and tell me stories I already knew, but I listened because she was so enthralled.

'She promised him a great-grandchild. He left some flowers and an unsigned note written in his perfect handwriting beside her grave. I never mentioned the note to him. That was between them, but I kept it and read it after he died. He apologised for the bad start. Despite being well into his nineties he still learnt his lesson, that's how I know he would have liked you.

'This chair is where he did his thinking. For all his faults and stubborn ways, he wouldn't have made the same mistake twice. He always knew what was right in the end. Mum would take me to the Anzac Day marches. In the eighties protestors began heckling them, most of their abuse was aimed at the Vietnam Vets. Grandpa hated it and the next year, he marched with them. Local papers tried to make a story out of it. He said to me he understood the fuss, that's why he did it.'

'Sounds like he had an answer to everything.'

'Because he lived so long. When I was young I saved my pocket money and bought an old gun from the surf shop in town. I began to paddle out to the reef when it broke, but I was too scared to take off. He sat here watching me, in this chair. I didn't want to let him down. We'd sit and talk about it and he'd tell me about the many times in his life when he felt the same way and got through. Then he suggested I get Nat to come out with me.'

'Nat the Bos, huh.'

'Yeah, I nicknamed him that.'

She raised a smile. 'I know.'

'Grandpa used to drive us to different breaks on the weekends and watch. He knew how good Nat was. I hadn't told Nat about the wave on the reef and when he found out, he punched me so hard, gave me the worst dead-arm because I'd kept this secret from him. Then one day the swell got big enough again and the wave started breaking. After school we paddled out together and Nat just pulled into this fifteen foot smoker, simple as that.'

'Grandpa knew getting Nat out there was the right answer. There's nothing he could teach me about surfing, still he had the answer.'

'So what did you do?'

'I was so pissed off I paddled into the next one and got the rush of my life. I'll never forget that wave. Think the wax is still embedded under my toenails. I'd stared down my biggest fear, now I have to face another. That's all this is. That's the way Grandpa would see it. The answer is we have to go. Doesn't matter where he is in the world, we can't stay here. We both know that.'

'Babe …' she said, slowly brushing her hand over his hair. 'You know there's another way.'

The heaviness rose in his head, he shut his eyes to ward it off. 'No. We've spoken, remember. We do this our way.' He thought of his wife and parents. 'I can't make the wrong decision, not again.'

Isabelle had this ability to know what he was thinking. He couldn't quite work it out. Guilt must have betrayed him because, with her hand, she turned his chin to face her. 'What Lucas? What do you mean?'

He paused, swamped by overwhelming sadness. 'I should have been with them that day. I'm responsible.'

'Lucas, that's crazy. It was an accident.'

'I should have been driving.'

'Well … it's lucky you weren't.'

'No it's not. Sue had bought tickets to a show, booked a motel weeks earlier. Had it all planned, I let her down. They died because I let them down.'

'I always wondered why you weren't with them.'

'I stayed here. We rarely get big ground swells in summer, if we do it drops off in a day or two. Horry, Nat and I had surfed since sunrise. Sue wanted to leave after lunch and I fell asleep on the bed. She woke me, sometime in the afternoon. I've tried to remember exactly when I last heard her voice. She sat on the bed and stroked my forehead, said we had to leave. I told her I was too tired to go.' In an effort to alleviate the strain, he rubbed his hands down his face. It didn't help.

'Truth is, the swell began dropping and I knew the reef wouldn't be working the next day when we were due home. Time and tide wait for no man, they say. The water was warmer and Horry and Nat had planned to surf that evening on the push of the incoming tide. Melbourne's the last place I wanted to be.'

'Luke. Darling. You can't say it's your fault.'

'If I was driving we'd have stopped for food or left later, something would have been different. Anything. They would have lived if I wasn't so selfish.'

'But you're the most unselfish person I've ever met, don't be—'

'No I'm not. I made a decision that day that haunts me, follows me everywhere. My grandfather knew, never said a thing. Just helped me through before he passed.

'I couldn't surf for two years after the accident. You have to know this. You have to understand how I think. Sue understood. She joked that she came second to my surfing. Did she come second? That day she did. I loved her every bit as much as I love you, but I was a different person back then and now I think maybe our marriage survived because she accepted my surfing. What matters most is she was right and I can't take anything back. That's a part of me I can no longer tolerate.' The heaviness cemented in behind his brow. Clyde sat quietly, picking up on his master's mood.

'Sue was on life support.

'She'd sold my ticket to a girlfriend from Melbourne, who tried to call me. Then she rang the pub, luckily got onto Steve. He came to the house and of course, we were out surfing. The swell was so big he couldn't get his boat out, so he chartered his mate's plane to circle the reef. We thought they'd spotted a shark.

'Steve was beside me when I made the decision. I held her hand. It was just like holding a piece of fruit picked from a tree. You can't replace it.

'She'd bought a blue dress for the theatre and when she came to me that night in the forest, I saw that dress. She led me back to you. I don't believe in ghosts or God. But I do believe that there's an imprint someone you love leaves in your mind, it's as real and powerful as any of the beliefs other people hold. She helped me through that night. I owe it to her to become a better person for you. I can't be that selfish guy no more. Watching you surf gives me a joy I can't describe, makes me happier than being out there myself.'

'I understand now, Luke.'

He touched the scar tissue on his cheek, a recently formed habit. He felt a lot older since the crash.

'This is a second chance for both of us,' she said.

'I know, but they may never catch him. We've made the right decision. Steve rang before. Got us that house in Port

Lincoln for as long as we need it. We can settle down, become South Aussies.'

'Something new I guess.' She tightened her grip on his hand. 'I'm glad we came back. You needed to say goodbye.'

———

After all the books and all the years of studying the Mafia, the island did not provide a sense of fear Ingliss assumed he would feel in this land. Rather, everywhere he went in Gela, Sicilians treated him with respect.

Like a guest.

A humbling feeling.

He was in the bathroom brushing his teeth when his phone rang. He found it beside the bed and answered.

'I have news,' Meyanne said. 'Spinali's yacht docked early this morning at Licata. You remember the port we visited?'

'Yes I do. West of here. Could they be moving him out today?'

'I have been notified that is the case. An officer is on his way to pick you up.'

'Why not you?' Ingliss asked.

'I'll be assisting the arrest. You will be notified once he is in custody. We must follow protocol. Pack your bags. We'll be taking him straight to the mainland.' Meyanne hung up.

Finally, after five extensive days in Gela and all the reports and photos showing the operation was proceeding.

Ingliss dressed, packed and checked himself in the mirror, studied his whiskers. No time to shave so he just splashed his face and headed down to the lobby. Several times throughout the week he walked the length of the Lungomare across the waterfront of the city, up the Via Francia, past the Condos wearing a straw hat to ward off the fierce sun, despite knowing there was nothing he could achieve.

A car arrived. Agente Scelto (Senior Officer) Gatto

introduced himself, a plain-clothed man in his mid-thirties with poor English. Ingliss threw his bags in the boot and they drove not five hundred metres up the waterfront where Gatto parked at a café Ingliss knew well.

'Officer, what are we doing here?' He pointed to his watch.

'Hurry hurry … ah … *fa presto.*'

'No, no, *mangiare*, we eat, we wait.'

'What?'

'Sì.'

They ate, filled in over two harrowing hours with coffee and very little small talk. Ingliss rang Meyanne several times only to be told the operation was proceeding. The officer smoked nearly half a packet of cigarettes until he received a phone call just before midday.

Gatto spoke Italian into the phone, and not for the first time that week, Ingliss regretted taking French in school.

'Sì sì. *Est,*' Gatto said, as he hung up.

'*Est!*' Ingliss said. '*Est* … east. They're moving him east?'

'*Si trasferire.* (Move.)'

'East? Why east? Meyanne said west, west. *Ovest!*'

'*Aeroporto.*'

'An airport? Are you saying there's an airport east of here?'

Ingliss didn't wait for an answer and rang Meyanne. 'What the hell's going on? You can't let him get to an airport.'

'Inspector. We have him under arrest. Your driver will take you there now.'

Ingliss closed his eyes, pressed his fingers tight over his eyelids so as not to let the emotion building up inside, escape. After eight years, almost a fifth of his life he could finally bring this killer home to face justice. He pictured Sam Benson and Craig Welham, whose families would know their killer. Benson's boy, who had grown up without knowing his father. Isabelle, he could finally deliver her the peace and happiness she deserved in life. Then he pictured Maureen, his wife, the only person who knew the depths of his anguish. She would warn him of complacency. *"Wait until he is back in Australia, locked away for life,"* she would say.

Tyres screeched.

Gatto drove like Meyanne, only a younger, faster version with a siren. Ingliss tried to ward off the nerves, wondering if he'd die at the hands of this maniac before he finally saw Caruso under arrest. But like Meyanne, Gatto was in firm control of the surrounding traffic as he raced north to the highway. They took a roundabout almost on two wheels, turned east onto the highway, out past the refinery. The traffic was banked up, so Gatto raced down the wrong side of the road. They crossed a bridge, the roadblock was perfectly executed at a clearing with a bus depot on the left, terminals to the right. Slow, warped spinning lights of the dark blue, red striped Carabinieri cars blocked the road. Alongside were two black Mercedes, doors hanging open. The traffic simply drove around the roadblock like ants would do. Gatto skidded in front of the cars.

He nodded eagerly at Ingliss. *'Sì ... Sì ... arrestato ... Sì.'*

Ingliss tried to remain calm as he got out, drawing in the warm Mediterranean air. He counted five men lying face down on the bitumen, handcuffed. A dozen or more officers stood by smoking, chatting loudly, guns drawn. He looked for Meyanne amongst the surrounding faces, all uniformed strangers. Three of the men on the ground were overweight. The fourth was bald. The last man was broad shouldered with large, long arms handcuffed behind his back, tall, dark cropped hair.

Caruso.

The officer standing over the captive saw Ingliss approach and raised his gun. *'Ehi, ehi,'* he yelled, then backed off when he noticed Ingliss's outstretched badge.

'Iddu è cu mia,' (he is with me) Gatto called.

'*Sì.*' The man nodded. Ingliss reached down, lifting the head by the hair. He studied the anonymous face in horror, the man gave a sly grin. Ingliss slammed the face into the bitumen.

'Where the hell is Meyanne?' he yelled.

22

Horry called them fire nights. He built a pyre several feet up from the last of the tiered steps created by king tides, which had claimed back large sections of the beach. Flames quickly rose, fanned by the howling onshore strafing down the Bluff. Surrounded by his mates, Lucas welcomed the heat on this cold night of late winter.

Patto spoke. 'How can we help, what can we do?'

'Nothing mate, Isabelle and I have made our decision.'

'You don't have to do this.' Patto glanced up toward the house. Connie and Isabelle were in the kitchen. An orange glow licked one side of his face.

'She doesn't deserve what's happened,' Lucas said.

'Neither do you.'

'That's just not the way it is, Patto.'

'Sorry mate, but—'

'Don't be,' Lucas said, 'you've always called it as you see it. Now's not the time to apologise.'

Patto swallowed a mouthful of beer. Steve, normally the devil's advocate, remained uncannily silent.

'How long you going for?' Nat asked.

'Who knows, just wanted to tell you guys all that we've enjoyed has come to an end.'

Head down, Nat kicked his foot in the sand. Lucas feared he would struggle the most. They'd caught a million waves.

'Jarred and Dave, they been back?' Lucas asked.

'Every swell we've had over winter,' Nat said, 'both getting waves, too. Don't know if they've got jobs anymore. Said to say thanks for fixing up the fines.'

'You look after them out there,' said Lucas.

'No probs, mate.'

Through the ensuing silence, Patto cracked the esky open and passed Horry a beer. 'Nah, I'm right,' Horry said. Thumbtack put out his hand.

'Do you really think running's the answer?' Nat said.

'There's no answer,' Lucas assured him. 'There's only living, we have to find somewhere to live in peace.'

'It's a tough decision,' Horry said, kneeling in the sand stroking Clyde's back. 'When I was young my country made the toughest decision of all, look at it now. We both remember your grandfather telling us that at the time. He'd say if this is what you want for you and Isabelle, then it's right.'

Steve patted Horry on the shoulder.

'We're leaving tomorrow,' Lucas said, 'maybe forever. Nothing can take away our years together, good and bad.' His eyes moved to each of the men. 'One day when we're old, we'll look back on this and just like the accident, this will be something we overcome together.'

Nobody spoke. Flames crackled, sparks drifted high on the wind.

Lucas turned to his little mate. 'Heard you've been making the odd trip to Melbourne?'

'Yeah,' Nat replied, sheepishly.

"I want you to know she's okay with me.'

'Yeah, she told me yous were good.'

'There's something else you should know. She went up to that cliff top on her own after him. That took real guts, mate. Maybe you two have got more in common than you think, you're welcome to bring her down here for weekends.'

'Already done that.' The men chuckled, the mood lifted a notch.

'What are you going to do for money?' Patto asked.

'The agents got some people interested in Gloucester Street. Hopefully it's tied up in the next week or two. Signing contracts in the morning before we leave, that way we only have to get to a figure and it's done. Means we don't have to come back. Tom's thinking of buying the shop too, venders terms, we'll get the deal through, should be right for a while, might even get a job, eventually.'

'You ... a job?' Horry said.

Lucas grinned. 'Something different.'

'You'll be forced to do a job in a place you don't want to live in. I know you too well, mate.'

'Nothing I can do about it, Horry. We're leaving tomorrow.'

———

Later that evening Clyde scraped at the glass door, then stopped, his paw dangled mid-air, eyes pleading.

'Do I let him out?' Isabelle asked.

'Yeah sure,' Lucas said. 'If he wants to go.'

She unlocked the door, the dog slipped through. 'Want a red?'

'Why not?'

She was fixed on something through the kitchen window, seemingly mesmerised by the night. He put his sketchpad down, walked over, placed a hand on her shoulder.

'Huh!' She gasped, a hand flew to her heart.

He hadn't meant to startle her. 'Hey, you sure you're okay with this?'

'I'm fine, just the fire, has that magnetic effect.'

Embers, left to die in the sand, glowed. He massaged her neck, she leaned her head forward. 'That's nice. I feel like my muscles are constantly wound up like a ballerina in a jewellery box.'

Lucas rubbed deeper, concerned. One day her muscles might wind so tight they'd play a downhill spiralling tune until she eventually suffered from one of the litany of modern day diseases, fuelled by stress, eradicating both mind and body from within.

Many people grew old before their time.

She poured two half glasses, carried them over to the couch. He followed and rested his sketchpad on his knee and continued drawing.

'How do you keep your hands so light?' she asked.

'Old school, I guess. My first teacher at Uni was a Greek named Mr. Papadakos. He was right into astrology, put a lot of emphasis on sketching freehand. "You have to learn to dance on the mount of the moon, " he'd say.'

'Mount of the moon?'

'Bottom of the palm, under your little finger. Psychics refer to it as the mount of the moon, takes the weight off the fingers.'

When he finished the outlines, he shaded the windows in. 'What do you think?' He turned the pad around so she could see the drawing from the bottom of the page. 'Steve wants to buy his auntie's land on the other side of town, great views of the ocean and the golf club. There's an outcrop of rock in the middle, it's actually a dry creek bed except for when we have a very wet winter, then a waterfall forms and the site has potential for an idea I have. This may be the last home I design in the area, might become a bit of a statement, Steve can afford it.'

'How are you going to build it if we're not here?'

'Patto will build it. I'll show you my inspiration for this design.' He opened up the book, flicked through the pages until he found the one he was looking for. 'This is a Frank Lloyd Wright home in America called Falling Waters. He's the greatest architect of the twentieth century and this is possibly the most famous home in the western world. Imagine putting something like this on the Great Ocean Road.'

'Aha. Why does it look like a wedding cake?' She sipped her wine, an attempt to smother her smirk, but she couldn't hide the dimples below her cheeks.

'Oh, cause he liked wedding cakes, stop takin' the piss, you just can't say that about a house like this.'

'I'm sorry.' She giggled. 'Seriously, tell me about it. A cake-house built over a waterfall. You'll give me wet dreams.' She rocked forward laughing delightfully.

'Be serious.'

'Okay, okay, all right,' she said, trying to control herself with a hand over her lips.

Her phone rang from the bedroom. 'Hang on.'

She headed off to the room and re-appeared with the handset, a troubled look. 'Think that was John, missed the call, he might ring back in a minute.'

'What's the matter?'

She stared at the handset.

'Isabelle … Isabelle?'

Her face drained of colour. 'I can't do this, Luke.'

Urgency engulfed him. 'Grab the bags, I'll get Clyde.'

He slid open the glass door, night entered, with two fingers in his mouth he sucked in a lungful of air to whistle, and froze. Clyde lay motionless on the deck. Carlo Caruso pointed a gun at Lucas's stomach.

23

A blood-curdling scream almost rattled the windows. Isabelle stood rigid, staring wildly at Lucas, at Caruso. The phone dropped and bounced on the floor, then settled. Despite the cold, Caruso wore only a tee shirt. Muscles brilliant and frightening.

He raised the gun a little more. Lucas moved back, eyes on the weapon. Caruso stepped inside.

Isabelle placed her hand over her mouth, muffling unearthly screams until empty lungs heaved in each tumultuous breath, then only silence. The rise and fall of her chest, sharp, disbelieving wide eyes, full of alarm. He wanted to run to her, to hold her, tell her this was an evil dream. Caruso gave a steely, patient look. With raised hands, Lucas stepped away further into the living room. The mobile rang again from the floor. Caruso strolled over, crushed it beneath his heel.'

He motioned with the gun, this time toward the couch. 'Sit down, please.' His tone, deliberate.

Lucas's legs refused, desperately he concentrated on Isabelle, a stare of dread returned.

'Hurry up.'

They both moved, slow, sitting a full cushion width apart.

Caruso reefed the landline from the wall beside the fridge. Lucas took a chance to gently touch the back of her hand. It was cold. With the butt of the gun, Caruso struck down hard on the wall unit, tearing the wiring out before striding back to the middle of the room.

———

Beneath the plastic exterior, old mannerisms were unmistakable. She feared for Lucas, her love, her everything.

Then defiance rose, loathing and hatred surfaced, predatory eyes moved to her knees. She tugged down the hem of her dress.

He bowed forward, wrapping his fingers around her wine glass, eyes always looking up, the grin, suffocating, reeking arrogance. This room held no threat. He was so close, she wanted to lunge at him, dig her nails deep, peel back the skin. In this face she saw none of the fake altruism she had come to know in their time together, nor the uncomfortable look of a past lover. Nervous tension one might feel when one saw an old partner in a new relationship in a more traditional life where people didn't split up because of murder. Purposely she breathed out, wishing she could air her hatred over him.

He sipped the wine. 'You've lowered your standards.' He placed the glass back on the table, eyes never leaving hers. She searched those eyes, those inner eyes.

What was it? The nose was too slender, too perfect.

She swallowed hard. The eyes, eyes that once showed her fallacious caring.

He was a lie, a well-honed ruse, a travesty of misguided lust.

Haunting memories flooded, bullet-riddled bodies, young Jack Benson's face, tender years ripped away by this criminal who murdered his father, this criminal, all of a sudden back in her life.

He was here for a result.

Another crossroad in her life.

Her life.

Perhaps the only bargaining tool left to help Lucas, her soul mate.

If she left, would Lucas be allowed to live?

The police said they were close. How wrong they were, again.

She looked hard, eyes creased.

Was it doubt?

Carlo pulled his gaze from her and picked up the book, casually flicking through some pages. 'I appreciate good architecture, Lucas. Lived in a Ray Kappe in California. You know of his work?'

Lucas remained quiet.

Murderous eyes danced back and forth, an unnatural tension hung in the corners, their sharpened edges. No crows feet. The hair, so fake, bristly. Not Italian.

This man had adored the person he used to be.

You had no say in your face. You hate it. Isabelle held back her words.

The surgery hadn't been necessary for the reasons of age or irregularities. The face, a mere parody of the man she once knew.

She smiled inwardly, a tiny consolation, present nonetheless.

He spun his head around the room. 'This is nice, Lucas, blends with the landscape.'

'You're not here for my work.' His first words, defiant.

'You're not wrong.'

In the fleeting eyes, Isabelle was now sure there was a hint of doubt. Never before had she seen that.

Unsure about what?

"You have a hold on him," came Ingliss's words.

The eyes fell on her again.

Why?

Was he seeking approval?

Approval?

He hates his face.

So apparently devastating for such a man of confidence. To know this face was something so badly crafted as to seem an intentional mockery. Courage surfaced even more, a cold sense of comfort.

'I'll come. If you don't hurt him, I'll come.'

The evil, malicious grin only widened. 'I know you will. I'm not here to hurt him. I need you to leave us alone.'

'I don't believe ... how can I believe you?'

'You have to trust me.'

Isabelle tried to speak, her throat failed.

'There *will* be an outcome tonight. Everything depends on you doing as I say.'

She swallowed hard. 'Wh ... what ... are you going to do to Lucas?'

'We are going to talk. His life depends on you, Izy.'

Don't you dare speak that name, she held back from saying. 'No ... no,' she whispered. 'I can't trust you.'

'In the study. Now!' He motioned with the pistol. Her mind snapped to attention.

The study. Lucas's phone.

She gave Lucas a lasting look. He nodded, gently.

'Go,' he whispered.

Slowly she rose, walked grimly toward the study, a weighty lump in her throat, legs wanted to buckle. Heavy footfalls followed, she wanted to turn, to run at him but she was trapped, helpless. Carlo stood at the doorway with the gun pointed at Lucas. She moved in front of the phone charging on the desk.

Carlo stretched out his hand. 'The modem please, and that mobile.'

Her heart sank. She unplugged the modem, slid both items over the floor toward him. He stomped them into the hardwood.

'Lock that outside door. Twist the key in the latch and throw it over.'

Isabelle twisted the key, tested the latch and threw the key in front of him. He picked it up.

'Don't do anything before I come to get you, and—'
He glanced at Lucas without continuing the threat, then
went to close the door.
'Wait … wait, I told you I'll come. Please Carlo, there's no
reason to harm him.'
'I know, do not move from here and you have my word.'
He closed the door.
She was back.
Alone, and helpless.

———

Maddigan sat, hunched forward, hands pressed between his
thighs. Carlo rubbed the stubble on his chin.
'Bit more relaxing with her out of the room, don't you
think?'
Maddigan's eyes rolled up.
'Good,' Carlo said. 'The time has arrived to discuss this like
men.'
'What are you going to do with her?'
'She is no longer your concern.'
'Isabelle is my only concern.'
'Your concern is your life, Lucas, the bane of every living
creature. The world will have you believe people give up their
lives for each other, well that's all bullshit. You will not give
up your life for her.' He looked down at Maddigan, who
remained silent. 'Let me start with goodwill. I like dogs. Gave
yours a general anaesthetic, he'll be fine soon enough, maybe
a little drowsy but he'll live. We have a lot in common,
Lucas.'
'What would I have in common with you?'
'Philosophy.'
Maddigan shook his head, slowly.
'You have no clients,' Carlo said.
'You've been through my files.'

'Let's call it research. I admired the manner in which you spoke to me at your other home. Who in their right mind would want to deal with the public? They need people like us to tell them what's good for them. Despite your troubles, you are your own man, I like that about you.' He looked down at the photos once again. 'Your family?'

Carlo waited, allowing the man to gather his thoughts. When it became clear Maddigan wouldn't offer a reply again, he picked up the photo of the wife. 'Must have been the hardest time, she was a beautiful woman.'

Maddigan bowed his head, clenching fists. 'Put that down.'

Carlo relished in the man's pain, placed the photo back carefully in the same position and wandered over to the window. The translucent blind was half pulled down. Outlines of trees waved in the dark.

'Do you ever think of the man who killed your family? Any thoughts of revenge?'

'What has that got to do with Isabelle?'

'Everything.'

'He got seven years.'

'Thirty-eight months.' Carlo let his words sink in. 'Good behaviour, can you believe that? Some system, huh. They even gave him a licence again.'

'How would you know?'

'Research Lucas, he was still a pathetic drunk. The system's not working for you. This system tells you the lives of your wife and parents are worth a little over one year in jail for each. He showed remorse, they said. His wife had just committed suicide, they said. Can't you see the system has let you down? How can a man not want revenge for such an act? This is perplexing to me. Why do you not seek vengeance for your family?'

'I have accepted it. I don't want to lose what I've got.'

Carlo tapped his boot on the floor. 'You don't want to lose what you've got. I like that answer. We're moving forward. I would have destroyed that man's entire family because in my world, family is everything, that's why I'm here. I can see you possess the same values, just not the same reasoning. Why, I wonder, are we so different? I mean, we both love the same woman.' Carlo waited to see if his words would entice a response. None came.

'Why can't you harbour vengeance?'

'You wouldn't understand.'

'Try me?'

'I have flaws. Vengeance is not one them.'

Carlo paced, listening, nodding. 'I've seen you surf those waves, the size, the raw power, it's exciting. I watched you for days, just before ... just before you stabbed me.' He held out his arms. 'That's a different type of strength you guys have out there. I respect that. What would happen if your mind is poisoned with hate or heavy with burden out in that ocean?'

'I would not be able to commit myself. Hesitation kills.'

'I know it does.'

Maddigan stared past him, Carlo turned, met the eyes of the grandfather in the photo.

'The war hero, did he teach you that?'

Maddigan gave a look of surprise.

'I have found research to be so important. Makes everything go to plan. How is your mind now, Lucas? Is it burdened by the fact you are screwing my woman? Poisoned with thoughts of what you want to do to me?'

'No.'

'No?' He turned his back. No movement came. 'I came here once, looking for vengeance. You gave me this limp. No man has ever done to me what you did, and lived. In that forest you showed me a side of you I would never have thought existed. Karma, whatever you call this whole one with the ocean and earth thing you got happening here. Something protected you. And it was more than just a knife. While my foot was healing I changed my whole way of thinking about you. I forgot the basic principles my father taught me. I came to your house with vengeance and anger, I should have come here to talk with you, like men. My father is an extraordinarily powerful man. Men who came to my father's house with vengeance always earned swift reprisals, others came to negotiate, to reason. They would bring gifts.' He shrugged. 'Sometimes, just a bag of avocados for my mother, a gift is a gift, a mark of respect to show they were rational men.' He raised his index finger to highlight his point.

'You took some injuries too. We can start again, you and I. But we both must be rational. We both have to be prepared to give a little.' He faced Maddigan again.

'I know my limitations. I couldn't surf those waves out there and you … could you kill a man, Lucas?' He paused again, letting the words sink in. 'Undoubtedly you know that much that about me, but I'm changing, I have to for Izy.

'Can a man like me change?

'Of course, that's why you're still alive. I don't want to take any of this from you. Despite your troubles, you've built a life for yourself here. From Sydney we look down and wonder why anyone would live in such a cold shithole. Now I can see why you live here, I don't want to ruin this for you.' He lowered his tone, expressing sympathy by almost whispering, offering enlightenment to this helpless man. 'I know what you've gone through, I have empathy for you.'

'Empathy?' Maddigan said.

'Empathy.

'On my travels I began to take note of how normal people lived. I studied them in bars and cafés, in parks, I'd watch for hours, just like a sport. People watching I liked to call it. People outside of my world, driving cars registered in their own names, the simple things, holding hands with wives and children. I found I wanted some of that normality. Not all of it … just some.' He strolled back over to the window. 'You can have all of this.' He spread his arms wide, spinning on his heel. 'My father taught me when to be fair, when to be hard. I'm being fair to you now.' He leaned forward and stressed. 'You don't have to die.

'This is a rebuilding phase for me. I have to show Isabelle that I have not only come back for her, but I have changed also. You *will* let her go, Lucas. She is not for you, but I must have a guarantee this conversation goes no further than this room.'

Maddigan's brows turned in, a look of worry, alarm, strained confusion. 'How can I provide you with any type of guarantee?'

'It's not about you providing the guarantee, that's already been provided. My guarantee is my gift to you.'

'I don't understand.'

'I thought long and hard about it myself, Lucas, but in the end I figured it out. I resolved it, as you architects would say. The soil around here was so easy to dig. Sand, all the way to China as my mother used to tell me.' He chuckled at the memory. 'I imagine you know that. What I thought was going to take me at least a day with my foot the way it is, took only a couple of hours to dig.'

'What are you talking about?'

'My gift.'

Slipping the newspaper clipping from his front pocket, he tossed it on the couch beside Maddigan.

'Read it.'

Maddigan spread it out, scanning the page. Wary eyes flicked up.

'Bottom right hand article.'

Maddigan read, took some time, perhaps he read it again.

'You're lying. How do I know this is not one of your tricks?'

'You mean like Sicily? A den of corruption over there. This comes from the media, bunch of self-righteous arseholes not even I can buy.'

Maddigan's eyes hardened. 'Kernot, you … you killed him.'

'I can see it now. I can feel it, Lucas, vengeance. You can't convince me you wouldn't want that man dead because that part of human nature is the same through all men. It's only *the doing* that's the difference between us. We're men, Lucas. We all have two wolves inside us. The wolf that wins is the wolf we feed. I can see the wolf of vengeance rising in you now. The part of you that is pleased the man who killed your family is dead. You can't deny it. You just didn't have the guts to do it yourself. I took care of that for you, another token of my goodwill.'

'What … what have you done?'

'Buried back from the beach on the other side of that cliff is my guarantee that I get what I came here for.'

'What?' Maddigan's lips hardly moved.

'Kernot would have driven pissed again, killed someone else, don't feel sorry for him. The body's down a long way, no-one will find him, unless of course the cops are told the exact location. Your DNA will match hair samples I left on the man's kitchen floor.'

'Hair samples?'

'Those clothes hanging off the end of your bed, one anonymous call, they'll be down here like the plague.'

'I will have to tell them what happened.'

'Say what you want. Cops only believe what they're trained to believe. Evidence, DNA, the location of the grave, there's certainly motive.'

'I was away at the time.'

'And who can verify that, Isabelle? She'll be with me.' Carlo raised the gun. 'Forgot about that, didn't you, oh, and let me guess, Ingliss told you to get off the grid.'

'She will never go with you.'

'Understand this, Lucas, I always win. The media, the public, the cops, no-one believed her last time, that's the real reason why she ran to Perth. Imagine if someone as fragile as

Izy is linked to another murder. Nobody goes for conspiracies anymore, that's so nineties. The media are the modern day judge, the jury is their pathetic readers.'

Maddigan's shoulders slumped. Carlo knew the man's mind was at an impasse. Research had proved a powerful tool.

'You will tell her to come with me because you will tell her you don't love her. Think about it, Lucas, you expected to die, now you get your home, your friends, the arsehole who killed your family, even your life. Take the deal, Lucas.'

Maddigan shut his eyes tight, held his head in his hands. 'You're insane.'

Carlo was taken aback. 'Don't you push me. You got lucky once. I could snap your back like a twig. I'm letting you live. You're a man of intelligence, you don't have a choice.'

Carlo strode over toward the large window, heal to toe, enjoying the mood once again. Below the level of the blind something caught his attention at the foot of the deck. He moved closer, running an eye along the line of timbers. They stopped abruptly at the shape of a half rounded form jutting up from the top step.

A head?

The window exploded.

24

Carlo was thrown off his feet. Another blast came through the empty window. He sprung up on one knee, wary for the next shot. He fired twice out the window. Movement came from behind, Maddigan fled down the passage.

His face stung. Warm blood trickled down his neck, he felt his cheeks, glass fell, relief came. He hadn't been shot. Quickly he moved over to the sofa, crouching behind it. The blasts were from a shotgun. Un-nerving silence filled the room, ruptured only by the night air flapping the blind.

He checked behind, fearing the gunman might have moved around to the rear deck. No-one.

Who was the shooter?

Unlike the farmhouse there were no guns here. He had searched every cupboard, every nook where a weapon could be hidden.

A shadow cast over, followed by a whooshing sound as a blow blackened his mind. Instant pain jolted his senses back and he spun, letting off a blind shot. It lodged in the wall above Maddigan, the golf club held high across his shoulder poised for another strike. Maddigan swung down at the gun, Carlo pulled back just in time and drove his fist into Maddigan's leg. The knee buckled, he cried out aloud as he fell, dropping the club. Carlo grabbed his throat at arm's length, placing the tip of the barrel between the architect's eyes.

The door burst open. Isabelle screamed, eyes wide, filled with terror. 'No … no,' she shrieked. 'No. Carlo. No … I will go … I will come.' She sobbed, sliding down the wall.

'You told me … you won't hurt him … please … please … please, Carlo. I will come … I will go anywhere. But—

Dark eyes shifted up to her.

Obedient eyes.

He hasn't fired.

Why?

Fear?

Isabelle held his stare. Jaw muscles tightened.

She knows he can't do it in front of her, in the forest it was so different.

Lifting her head she arched her back and felt for the wall, sliding up to stand almost fully, eyes bearing down.

'But, you must keep your word, Carlo.

'I will come, you gave me your word, and I give you mine.' Her voice, unwavering, firm. 'Things will be back the way they were, I promise.' She paused, then stood tall. 'But only on my terms.' She didn't even look at either the gun or Lucas. Instead she held a lock on Caruso.

'No Isabelle.' Lucas's words were spoken in barely a whisper.

She ignored him. 'I knew you were coming.' She took a breath. 'I felt the excitement once again, Carlo.' When she said his name, she said it provocatively. Lucas watched in awe.

'I will go … wherever you want me to go. It's just you and me, now, he doesn't matter anymore, it's always been about you and me, we can go anywhere in the world, do anything, as long as it's together. But if you hurt him, Carlo.' She hardened her tone with control. 'I know I will be forced to come. And I promise you, I will make your life a misery.'

Caruso listened.

She lifted her head more, eyes fixed. 'You will regret hurting him with every breath you take, you have what you came for, think of what you will take away, I will bear your children, pray with all my heart for boys to make strong, stronger, better men than you. And when they are *real* men, I will turn them against you and your family each second I live. And our lovemaking Carlo—' her mouth twisted, measuring each word '—I will rot from the core like a cancer. Eventually you will hate me more than life itself. That is my word, Carlo. I will make sure you live it.'

Seconds passed. Air escaped from Lucas's chest, he followed the hollow emptiness as the barrel lowered.

'You will leave now.'

Isabelle nodded.

He reached behind his back, produced a white envelope from his pocket, the unmistakable bulk of cash was inside.

'There is a note, follow every word.'

She took the envelope. 'I understand.'

Caruso glanced over his shoulder, checked the open window once more then stood, taking one last look at Isabelle before disappearing down the stairs.

Lucas reached for her hands, she pulled her arms back, standing her ground. A stranger.

'You saved my life.'

'But not mine.' She spoke quietly. 'I'm sorry, Luke.'

'No … no … this is not over yet. That's Horry outside. I know it's Horry. We can end this now. We can stop him.'

'Lucas, you saw him. You can't go out there.' She gripped his arm.

'I have to go. Shut the study door. Crawl under the desk, don't move.' He hesitated, 'He's framed me for a murder. We *cannot* contact the police. If I don't come back, then you take that money, get as far away from here as you can. Disappear again. I know you can do it. Do you understand me?'

She placed her hands on his cheeks and pressed.

'A murder? What are you talking about?'

'Can't explain, just promise me. Make sure this time. Make sure he never finds you.'

She nodded, crying, then pulled him close. 'I promise. I love you more than anything. Come back to me, Luke.'

He kissed her trembling lips, fearing he'd never see her again, then ran into the kitchen, grabbed the carving knife off the rack and raced onto the deck. Clyde was lying almost still, trying to scrape his paws on the timber, a desperate whine rose. Below, gunfire filled the night.

———

Burdened by years of salted air, roller bearings screeched as Carlo eased open the downstairs glass door. He slipped the nose of the Glock through. A blast shattered the door. He reeled back, moved to another window on his right and saw a man crouched in the sand, perhaps thirty metres away, the shotgun still levelled at the door. Carlo fired three shots through a small opening, then ducked. Glass blew out, it rained on his head. He sprang out the door, dived behind the boat, another shot splintered wood off the bow.

Using the boat for cover, Carlo fired back. The man held his position, blowing a hole in the side of the boat, another blast hit the post beside him. Carlo was low on bullets, he'd left his bag hidden in the scrub beneath the Bluff. Not in his wildest dreams had he expected to need more bullets, or even the other gun. Maddigan ran down the stairs. Carlo saw his chance and sprinted away from the gunman toward the fire pit, letting off the last of his bullets. A blast returned, pellets slammed into his side, he swayed, but kept his legs pumping through the heavy sand. He'd been hit, but from well outside the killing range of the shotgun. The shooting stopped.

Why?

He glanced behind, Maddigan chased.

Ignoring the pain he kept running, thick, heavy sand drained his strength. Maddigan pounded behind. They entered the scrub beneath the Bluff, pace quickened on firmer sand and without breaking stride, Carlo scooped the bag up and sped toward the base of the cliff where the old foot track was carved into the face. The gunman would have the other track covered. Maddigan was right behind. Carlo couldn't stop to reload. Saltbushes clinging to the face protected him from view, and gunfire. He began the climb.

His side ached, warm moisture soaked his shirt.

Blood.

Still he climbed as fast as he could. The gunman had disappeared. Carlo knew he'd be heading up the back track. A hand clung to his ankle, he wrenched it free, kicking downward. Pain jabbed his right side, but he kicked hard again only to have the foot grasped tight. Maddigan hung on, a knife raised in the other hand, but before the knife was thrust into his leg he heaved with all his remaining strength, breaking the hold and driving the boot onto Maddigan's head. The knife fell. He stomped hard on the fingers, a cry of pain followed and with one more swift kick, Maddigan was sent tumbling into the bushes below.

Carlo moved freely through the hardest section of the climb. The scrub thinned, he made up ground over the last few steps and reached the top where the track along the Bluff would lead him out of this place, forever.

Just as he was about to unclip his bag, the gunman appeared, the shotgun raised. Carlo pounced on the gun, shoving the barrel upwards. A shot rang out, each man with two hands on the weapon. Despite his injuries, Carlo drove the man into a bush. He wrenched the gun back, but the man refused to surrender his grasp.

Carlo smashed his fist into the side of the face, then recognised him.

The baker.

Horry's head reeled back. Carlo thumped him again, the eye split, still Horry held onto the gun. Carlo anchored his feet and yanked hard, turning Horry so his back faced the edge. He pushed, step by step toward the drop down to the ocean. Carlo grinned at the terrified man. One more step. The scrub behind rustled, snapping jaws lunged through the air, saliva glistened, teeth locked onto his shoulder, ripping flesh. Carlo was spun around by the sheer power of the dog. A hand found the baker's arm. All three toppled over the edge.

25

Lucas ripped off his shirt and dived into the ocean, desperate to reach the rock pools, a hard swim against the current and waves.

Horry would surely be floating upside down, dead. He tried to block the thought.

Once he cleared the shore break, he swam parallel to the Bluff face until he found the rim of the pools beneath the high tide. Too many lengthy minutes had passed.

'Don't die on me, Horry.'

Barnacles surviving on the jagged ledge tore at his cold feet; he ignored them, bracing his legs against the relentless waves, yelling Horry's name over a dark surface. He readied himself to jump in, an arm rose, then another between the troughs. Moonlight picked out a fluent stroke, waves crashed over, but despite being pushed toward the cliff, Horry swam strong.

'HORRY!'

No sign of Caruso.

Or Clyde.

'Horry, come on!' he yelled over the wind. Before he came to St Claire, Horry could hardly swim. Now, almost twenty years later, this man from inland South Africa was as much a waterman as any of the local crew. He reached out. Horry grabbed the hand. Lucas hauled him up onto the rock pool, keeping an eye out for Caruso.

'Horry, you okay mate?'

Watery blood streamed from his brow. Despite his exhaustion, Horry laughed, a crazy laughter of relief. 'Ja, I'm all right, nothing like cold water to ice the pain, hey.'

'Where is he? Did he come up?'

'No mate, I waited and waited to push the bastard down again. He didn't surface. My knee hit his chest when we landed. We did it!' He puffed. 'Can you believe it?' Horry leaned forward over the wall of the pool, wiping his face. The permanent grin broadened.

'We have to make sure.'

'I shot him too, Luke, he's dead. We must find the body, it's all been worked out, mate.'

'What? What's been worked out?'

'He's going out deep.'

Lucas glared at Horry. 'What—?'

'We have to get rid of him. Me and Steve discussed it. If he ever came back, this is what we have to do. If he's found to have died here, think of the media, the investigations, think of Isabelle. His family will want answers, we can't give them any.'

Lucas sat on the jagged rim absorbing it all, the black star-lit sky, the cliffs, dark waters shifting by. Against all his beliefs he knew Horry was right. 'Let's go in, get some lights. The body will wash up either along the beach or on the rocks past the house.' He turned to this strange man who had risked his own life to save theirs. 'How did you know?'

'The bird, mate. Saw the bird a couple of days ago, and again yesterday over that cliff.' Water escaped his lips with each word. 'Just like last time. Yesterday, after I saw it again I went back home, grabbed the shotty and walked the track, but didn't see anyone. Thought I must be mad, must be wrong. Didn't really believe he'd be up there because you told us that cop had tracked him overseas. Didn't know what to think, just planned to hang around for a few hours, then go home, ja.'

Lucas simply shook his head in amazement, slinging an arm around him.

'Isabelle, she okay? Heard a shot inside the house.'

'She's on the beach, mate. She's fine. You saved both our lives tonight. Thought you were dead. Don't you ever die on me again, Horry.'

Horry's teeth gleamed in the moonlight. 'It's over, mate. Clyde? You seen him yet?'

'Not yet. He's a good swimmer. He'll be alive,' Lucas tried to believe in his own words. 'Come on.' They stood and called the dog at the tops of their voices, but Clyde was nowhere, so they walked the rim to the front of the rock pool, hoping he might already be on the beach. Horry's jeans slapped loudly with water.

Lucas said, 'You look like that drowned rat I hauled out of Fishhook Bay all those years ago.' Nothing had changed from the first time they'd met. The two thoughts – one of the present, one of the past – lodged in Lucas's memory like bookends guarding the most valuable times they'd spent between.

———

Slimy hands reached out from all directions. He brushed them away, realising they were only rubbery strands of kelp. Weight of the cold water pressed, he searched for light, lungs ached, panic broke out and he kicked and kicked, striking at nothing except more kelp. Finally he touched sand, solidity amidst chaos. He pushed hard off the ocean floor and broke the surface, heaving a lungful of precious air, and water. The ocean filled him again and he was back under. The wave rolled on, he found the surface, more air.

Pain rang out from his sternum. The baker hit him hard on impact, he had to get out of the water. Relentless waves pushed him down. Too much energy was spent just treading. Unable to feel the bottom, he began to swim toward the dark cliff face until, during a patch of calmness, he heard a noise over the surface. Voices. He kicked, lifting himself above the waves.

They stood only a short swim away in deeper water.

How?

The rockpools.

With renewed effort he swam breaststroke. Waves seemed to crash with much less vigour. He wasn't fighting the wind or current anymore, only jabs of pain from his shoulder and chest with each stroke. A larger wave swamped him and as he resurfaced, the voices became louder, calling the dog. He adjusted to the cold, became better at judging the waves.

Almost there.

———

'You go first,' Lucas said. 'I'll follow, in case you get tired.'

Horry dived in. Lucas heard the water change behind and braced for another wave to surge, when he felt the hand.

'HORRY!' he yelled before he was dragged beneath the surface. He tried to dive, first instinct was to break the hold on his neck by kicking and twisting to reach deeper water, but the hand clutched tight. In wild desperation his fingers searched through layers of weed-covered reef on the wall adjacent.

Nothing.

Frantically, he reached up grasping Caruso's ankle, trying to unbalance him off the ledge above. It wouldn't budge.

'NO!' Horry screamed. The baker had hauled himself back onto the wall, and when he lunged, Carlo backhanded him into the centre of the rock pool. He held Maddigan under until the struggle left, the hand went limp, releasing the grip on his leg. He judged another minute to make sure and let go, the body sank. The baker scrambled back up onto the ledge and attempted to throw a punch. Carlo easily moved aside, grabbed the man's throat and cocked his fist.

But the baker peered past him.

Lucas clubbed the back of Caruso's neck again and again. Bones crunched under the weighty shell. Caruso fell to his knees. Lucas struck harder and harder, blood spilled from an open wound at the base of the skull. Caruso's back jerked up in a spasm. With both hands, Horry grabbed the head and slammed him face down onto the ledge of the rock pool. Caruso spun over, blood poured, the murderous hand reached for Lucas, but the great strength that held him under moments ago, was gone. Fingers loosened, the arm dropped, Lucas sent blow after blow down, the insides of the hard abalone shredding his palm. Then he brought the back of the shell down twice more into the thick of Caruso's neck. A dull crack sounded above the lapping waves.

Desperate eyes softened their gaze. Lifeblood flowed from Caruso's mouth, whisked away on the current. Lips moved, a hideous gurgling was heard. Lucas could have mercifully pushed the man's face to one side and drowned him, instead he lifted the head above the water, knelt closer and spoke.

'This ocean will flush your filthy blood, but you will not stain my reef.

'And Isabelle, she's all mine.' He let go of the head. 'Can I kill a man? An old man knew that answer.' Lucas lifted the shell high and bludgeoned Caruso's skull until Horry finally dragged him off.

———

From the beach Isabelle recognised the two men as they waded in from the surf.

'Lucas … Lucas!'

He dragged something. A figure. He let go and rushed to her, but she couldn't take her eyes off the body.

Face down. Dead.

She ran into the water, hugged Lucas, crying and digging her fingers into his back, smelling his hair, his neck, his skin, weeping with joy as the corpse bounced back and forth on the shoreline.

'It's over ... it's over, Isabelle. He's dead.'

She grappled him, fearing the body would get up.

'Is he really—?'

'As a doornail,' Horry said, gasping, wading through the shallows.

'Horry!' She ran to the South African, wrapping him in her arms, kissing him. 'Thank you ... thank you, Horry.' The words seemed so hollow. 'How can we ever ... take a look at you—' She wiped the blood from his eye. 'You're the bravest man I've ever known.'

Horry blushed, she could tell by his grin. She kissed him again, he laughed back.

'Let's get you inside. We have to call the police.'

'Isabelle.' The smile left, he gripped her shoulders, his chest pumping with each breath. 'You're not going to want to hear this.'

She realised his tone, her mind seemed slow to react.

'This has to stop here.'

She turned to Lucas. 'What's going on?'

But he was gone, sprinting down the beach toward the dark shape lying on its side in the water. Isabelle and Horry followed.

'Clyde ... Clyde!' Lucas dragged him out of the water, knelt down and stroked the dog's head.

The dog whined, spewed water, legs scratched and scraped. Within seconds he bravely managed to roll over and stand up. He took a few wary steps, exhausted, disorientated, yet he shook himself off and staggered toward Horry who put him in a gentle headlock. 'You know what you did up there, boy.' Horry brushed the water off his back, tenderly. Clyde licked his face. 'We Afrikaans, huh. We stick together, eh boy.'

Isabelle watched on, unable to take Horry's comment off her mind.

———

Horry left in the Porsche and arrived back at the house half an hour later. Soon, the lights of the Princess Jenny slipped beneath the Bluff, bobbing on the swell. It stopped offshore.

Within minutes a motor could be heard. An aluminium tinny approached from the darkness, the engine cut, the boat rode in on a breaker. Lucas and Horry grabbed the rails and hauled the boat up onto the sand.

'Few hungry Noahs out there on the way in,' she heard Thumbtack say as he climbed out. He stared past the two men at Isabelle, further up the beach. She saw the face. Thumbtack grinning. So haunting. So real.

'Don't have to worry about this one no more,' he called to her. 'St Claire looks after her own, ya know.'

So the locals say, she thought to herself as the wind lifted and swirled like arms touching all around her.

In the time Horry was gone, Lucas explained they were dumping the body in a thousand foot of water over the continental shelf. His words rang in her mind,

"If Horry's sure, then so am I."

Thumbtack grinned back. She couldn't see the tear drop below the eye, but she knew it was there, always there, so many times before she woke. The apparition, a clown, no make-up, always standing over Carlo, grinning in front of the darkest ocean. The boat, rolling in on snow white, pristine caps. Carlo, face down. Always in her dream he was face down.

Clyde nestled in, nudging his nose under her elbow, she didn't mind his wet fur.

Her knees hollowed out in the sand, she placed her hands over her face, lucid tears of happiness flowed.

The many faces, the markings, all suddenly melded into one face, always laughing back at her.

Thumbtack, his little boat.

This house. This beach.

This man she would forever love, brave Horry and Clyde.

For all the wrong, this was right.

They flopped the body into the tinny. Lucas and Horry held the rails. Thumbtack tossed the legs over and climbed back in. The two men silently steadied the boat through the waves. Thumbtack brought the engine back to life. The beam of light danced on the swell, just inside the reef where the mighty wave they called All Mine broke only on rare occasion.

Isabelle had seen it all before.

Her dream had come true.

Her dream of happiness.

The End.

PETER EDWARDS

Acknowledgements.

Thank you to my early manuscript readers who gave me the confidence and encouragement to complete this work. Dave and Anne Blackie, Julie Rennie, Kevin and Rosina Rennie, Chris Haddock, Olivia Scott, Denise Hurley, Lisa Edward, Bronwyn Bliszczyk and Jude Reeves.

My friend for forty years, Tim Howells, was also my first reader. Punishingly, he read this work at 360,000 words in a three-book structure, then again at 190,000. Tim passed away before I could complete All Mine in its current form. He enriched the lives of anyone fortunate enough to know him and provided me with great encouragement to pursue my writing.
R.I.P. mate.

Thank you to Julie Rennie for your guidance in publishing this extract, along with Jude Reeves, Janine Grant, Chris Haddock and Lynne Pitcher (from MCG signs in Torquay) who all offered advice on the cover design.

I am forever indebted to three amazing ladies.
My patient and amazing editor, Serena Sandrin, and Louise Cusack and Raewyn McGill who both provided insightful manuscript assessments. I have learnt so much from each of you and cannot begin to repay you enough.
Without your help I'd still be floundering away, totally lost at sea with Carlo.

Like John Ingliss, I felt like a guest on my travels throughout
Sicily where I met an extraordinarily helpful young man, a
teacher name Paolo Parisi who taught me the correct Sicilian
dialogue unique to the Province of Caltanissetta. Sicily is a
beautiful island full of intrigue, great food and wine and
friendly people.
Thank you Paolo.

And if you are ever in the ancient city of Catania on the east
coast, call in and see my friend Jacopo in the Hoppe Beer
Shop on the Via Carcaci. Tell him Peter the *scrittore* from
Australia sent you and you will be looked after.

A final word from me.

I began writing this book over five years ago with an idea to set a thriller along the ocean side of the Great Ocean Road. Lucas entered first as the owner of the property. Then came Horry and Clyde. Still don't know the origin of Horry's name and Clyde is based on my own Ridgeback/Greyhound cross, Sue who spent everyday of writing with me, only contributing her looks. Then Isabelle moved into St Claire and when I asked her, 'what are you running from?' Carlo simply appeared and took over. He was a lot of fun to write and led from the front. Oh, and don't Google the I.D. program, Iceberg. I had to find a way of identifying Carlo, so I just made that up.

Thanks for reading and check out the prologue and chapter 1 of Bushmore's Dark Secrets on the next page.

Pete, 2015.

Website: allminestories.com
Email: allminestories@bigpond.com
Follow me on Instagram
peteredwardsallmine
Liked my book, then please like my page,
www.facebook.com/PeterEdwardsAuthor
Twitter: Peter Edwards@allminestories

PETER EDWARDS

BUSHMORE'S DARK SECRETS

PROLOGUE

My son Jack fell a long way last night. Nurse Blaxland called soon after breakfast. He wasn't expected to make it through the day, so our family gathered at Jack's holiday home and travelled to the district hospice together.

His brother Tommy visited along with Jack's dearest friends, Nick and his partner Cherub. His three children, young Jack, Lucy and Denise all said their heartfelt goodbyes while I was out of the room. He conditioned them as best he could for his impending death, telling them his passing would become an important part of their lives, but was adamant he didn't want his children to see him finally succumb. Although my grandchildren wanted to be present, they knew there was no further discussion to be had. Once my son made up his mind it was final.

I watched his laboured breathing. Even my eyes hurt, such was the pain of seeing my eldest boy die. The only thing this disease hadn't taken yet was his soul.

He cut his visits four weeks ago and things have been nice and quiet since, but before that time Jack accepted his many friends with all the typical bulldog tenacity he displayed throughout his life. I reckon half the golf club came through to pay their respects along with yachtsmen and business associates from around the country. They stood alongside plumbers who had worked with him and for him over the years. Many of Melbourne's leading thoroughbred racing identities came too; jockeys, trainers, even other owners. Most were people from the other side of money who he rarely spoke of to me. I'm just an old retired plumber with a crook back and a liver as useless as tits on a bull, but I was touched deeply by how they all spoke of my son.

The door opened, his wife Wendy entered and sat down. Her face drawn, her eyes dry. Relief will be a welcome stranger for her, too. We held one bony hand each listening to the rasping of air into tired, spent lungs. He cracked his eyes open and raised a finger, pointing to the bag on the chair beside Wendy.

'Take a look,' she said.

I opened the bag and saw the back of a thick, yellow clip folder full of paper, about a half ream in thickness. I ignored it and slid out the leather satchel with his MacBook inside, although I wondered where he'd find the strength in those fingers to push the keys. I passed the laptop over.

'No,' he mouthed.

'No?'

'No.' The finger moved down.

'The folder?'

I held it up, the lips moved, air hissed. 'Yeah, Dad.'

Wendy nodded and I opened the folder and read the first page.

<h2 style="text-align:center">ENOUGH ROPE
BY
JACK GILLINGS</h2>

'Shit Jack! No … no.' I glared at him in disbelief. For a brief second I saw a monster. Then I looked harder and saw my son, Jack. It was still my beautiful boy beneath those eyes, sunk deep behind the protruding cheekbones below them.

'Jack … how did this get in here?'

I turned toward Wendy. Surely she didn't know. But I could tell from her compressed, flattened out lips that she did. She kept a strict eye on what came and went from her husband's room.

'Linda,' Wendy said.

Then I recalled Jack's secretary had paid a visit yesterday afternoon.

'You've read this?'

'Not this one,' Wendy said. 'I ran my eyes over an edited version, one with a happy ending he and a publisher worked on sometime around the late nineties. They changed a lot of stuff, to make a better story and all that but Jack pulled the plug. Couldn't go through with it. This is the original manuscript he wrote back in '83, the year after it happened. He kept it in his safe.'

'Why … why now? We left all this behind.'

'He never could,' Wendy said. 'We've been speaking. He always thought he'd have the time to maybe … maybe find the right moment to give it to you. Other times I thought he'd never really get around to it, but these last weeks, this illness has changed his mind. He wants you to know everything. The truth.'

'And Nick?'

She shook her head. 'Jack said it's for you to read, then he wants you to destroy it. I have always asked him never to show you but he's made his decision. You know our Jack.'

'We buried this years ago … when we left that town.' I looked to my son and he said one more ghostly word, 'Read.'

I pulled my glasses from my pocket and slipped them on. The first page was blank except for his handwritten words,

FOR MUM, DAD AND TOMMY.

CHAPTER 1

My name is Jack Gillings. I am sixteen years old at writing and directly responsible for the deaths of two people. I live with my family in the coastal town of St Claire, on the Great Ocean Road in Victoria's southwest. We moved here just under a year ago, but I grew up in another country town called Bushmore, slightly inland about a half hour drive to the northeast, high up in the Otway Ranges.

In Bushmore, we lived at 19 Pinehurst Avenue. St Patrick's Secondary College was my school, but not by choice. I wanted to be at the Bushmore High School where my mates were and where the girls went.

I hated my school with a passion.

Christian Brothers ran St Pat's. When it came to being strict, those weirdos were full on. Our first punishment of every morning was that classes began at eight forty, sharp, twenty minutes before my mates began their lessons at high school. Then they'd try and control your life at every turn, even coming to and from school. Teachers would deliberately drive past the bus stop and if we weren't wearing ties or blazers, then lookout. Hell … you might've just loosened your tie to get a bit of relief from the heat, or your socks were down, scrunched around your ankles, it didn't matter. We'd get detention. They even used spotters, usually senior kids to report us for so called *uniform crimes* on the bus. They'd ram religious education down our throats every day. Then came the daily grind of two to three hours of homework, and a minimum of three, sometimes four hours on weekends. As if six and a half hours a day stuck in school, five days a week for six years of my life wasn't enough time for them to do their jobs properly. It seemed to be enough time for high school teachers – none of my mates copped any homework at all.

Each morning I'd try and smash out my homework while stuffing down breakfast in my room, because there was simply too many fun things for a fourteen-year-old to do after school in Bushmore. I'd either be motorbike riding, hanging out at my mates houses, playing the pinnies in the pinball parlour or even roof-rocking teachers houses after dark. Anything but homework.

English, History, Geography and P.E. were the only subjects that interested me, all the rest were totally unnecessary for my future. I'd already decided to be a plumber like my dad. I knew the job inside out. I'd been working with him for most of my life and my oldies both agreed I could begin my apprenticeship with Dad after year ten. Meaning, at the time of the events in this story, I only had another year and a term to go.

And that's where I have to begin. A little over one year ago on the second last day of mid-term in 1982, when Tony Debono clobbered me good and proper on the school bus for the final time.

Each morning I'd walk to Ackley Street, three streets away from my home and catch the bus from there. Debono hopped on the bus at Pinehurst Avenue. I know it might sound strange – Debono and I lived only three houses apart – but there were two reasons why I walked to Ackley Street every morning.

Firstly, Debono was a year older and had picked on me since our late primary school years. Before that time we grew up together, messing around in the street and at each other's houses. Then he changed and became an arsehole and now, I didn't even want to stand next to him at the bus stop. The second reason was so I could walk Rex, my border collie in the mornings. *"Your dog, your responsibility"*, Mum always said. Once I was on the bus, Rex would make his way home and then walk with my younger brother, Tommy to the primary school.

To avoid Debono, I'd try to find a seat as far down the back of the bus as possible. If he passed me down the aisle, I risked being clipped on the way through. Most times it was only a slap under the chin or over the side of the head, the odd knuckle grind through the hair, that sort of thing. Not enough to hurt too much, just enough to piss me off and push my boundaries as far as he could. Sometimes I'd be lucky and find a corner spot in the back seat where he couldn't reach me. Other times I'd kick a skin nut (year seven kid) out of a window seat and made him sit next to the aisle.

But on that particular day the second school bus had broken down, meaning the kids from Beaconshire – the nearest town to ours – filled the back of our bus. I'd been forced to take up an aisle seat half way down. Debono got on and began calling out stuff and whooping and hollering to his mates down the back. He hardly had any mates in Bushmore, yet he seemed to get along with the kids from Beaconshire. (I figured they didn't know how much of a dickhead he really was outside of school.) Then he saw me, and that stupid grin widened. He wore a gold stud in his left ear. What a tosser. He'd have to take it out before school otherwise he'd get detention, but most kids had sussed him out long ago as a spotter which explained how he got away with wearing the earring on the bus.

As he approached me down the aisle, I had my hands ready to cover my ears where he clipped me last time.

'Gillo,' he said in a smartarse voice. I watched him carefully as he passed, thinking I was in the clear because he had his eyes up, grinning at his mates down the back. Then the left hand shot out and palmed me on the forehead, ramming my head into the chrome steel bar that looped over the top of the seat. The blow knocked my senses around a bit and I saw red. At almost fifteen years of age, I'd had enough.

'Fuck you,' I screamed and went totally ape shit. I leapt into the aisle and punched the back of his head so hard it sent him stumbling forward. I shook my hand, the centre knuckle felt like it might be broken. He tried to spin around but with his school bag on his back, the aisle was too narrow. I had one chance to keep going so I ignored the pain and with both hands reefed his head by the hair, dragging him down onto the floor of the bus. I stomped on his head and as he tried to get back up, I bent down and thumped him one more time right in the earhole before the bus brakes squealed and the big hands of George, the Greek bus driver hauled me back up the aisle by the scruff of the neck.

Voices were egging me on yelling, 'Gillo Gillo.' Others urged Debono on but the fight was over in a flash. Of course I knew George would report us both; I didn't care. It felt good to be cheered and this prick had been bullying me for way too long. I liked George. He knew the history between Debono and myself and made me sit up the front and sent Debono to the back for the rest of the journey. I'd kicked his arse and that was worth the Saturday morning detention we both knew was coming our way. Debono was bigger and stronger than me and I knew I was in for it and would spend the school holidays looking over my shoulder each time I left the house. But as I said earlier, that was the last time he ever belted me because soon after, Tony Debono would be dead and I was responsible.

allminestories@bigpond.com

www.ingramcontent.com/pod-product-compliance
Lightning Source LLC
Chambersburg PA
CBHW032342280326
41935CB00008B/415